Heidegger and ethics

Heidegger denied that his enquiries were concerned with ethics. *Heidegger and Ethics* questions this self-understanding and reveals a form of ethics in Heidegger's thinking that is central to his understanding of metaphysics and philosophy.

In our technological age, metaphysics has, according to Heidegger, become reality; philosophy has come to an end. Joanna Hodge argues that there has been a concomitant transformation of ethics that Heidegger has failed to identify. Today, technological relationships form the ethical relations in which humans find themselves. As a result, ethics is cut loose from abstract universal moral standards, and the end of philosophy announced by Heidegger turns out to be an interminable interruption of the metaphysical will to completion. In order to realise the productive potential of this interruption, the repressed ethical element in Heidegger's thinking must be retrieved.

Discussing the relations in Heidegger's thought between humanism and nihilism, between anthropology and homecoming, and between history and violence, *Heidegger and Ethics* reconstructs the ethical dimension of his work and offers new insights into the role of ethical enquiry in current philosophy.

Joanna Hodge is Senior Lecturer in the Department of Politics and Philosophy at Manchester Metropolitan University.

Heidegger and ethics

Joanna Hodge

London and New York

First published 1995
by Routledge
11 New Fetter Lane, London EC4P 4EE

Simultaneously published in the USA and Canada
by Routledge
29 West 35th Street, New York, NY 10001

Typeset in Times by LaserScript, Mitcham, Surrey
Printed and bound in Great Britain by
Mackays of Chatham Ltd, Kent

British Library Cataloguing in Publication Data
A catalogue record for this book is available from the British Library

Library of Congress Cataloging in Publication Data
Hodge, Joanna, 1953–
    Heidegger and ethics/Joanna Hodge.
    p. cm.
    Includes bibliographical references and index.
1. Heidegger, Martin, 1889–1976. 2. Ethics, Modern – 20th century.
I. Title.
B3279.H49H5   1994
171′.2 – dc20   94–10240
                                                        CIP

ISBN 0–415–03288–1 (hbk)
ISBN 0–415–09650–2 (pbk)

In memoriam
Alan Hodge
1915–1979

Contents

Abbreviations

Unless otherwise indicated, references to Heidegger are to the following editions:

BPP   *Basic Problems of Phenomenology*, translated by Albert Hofstadter, Bloomington: Indiana University Press, 1982, revised edition, 1988.

DT   *Discourse on Thinking*, translated by J. Anderson and E. H. Freund, New York: Harper & Row, 1966.

ED1   *Erläuterungen zu Hölderlins Dichtung*, Frankfurt am Main: Klostermann, first edition, 1944.

ED2   *Erläuterungen zu Hölderlins Dichtung*, Frankfurt am Main: Klostermann, second edition, 1949.

EGT   *Early Greek Thinking*, edited and translated by Frank Capuzzi and David Farrell Krell, New York: Harper & Row, 1975.

EM   *Einführung in die Metaphysik*, Tübingen: Max Niemeyer, 1953, third edition, 1966.

FD   *Die Frage nach dem Ding: Zu Kants Lehre von den transzendentalen Grundsätzen*, Tübingen: Max Niemeyer, 1962.

GA   (followed by volume number) *Gesamtausgabe*, Frankfurt am Main: Klostermann, 1977–.

HW   *Holzwege*, Frankfurt am Main: Klostermann, 1950, fifth edition, 1972.

ID   *Identity and Difference*, parallel German and English edition, translated by Joan Stambaugh, New York: Harper & Row, 1969.

KPM   *Kant und das Problem der Metaphysik*, Frankfurt am Main: Klostermann, 1950, fourth edition, 1973.

MFL   *The Metaphysical Foundations of Logic*, translated by Michael Heim, Bloomington: Indiana University Press, 1984.

PLT   *Poetry, Language, Thought*, edited and translated by Albert Hofstadter, New York: Harper & Row, 1971.

QT   *The Question Concerning Technology and Other Essays*, translated and introduced by William Lovitt, New York: Harper & Row, 1977.

SB   *Die Selbstbehauptung der deutschen Universität*, Wrocław: Korn, 1935.

SD   *Zur Sache des Denkens*, Tübingen: Max Niemeyer, 1969.

SG   *Der Satz vom Grund*, Pfullingen: Neske, 1957, fifth edition, 1978.

SZ   *Sein und Zeit*, Tübingen: Max Niemeyer, 1927, ninth edition, 1963.

US   *Unterwegs zur Sprache*, Pfullingen: Neske, 1959, sixth edition, 1979.

VA   *Vorträge und Aufsätze*, Pfullingen: Neske, 1954, fifth edition, 1985.

WHD   *Was heißt Denken?*, Tübingen: Max Niemeyer, 1954, second edition, 1961.

WM   *Wegmarken*, Frankfurt am Main: Klostermann, 1967, second expanded and revised edition, 1978.

WP   *What is Philosophy?*, edited by Jean T. Wilde and William Kluback, New Haven: College and University Press, 1958.

Chapter 1

Preamble
On ethics and metaphysics

> In so far as human beings exist, so philosophising occurs in a certain form. (*WM*: 121)

Heidegger himself writes very little about ethics, and then only to state that ethical questions are not his concern. Thus it might seem inappropriate to trace out a contribution to ethical enquiry in his writings. His endorsement of Nazism in 1933 might seem like another good reason for doubting his ability to contribute to ethical reflection. However, in this study I claim that the question of ethics is the definitive, if unstated problem of his thinking. In the first part of this chapter, I discuss the questions of politics which arise in relation to his work. As a result it is possible to identify a series of interconnected splittings in conceptions of politics, of history, of time, the past and the future, and indeed of the present and of philosophy itself. These splittings sustain the precarious distinction between ethics and metaphysics, which, viewed more carefully, also reveals that there are forms of ethics and metaphysics which do and forms which do not bring into question their own conditions of possibility. In the second part of this chapter, I discuss the relation between ethics and metaphysics in Heidegger's thought with regard to a movement from the earlier proposal in *Being and Time* (1927)[1] to retrieve the potential of philosophy by destroying the tradition, through the protracted encounter with Nietzsche, into the postwar declaration of an end of philosophy in a recovery from metaphysics. I seek to show that if that recovery is to take place, there must not just be a step back into the ground of metaphysics but a step forward into the transformative powers of ethics.

Through these discussions, of politics and of the movement of Heidegger's thought, it becomes possible to identify a splitting between three versions of ethics. There is the version of ethics as a history of ethical enquiry, made up of the foremost contributions to ethical thinking: those of Plato, Aristotle, Augustine, Luther, Hume, Kant, Schelling, Nietzsche, Freud. While for Heidegger the completion of metaphysics is not the occasion for the advent of ethics, his texts can also be read as opening up a possible retrieval of ethics, as a textual tradition, especially out of the writings of Nietzsche, Schelling, Kant, Aristotle and Plato. The themes to be retrieved are *Gerechtigkeit*, responsibility, evil, autonomy, and the relation between theoretical and practical reason. There is a second version of ethics as the more abstract specification of a concern with the well-being of human beings and with deriving rules of human conduct. Neither of these versions is the central concern of this study. The former sets up for investigation an interplay in Heidegger's enquiries between his readings of the texts of the tradition for their ethical content and his own distinctive formulations. Heidegger himself explicitly rejects the second version of ethics as a focus for concern, since it takes the question of human flourishing in isolation from the wider context in which human beings find themselves. This is a restricted conception of ethics, by contrast to which I seek to find at work in Heidegger's enquiries an unrestricted conception of ethics concerned not just with human beings, but with human beings in relation to difference and to otherness. This is the point of analysing *Dasein*, rather than human being, showing that human being is essentially relational, and not just in relation to itself and to other human beings, but in relation to both known and unknowable otherness. *Dasein* is a form of self-relation which is systematically connected to others of the same kind, others of different kinds, and to the ground of possibility of there being such differences and otherness at all: to being. I seek to show that there is an ethical dimension to Heidegger's thought in advance of any division between ethics and metaphysics. It is this unrestricted conception of ethics, concerned with identifiable and unknowable others, that informs this study.

Since Heidegger's involvement with Nazism is commonly rehearsed as an objection to supposing he might have anything to teach us about either ethics or politics, it is perhaps important to distinguish, as Pöggeler seeks to do, between different kinds of involvement in Nazism.[2] I incline to the view that Heidegger was not an anti-Semite, but was both culpably self-deluding in 1933 when he took over the rectorial position at Freiburg and distorted his involvement after the war in a vain attempt to retrieve his academic career. I believe there is no excuse for intellectuals who endorsed Hitler; there is no excuse for endorsing Hitler and refusing to read Hitler's *Mein Kampf*, thus avoiding the encounter with Hitler's views on biology and race. However, I suppose that Heidegger did not share these views on biology. For Heidegger, the destiny of the German nation is bound up not with race but with language; and I suppose that after 1934, Heidegger adopted the strategy of survival, which I think cannot be judged by those who have not confronted such conditions. I take neither the view that Heidegger's endorsement of Hitler in 1933 was a direct consequence of his philosophy; nor do I take the view that it is irrelevant to his philosophy. Indeed, I think that Heidegger's pessimism about the future is a consequence of his having been proved so totally, hideously wrong in his judgement with respect to a future under Nazi rule. However, the question of Heidegger's personal complicity with Nazism occurs at a different level from that at which my analysis takes place.

I identify in Heidegger's thinking a kind of ethical articulation which occurs before a division between the formation of individuals and the formation of collective identity, in advance of any division into ethics and metaphysics, into moral and political philosophy. There is a kind of meta-ethics which takes place in advance of any division between ethics and politics, if these are understood as concerned with the formation respectively of individuals and of communities, as independent processes. A metaphysical understanding of such identity supposes it to be determinate and determinable. Ethical enquiry by contrast would suppose that such identity is a continuing project of renegotiation between scarcely definable forces, to which Heidegger refers as an 'originary *polemos*', a conflict taking place in advance of all other processes. The identity of Martin Heidegger is similarly in process, not given; and this study has a place in an ongoing struggle about the significance of Heidegger and about the possibility of a postmodern ethics.[3] Metaphysical construction results from posing and responding to questions about truth claims and about what there is. However, the essence of metaphysics, that it should take place at all in the forms in which does, is an ethical issue, for it poses the question about the mode of living within which philosophical questions can be asked and within which metaphysical systems are constructed. Heidegger's diagnosis of technical relations is that they make it redundant to construct metaphysical systems, since everyday life has taken on the form of a metaphysical system. The consequent erosion of the everydayness of everyday life is in part an erasure of the autonomy of the ethical mode of questioning. In the transformation of metaphysics into technical relations there is a diminution of the ethical element in an originary *polemos*. My claim is that Heidegger falls short of the possibilities of his own thought by proposing to retrieve the tradition and to step back into the ground of metaphysics, while failing to pose the correlative question: what is ethics? He fails to affirm the coterminous necessity of taking a step forward into the potentiality of ethics. I suggest that his Nazi adventure is a result of this failure.

In May 1933 Heidegger delivered an address as the newly installed Nazi rector of Freiburg University. In this *Rektoratsrede*,[4] he responds to Nazism by re-peating, not retrieving, the race-, class- and gender-bound Platonic division of labour between thought, soldiering and work; between thoughtful contemplation as self-constituting activity; military service as purposive activity; and activity determined by an end imposed from outside that process. Once this division has been adopted, the hierarchies of race, class and gender can be set up through the determinations of who may and who may not posit their own ends. The repetition performed in the *Rektoratsrede* assumes a pre-established distinction between individual and collectivity; the roles laid out in the *Republic*, of working, guard-ing and thinking, can then be distributed to already constituted individuals, to whom Heidegger addresses himself. More promising than this repetition is the dynamic within Heidegger's thought, taken up by Jacques Taminiaux and by Hannah Arendt, of an Aristotelian distinction between *poiesis*, a form of activity in which the agent is not also transformed, and *praxis*, a form of activity through which the agent itself acquires an identity.[5] This dynamic destabilises the view, also derived from Aristotle, that questions of order in the community can be separated from questions concerning the constitution of the self. While Aristotle discusses the politics of the community separately from questions of the self, this distinction between *praxis* and *poiesis* opens up the possibility of analysing the constitution of collective identities through the performances of collective agency. In the shift from the thinking of *Being and Time* to the questioning of technology, Taminiaux suggests that Heidegger moves from privileging *praxis* over *poiesis* in the analysis of *Dasein* to privileging *poiesis* over *praxis* in his explorations of the work of art, as making possible a revealing and founding of order. In neither of these formations, however, is there a subordination of the distinction between *poiesis* and *praxis* to a pre-given individuality and individualism. Heidegger thus indicates the possibility of deploying the terms *poiesis* and *praxis* in advance of any distinction between the ethical concerns of individuals and the political concerns of communities, assuming as given neither the distinction between ethics and politics nor that between individuals and communities. As a result, the terms *poiesis* and *praxis* can be shown to contribute to the emergence of a distinction between the personal and the political.

In a rethinking of political theory, which this study cannot hope to embark on, this division between the political and the personal, between politics and ethics, and the presumption that identity is defined by metaphysics in advance of ethical questioning, inherited jointly from Aristotle and from Plato, must be unpicked. In his lectures from 1942, *Hölderlins Hymne 'Der Ister'*,[6] Heidegger indicates the possibility of such rethinking. He addresses himself to the question of the political and to the meaning of the term *polis* for the Greeks and especially for Aristotle and Plato. Heidegger starts by confirming that the writings of Aristotle and Plato set up the terms in which politics in Europe is thought:

> If we are to ask 'what is the *polis* of the Greeks?', then we must not presume that the Greeks must already have known, so that all that is needed is to ask them. It is true that we have handed down to us from Greek thought the most wide-ranging discussions of the *polis*: the thorough dialogues of Plato on the *politeia*, that is everything pertaining to the *polis*, and wide coverage of Aristotle's lectures on 'political science', *The Politics*.

He then interrupts himself to ask a question about the adequacy of this thinking about politics: is there here an answer to the question concerning the nature of politics, or much more the first identification of a problem which is still un-addressed?

> Surely – but the question remains from whence these thinkers think the essence [*Wesen*] of the *polis*; the question remains whether the basis and basic concerns of Greek thinking at the end of the great Greek period were still sufficient for the questioning of the *polis*. Perhaps in these later discussions of the *polis*, there lies an inherent misrecognition of its essence, that the *polis* is the most in need of questioning and is kept and preserved in this need. If this is indeed so then we must think more thoroughly Greek than the Greeks themselves. It does not just seem so; it is so. (*GA* 53: 99)

This suggests that it is necessary to return to the context in which political philosophy becomes distinct from moral philosophy and metaphysics. Heidegger asserts that it is necessary to go beyond the Greeks, to think through the implications of the questions they opened up. He begins to do this in his questioning of technology, to which I return in the second part of this chapter. This questioning reveals that technical relations constitute a new context for human existence.

Technical relations as the context for human existence break that existence loose from the division into ethics and metaphysics, and from the related subordination of ethics to metaphysics, within which the entire tradition of Western political life has been held since its inception among the Greeks. The public life of the Greek city state, which provided a site for the articulation of political ideals, is transformed out of recognition in the modern world; there is no longer a secluded, private sphere of economy, meeting needs, as distinct from a public, political, symbolic world, concerned with producing meanings. The permeation of both private and public life by information systems and electronic gadgets fundamentally shifts human relations to each other, to the world and to the divisions installed at the beginning of the history of philosophy. These changes require a rethinking of what politics consists in. This questioning of politics requires a questioning of the division between ethics and metaphysics within Greek philosophy. This, in turn, presupposes a questioning of the division within ethics between a concern with the evolution of individuals into mature rationality on the one side, through which women, children, the impious and the barbarian are excluded from rational deliberation about the collective good, and, on the other, a concern with the processes of affirming and developing conceptions of collective well-being and collective identities in the gymnasia of Eurocentric and androcentric privilege. The status of the tradition which links current thinking about politics, ethics and metaphysics back to some supposed Greek origin is a central question for Heidegger, and for this study.

Heidegger's insistence on embedding philosophy back into the tradition out of which it emerges makes philosophy a specialist, elite, esoteric enterprise, open only to those with access to the relevant forms of training. It leads Heidegger to suppose that, with the loss of access to that tradition, the practice is irretrievable. The specificity of the European tradition has gone missing through the spread of the results of that tradition throughout the world. Heidegger is committed to the thought that philosophy is essentially a Greek and, by extension, a European practice. In his late lecture *What is Philosophy?*,[7] given in Normandy in 1955, he claims:

> The word *philosophia* tells us that philosophy is something which, first of all, determines the existence of the Greek world. Not only that – *philosophia* also determines the innermost basic feature of our Western – European history. The often heard expression 'Western-European philosophy' is, in truth, a tautology. Why? Because philosophy is Greek in its nature: Greek in this instance means that in origin the nature of philosophy is of such a kind that it first

appropriated the Greek world, and only it, in order to unfold itself. (*WP*: 28–31)

This is an odd view for someone who supposes that philosophy results from responding to a homelessness and ungroundedness,[8] which is irreducibly characteristic of human existence. It is furthermore unfortunate that Heidegger does not stress a distinction between philosophy having some inherent connection to the Greek language and philosophy belonging essentially to some 'Greek nation'. This latter view is meaningless, since at the time of the formation of philosophy in Greek, there was no Greek nation. It is dangerous, because it permits a mistaken slide from ascribing importance to the German language for philosophy to affirming a specific destiny for a German nation. This view led Heidegger into his endorsement of Nazism and is still in evidence in his responses to Hölderlin in lectures given in 1943 and in the 'Letter on humanism' (1947).[9]

Unlike Heidegger, I do not suppose that philosophy is a distinctively European practice, and alongside these highly abstract considerations, leading to bifurcations in conceptions of history, politics and indeed ethics, there remain the ordinary everyday senses of the terms. It is a metaphysical will to system that requires that the everyday use must be brought into line with the complexities and paradoxes generated by the attempt to think systematically. In the ordinary everyday sense of the term 'politics', I am politically committed to the thought that philosophy is neither 'Greek' nor 'European', that it is essentially neither specialist nor elite, nor esoteric. This commitment is in part a consequence of my exposure to various forms of feminist critique of privilege. I am thus critical of one version of the Platonic inheritance within philosophy. I take homelessness and ungroundedness to be features of all human experience and therefore suppose that the responses of ethical questioning and metaphysical construction in philosophical enquiry are, similarly, potentially features of all human experience. Indeed, I take the completion of metaphysics in the spread of technical relations throughout the world to be the occasion for the dispersal of philosophy to all human beings, in place of a more traditional exclusiveness; and I, amongst many others, am a beneficiary. The resulting transformation of philosophy is no less great than the transformation of the religion that was Judaism, when it split into Judaism and Christianity. I suppose that this split within philosophy between an esoteric, exclusive, bygone tradition dominated by caste and an open, ecumenical tradition is in process of formation such that its full implications cannot yet be determined. I take it that the successful installation of this split is a precondition for the flourishing of democracy. Moving on to a form of philosophising that is not esoteric and exclusive would be one mark of the actualising of democratic ideals.

PHILOSOPHY, POLITICS, TIME

Heidegger's lectures from 1935, his *Introduction to Metaphysics*,[10] are notorious for containing the phrase: 'the inner truth and greatness of the National Socialist movement'. There is at best confusion about this remark:[11] whether it was read out; when it was composed; whether it represents a break with Nazism or an affirmation.[12] A charitable interpretation suggests that Heidegger saw the development of Nazism in 1935 already as a disappointment of his hopes for national regeneration. Jürgen Habermas has consistently challenged Heidegger's stance on Nazism and one of his earliest publications is a response to the unremarked republication of this phrase in 1953, in the context of Heidegger's refusal to make any other public statement concerning Nazism.[13] Habermas rightly contests this sleight of hand of both responding and not responding to Nazism. However, Habermas's own position relies on an anthropology implicit in German idealism, which Heidegger reveals to be part of the problem to be analysed. Habermas develops his response to Heidegger in his later essay 'Work and *Weltanschauung*: The Heidegger controversy from a German perspective',[14] written as a preface to the German translation of Farias's *Heidegger and Nazism*. Habermas suggests that the endorsement of National Socialism in 1933 twists an individualism of *Being and Time* towards a fascist collectivism. I shall return to this in the final chapter of this study.

By contrast with 1953, the connection between Heidegger and Nazism is now widely discussed. The *Rektoratsrede* of May 1933, given by Heidegger as the newly appointed Nazi Rector of Freiburg University, various additional materials by Heidegger,[15] and the posthumously published *Spiegel* interview can now easily be found in translation.[16] There are now many discussions in English of the relation between Heidegger's political statements and his philosophy along- side three early studies, two in German and one in French, of the relation between Heidegger's thinking, his political thought and his conceptions of history.[17] There is an outstanding book by Rainer Schuerman on the political implications of antifoundational thinking, *Heidegger: From Principles to Anarchy* (1986).[18] There are detailed discussions of the connections between Heidegger's philosophy and the *Rektoratsrede* by Derrida and Lacoue-Labarthe who, while disagreeing with each other, identify Heidegger's susceptibility to Nazism as enmeshed in his capacity to teach us how to identify and resist fascism.[19] Both identify Heidegger's proximity to Nazism as more instructive about the eruption of fascism in Europe in this century than any amount of analysis of degrees of moral failure. For Derrida, Heidegger's endorsement of Nazism is an aberration from the critique of metaphysical generalisation and of humanism, which he takes to be a central component of Heidegger's thought. For Lacoue-Labarthe, Heidegger's endorsement of Nazism in 1933, and his use of the terminology of *Being and Time* in the *Rektoratsrede*, is 'neither an accident, nor a mistake'.[20] Both accept that Heidegger in 1933 is eager to appear unambivalently committed to the Nazi cause. For both, Heidegger's thinking poses a problem about the relation between philosophy as metaphysics and political engagement.

I shall not be discussing these readings; nor shall I discuss the debates concerning the degree of Heidegger's involvement in Nazism, since, whatever the degree of his involvement, there is in my view no necessary consequence for the status of his writings; nor any necessary corruption ensuing in the reader of those writings. Whatever the lack of frankness in his accounts after the war about the degree of his involvement, Heidegger's writings remain also philosophical texts – not simply texts in a legal process, given over to assessing guilt. My concern in this study is not with assessing degrees of personal culpability or degrees of fascist inclination in the works of Heidegger. I do not know how such judgements might be made. I am concerned with a relation between ethics and metaphysics in Heidegger's thought, and I shall discuss the political questions raised by this relation, but not the political, historical, biographical questions about Heidegger's affiliations. These questions take for granted a set of relations between politics and philosophical enquiry, and assume an understanding of what politics is, which Heidegger's work brings into question. I shall distinguish between two questions of politics which the issue of Heidegger's Nazism tends to obscure. There is a moral question about whether someone who makes un-acceptable political judgements can engage in philosophical thought, with its traditional objects of enquiry: beauty, goodness and truth. There is also a con-ceptual question about the conditions of possibility for political activity and political identities in the modern world. By distinguishing between these two questions it is possible to show that while Heidegger may be open to condem-nation in terms of the first, he also makes a vital contribution to the development of thinking about the second.

I think that it is possible to read and admire Heidegger without subscribing to all of Heidegger's commitments. Indeed, I think it might have been possible to be Heidegger, the thinker, without subscribing to all of Heidegger's commitments. Some of those commitments seem to me to be not just independent of his thinking, but at times even in conflict with that thought. I am then thus far in agreement with Lacoue-Labarthe, who writes in *Heidegger, Art and Politics* (pp. 100–1):

> I do not subscribe to the thesis of European identity nor to that of the homogeneity of the West, nor indeed to that of the unicity-singularity of the History of Being. . . . I no more believe in the phantasy of a 'proper/own body' of Europe than I do in the fiction of the people as work of art.

I would go on to question whether the formulation 'the unicity-singularity of the History of Being' makes sense, although I appreciate that Heidegger writes as though there were such singleness. A singularity is perhaps evident in the recep-tion of that history, but that does not prove this history of being to be a single structure. Indeed, it would seem possible to predicate neither singleness nor plurality to the history of being, which is both *Seinsgeschick*, the destiny or sendings of being, and *Seinsgeschichte*, the history of being resulting from those sendings. This history of being consists in understandings of the sendings of being, constructed from certain points within that double process.

I have a version of the same problem with respect to the supposed history of metaphysics, which, quite unlike the history of being, is not a self-sustaining series. It is one which is dependent on extraneous conditions of possibility. The use of the term 'history' for both a history of being and a history of metaphysics reveals an irreducible duplicity in the term 'history'. This duplicity is grounded in the ontological difference between being and what there is. There is a *Seinsgeschick*, which is a complete historical process, but not given to us in its completeness. There is also what arrives as a result of this *Seinsgeschick*, as history, which is available to us but is not complete. There is thus a kind of history that can be narrated, identifying incidents, forces at work and significant relations. There is another kind of history that can only be experienced, with a sense of a set of forces not just above and beyond human control but also above and beyond human comprehension. Heidegger diagnoses the age of technical relations as one in which these forces above and beyond human comprehension and control are presented as controllable by human beings, generating a potentiality for catastrophe on a global scale indicated on the individual scale in the fate of Oedipus. Through the erasure of the difference between these two processes, the plural sendings of being are being reduced to a single framework, a *Gestell*. Heidegger supposes that the completion of this process will bring with it unprecedented disaster, with no possibility of a re-emergence in a new beginning.

The splitting of the notion of history connects up to a distinction between metaphysics, which provides answers to the question of the being of beings, *die Frage nach dem Sein des Seienden*, and Heidegger's thinking, which responds (*entspricht*) to the claim (*Anspruch*) of being and has as its focus the question of being, *die Seinsfrage*. The first kind of history is metaphysically grounded, or at least carries various metaphysical commitments which can be made explicit. The second is entwined within the conditions that destabilise metaphysical commitment and prompt the need for self-questioning and for a questioning of relations between individuals and forces above and beyond their control. This latter form of enquiry I consider to be a form of ethical questioning, in positing an excess beyond the scope of its own competence. Metaphysical construction pronounces itself competent to survey and include all relations within the system constructed, even though those systems are always open to subversion by the forces posited by ethics as always in excess. There is an inverse problem for ethical enquiry, which, while attempting to hold itself open to both an acknowledged and an unacknowledgeable other, nevertheless tends to reduce the latter to the former, and therefore to reimpose metaphysical oppositions in place of ethical differentiation. Out of this series of distinctions, there arises a further distinction between different kinds of politics. Metaphysical political thinking focuses on conceptions of sameness, of predictability and of fixity. Ethical political thinking makes difference, the unexpected and alterability central. Within the latter, Heidegger himself shifts from supposing, in the 1933 *Rektoratsrede* and in the 1936 essay 'On the origin of the work of art', that political agency can hasten the emergence of a new opening for politics, to supposing that it is necessary to wait for an opening to take place within which a new order might emerge. This is the moment of acquiescence signalled in the later lecture *Gelassenheit* (1959)[21] and in the *Spiegel* interview.

There is an important difference between the temporal structure of metaphysical construction and that of ethical thought. For Heidegger, metaphysics has no future because it has come to an end. However, if metaphysics now has no future, it will always have been going to have no future, and thus will always have had a strange relation to history and time, which for Heidegger are marked by an openness to the future. While Heidegger can write about a 'history of metaphysics', it is a strange kind of history which at some point can come to an end. This 'end' poses the question of the 'beginning' of metaphysics. I suggest that it is only through a relation to the future that a moment of beginning can be specified; and that a relation to the future presupposes an ethical stance. Heidegger's identification of a beginning for philosophy among the Greeks is possible only on the basis that he declares philosophy to be coming to an end, making possible a new beginning and a different vision of the future. There is a contrast to be noted between metaphysics and this history of metaphysics that can be declared to be at an end, when viewed from the stance of an ethical commitment to a different kind of future. Metaphysics is a constant possibility for human thinking, which can be overcome through a transformation of what it is to be human, but which cannot be brought to an end. I suggest that metaphysics has neither beginning nor end, neither future nor past, nor indeed strictly speaking a history at all. Heidegger supposes that metaphysical construction has worked through a sequence of necessary stages culminating in the emergence of subjectivity as the standard for truth, identity and for theories of what there is. This sequence would logically culminate in the annihilation of human beings, who, as conditions of possibility for metaphysical construction, threaten to become superfluous checks on the articulation of systems of technical possibility. The completion of that system of technical relations requires the erasure of the ethical concerns which human beings bring with them to their involvement in metaphysical and technical relations. The future of human beings depends on preventing the completion of the processes at work in the transition from metaphysical construction to the full actualisation of metaphysical system in technical relations.

There are concealed ethical conditions of possibility for metaphysical construction. This relation provides a rewriting of Heidegger's perplexing descriptions of the revealing which is also a concealing. These ethical conditions are concealed and erased by metaphysical construction but reveal themselves again when that metaphysical construction becomes unstable. One central aspect of these ethical conditions of possibility, viewed from the human point of view, is that there be human beings. In technical relations the concealed conditions of possibility for metaphysical construction are to be erased. This constitutes the difference between metaphysics, as always unstable since reliant on a set of conditions in excess of itself, and technical relations, which project infinitely into an empty future. Thus the logic of actualising metaphysics as technology implies the elimination not of some but of all human beings, since human beings form a condition of possibility for metaphysical construction which in technical relations is to be erased. To prevent this logic of actualisation completing itself, a retrieval of ethics is urgently needed. Metaphysical questioning attempts to set out a view which is not specific to human beings; as though there were no point of emergence, no thinking process out of which it arises, no human being as the physical site for the occurrence of a thinking process, no history. In its most extreme form, the relation between what there is and history becomes that of Heidegger's distinction between the *Gestell*, the rigid givenness of entities, which he takes to be predominant in the modern epoch, and the *Ereignis*, the sudden decisive event of it emerging in that way. Heidegger sets out these two elements in his postwar thinking as sharply disjointed, disconnected one from the other, but he does not remark that this extremity of disjunction is itself a symptom of the context he is diagnosing: the actualising of metaphysics in the spread of technical relations throughout the world. Because the contemporary world is the domain of *Gestell*, of the rigid framework, the thought of transformation appears strange, external and utterly unimaginable, an unknown *Ereignis*. The thought of a trans-formation inaugurating some more human future is blocked off. Access to the future, the temporal dimension privileged in *Being and Time* above present and past, is blocked. In revealing this, Heidegger reveals the suspension of the ethical dimension in metaphysical construction; he performs a reduction of ethics and reveals our ethical need.

Heidegger's history of metaphysics is a history which has a dynamic external to itself, constituted by Heidegger's ethical commitment to anticipating a new beginning. Thus, this history of metaphysics is not complete in itself. The transition from one epoch of being to another is not internal to the relations specified within metaphysics. The transition from one metaphysical formation to another is not interiorised in the articulations of the history of metaphysics. In parallel to this, metaphysical construction takes place within history but as though detached from historical process. There is no recognition at the moment of metaphysical construction that there are restricted conditions of possibility for that metaphysical construction. However, in his claim that these conditions no longer pertain, Heidegger reveals the historically limited nature of metaphysical construction, and reveals that such construction was never purely metaphysical, since it had particular historical conditions of possibility. Unconditional meta-physical construction has always been impossible. There must be a form of dwelling, a way of existing, an *ethos*, if there is to be philosophy and if meta-physical construction is to take place. That way of existing cannot get taken up into the metaphysical system without reserve and thus becomes an undeclarable condition of possibility for systems for which completeness is claimed, but which cannot account for the claim and therefore cannot be complete.

The pastness of metaphysics as a past that does not lead into a future is suggested by Heidegger himself. He proposes '*Die Vergangenheit der Meta-physik*', literally 'the gone-by-ness of metaphysics', as a better title for the notes he published as 'Overcoming metaphysics', in *Vorträge und Aufsätze* (1954).[22] In the preface, Heidegger distinguishes between an open past, connecting up into a present and a future, *Gewesendes*, and a completed past, *Vergangenheit*. Heidegger writes of this opening: 'Paths of thought, for which the past is indeed past [*Vergangenes zwar Vergangen*], while what is in process of having been [*Gewesendes*] all the same remains to come, wait until whenever thoughtful people go down them' (*VA*: 7). These paths of thought make it possible to detach what is still in process from what is over and done with. Metaphysics concerns itself with the completable and completed. Thinking is concerned with the open-ended processes still in play. For Heidegger, these potentialities laid down in the past can be retrieved and released into the future. Metaphysics, then, has definitively moved away into the past; it is not we human beings who have overcome metaphysics. However, metaphysics must always have been marked by this pastness, by a non-simultaneity with the here and now. This opens up a difference between the present as the here and now, in contrast to the future and to the past, and the present as a domain in which all relations are constructed. Metaphysical construction, by attempting to create a present as that in which all relations are contained, turns that present into a completed past. This present as completed past constructed by metaphysics is always closed off and not given in the here and now; and it does not open up into a future. In metaphysical construction the here and now is reified as an eternal unchanging present, thus erasing the difference between the two kinds of present and erasing both future and past. Metaphysical construction erases the difference between presence or perdurance, *ständige Anwesenheit*, and the present as a moment in the flux of time; it sets up that perdurance as capable of defying the erosions of time and the effects of the transition from moment to moment. The metaphysical model of time is one of a life viewed after death by other people. The processes are complete and definitive judgements are made. The ethical model is that of the living process itself, as marked by the irrecuperable moment of death. The former is a disowned model, where the stance from which the construction takes place is not taken up into the model constructed. The death is the death of the other. The latter is an ethical model. The former acquires the appearance of completeness by not attempting to account for its own possibility; the latter is emphatically incomplete and incompletable, but does address the question of its possibility.

I suggest that Heidegger does not celebrate an already achieved overcoming of metaphysics but diagnoses a need for such an overcoming, if human beings are to flourish. If the question of ethics is to be linked to the question of human flourishing, then such a question can be responded to only in the future anterior tense, when it will have been shown that human beings have continued to flourish. The question of ethics would then be irreducibly futural and equally irreducibly connected to the question: what is it to be human? Heidegger opens out the question, what is it to be human? He disconnects it from any determinate answer, as given in the various humanisms grounded in philosophical anthropology, that is in generalised theories of what it is to be human. Heidegger proposes that there can be no definitive answer to the question. It is a question which must be lived, in the form of the being which has its being to be, and which bears a relation to that being. Thus the question, what is it to be human?, is also irreducibly futural. The question of ethics, as a question raised for human beings, is irreducibly futural in two respects: both with respect to the future flourishing of human beings and with respect to the futurity of the experience of what it is to be human. Thus the question of ethics seems to be ineradicably marked by the temporal inflection 'not yet'. My readings of Heidegger's texts seek to challenge the suggestion that the question of ethics is therefore to be indefinitely postponed until the impossible time when it will have been shown whether or not human beings have continued to flourish, when what it is to be human might have been revealed through currently existing human beings experiencing as individuals or indeed as groups what it is to be human. I seek to distinguish between a logic of expectation presuming a knowledge of what that flourishing might be and of what it is to be human and a logic of anticipation for which no such knowledge is available. The latter logic presumes that it is necessary, in the absence of such knowledge, for human beings to behave as though it were going to be true that human beings will have continued to flourish. My claim is that it is possible to reject the logic of expectation without rejecting the logic of anticipation. Indeed only through a logic of anticipation is it possible to open out the ethical dimension of thought which I shall argue accompanies any metaphysical construction whatsoever.

This distinction between a logic of expectation and a logic of anticipation draws on Heidegger's own distinction in *Being and Time* between a stance of expectation (*Erwarten*) and a stance of anticipation (*Vorlaufen*) with respect to the future. The stance of expectation closes off that future and renders it a continuation of processes already dominant in the past and present; the latter stance opens the future up to the possibility of radical transformation. However, for all his insistence in *Being and Time* on the priority of the temporal dimension of futurity over presentness and pastness, in the 1930s Heidegger emphasises the dimension of having been as a correction to a metaphysical insistence on the present. This correction tends to elide the question of the future: the 'will have been' of the future anterior tense. However, the forgetting of being, which Heidegger identifies as resulting from a will to metaphysical construction, is no more one-sided than an insistent commemoration of being, which would be evident in a pure ethics. The opposition between forgetting and commemoration with respect to the past opens up a conflict between attitudes which it is possible to take up with respect to the future and with respect to the present. My argument is that philosophical enquiry and indeed human existence flourish only when the two extreme stances, a pure forgetting, towards which metaphysics tends, and a pure commemoration, gestured towards in the silences of poetic thinking, in which ethics comes to its purest form of expression, are held in balance.

I understand the end of philosophy as announced by Heidegger as the end of a cycle of philosophising that returns philosophy to a source at which an originary division between metaphysics and ethics takes place. Such a return presumes a return of being. However, that source is not some aboriginal historical event, but an everyday event in which distinctions are set out by people in their thinking and speaking. The return of being does not presuppose a return to some past origin. It is a retrieval in the present of that present as the moment at which distinctions are made. While Heidegger's talk of a completion of metaphysics in the twentieth century suggests that this return is particular to this century, I am inclined to think that such returns are recurrent and not unique. However, I take it that Heidegger is right in thinking that the return to this origin taking place in the current epoch puts metaphysics radically in question. For Heidegger, this disruption of metaphysics makes itself evident in, among other relations, the changing relation between philosophical enquiry and the tradition out of which it emerges. The overcoming of metaphysics makes ready for a new beginning, but Heidegger is increasingly pessimistic about it taking place. Notoriously, he supposed in 1933 that the Nazi upsurge was such a new beginning. He saw his error and surmised in the posthumously published *Spiegel* interview: 'only a god can save us'. This remark, mocked as hopelessly inadequate by some, picks up on a connection suggested in the 'Letter on humanism' (1947) between a loss of sense for divinity and the forgetting of the question of being. This language concerning the absent gods and the withdrawal of being makes it possible for Heidegger to identify a dislocation in what it is to be human.

While Heidegger seems to anticipate a reaffirmation of locatedness for human being, it may be possible that an ethical retrieval will require a dislocation of the presumption that human being should have a sense of belonging to particular geographical locations, with particular gods for particular communities. In the 'Letter on humanism', Heidegger writes:

> The home of historical living is closeness to being. In this closeness, there would emerge, if at all, the decision if and how god and the gods deny themselves and night remains; or how a day of healing might dawn; if and how, with the rise of this healing, an appearance of god and the gods can begin anew. This healing, however, which is only the space for the existence of divinity and which itself preserves the space for gods and the god, can come into appearance only if already and for a long time of preparation being itself has illuminated itself and been experienced in its truth. Only in this way would there begin out of being the overcoming of the homelessness, in which not only human beings but the essence of human being now wanders about. (*WM*: 335)

This healing is a making whole of a split constitutive of the Western philosophical tradition between questions about what there is and questions about how human beings are to flourish. This healing would make possible an overcoming of the sense of homelessness, which human beings experience when they can make no connection between what there is and their own existence, when there is no connection between metaphysical enquiry and questions of ethics. Heidegger writes of this healing in terms of a return of the gods and an affirmation of a relation to being. A return of being would bring a healing and overcoming, in a new relation between order and disorder, between change and renewal. It would reveal a transformation of what is it to be human. This would be a retrieval of ethics. This retrieval is not yet in evidence, but I hope to show that Heidegger makes a major contribution to opening out a domain of ethical questioning by revealing the obstruction preventing us from asking what it is to be human. He does this both explicitly and indirectly, and I shall show how he himself blocks the question of what is it to be human at a number of critical points in his thinking.

Heidegger's enquiries after the publication of *Being and Time* appear to turn away from ethical issues towards the questioning of metaphysics, away from the question of being, towards the question: why is there something rather than nothing? However, this second question opens out the question of freedom, which Heidegger explores in the papers and lectures from 1929 on, starting with 'On the essence/emergence of grounding/reason', 'Vom Wesen des Grundes'.[23] Freedom becomes a condition of possibility for ontological difference making itself known, opening up a gap between what is given and how it comes to be like that. Freedom becomes the site at which the difference between questioning entities and having a sense of being becomes available. Thus a theme central to ethics, freedom, here appears to be transferred out of the domain of ethics into the domain of abstract ontological enquiry. This can also been seen as revealing the ethical nature of ontology. From this essay, Heidegger goes on to discuss both Kant's and Schelling's analyses of freedom, leading into his lectures on Nietzsche. In between, in the 1935 lectures *Introduction to Metaphysics* (1953), Heidegger diagnoses a moment of violence in the constitution of any new world order, in his reading of the uncanny place of the apolitical in Sophocles' *Oedipus*. In Chapter 5, I discuss the relation Heidegger sets out between violence, homelessness and the uncanny, in relation to such a founding moment in which order is revealed.

This relation of extremity is not open to general inspection; and I neither suppose I have reached the site of such extremity, nor do I hope to derive from it a set of substantive ethical theses suited for contemporary conditions. However, I think it true that in the Nazi death camps the European tradition arrived at such a point of extremity; I am not convinced that we have managed to re-emerge. My central contention is that there is an urgent need for a retrieval of the notion of ethics, which is under way but not yet completed, and that there are elements of it to be found in Heidegger's work. This retrieval is needed if there is to be such a re-emergence. What I hope to show is that, as a result of an extreme refusal of an ethical problematic in Heidegger's thinking, it is to that extent possible to read it as a site for a retrieval of ethics. However, ethical construction is a collective undertaking; it is metaphysical construction which gives the appearance of being accomplished by isolated individuals independent of community. Thus, I cannot provide a definitive statement of what that transformation might consist in. The guiding thought of this enquiry is taken from the 1949 introduction to the 1929 lecture 'What is metaphysics?': 'the essencing of metaphysics is something other than metaphysics' – '*das Wesen der Metaphysik* [*ist*] *etwas anderes . . . als die Metaphysik*' (*WM*: 363). The use of 'essencing' here to translate '*Wesen*' captures two aspects of Heidegger's term: that it is verbal and that this notion of essence is one of process not of substantive states. I thus claim that this 'something other than metaphysics' is not, as Heidegger would seem to have his readers believe, '*das Sein*' or '*das Nichts*', 'being', or 'nothing', as the obverse of a realm of entities, of what there is, of *Seiendes*. This 'something other' is the possibility of a different stance in relation to what there is, a recognition of its temporary nature, in contrast to a false metaphysical presumption that its status is one of permanence. This is the human stance of finitude, not the impossible stance of eternity.

It becomes possible to suggest that it is not just human existence which is a temporary state. Both what it is to be human and the status of what there is can be seen as temporary and in transition. The difference between an ethical and a metaphysical form of questioning then becomes one of recognising or refusing to recognise the transitory nature of what is to be theorised; ethical questioning makes available in theories of what there is a recognition of its alterability. This alterability according to Heidegger results from shifts in the sendings of being, the *Seinsgeschick*. This alterability makes it possible for there to be different answers in different epochs to the metaphysical questions: what is there? what is truth? what is identity? Refusing the possibility of such shifts makes it completely mystifying how there could be distinct metaphysical systems which construe what there is in drastically different and incompatible ways. If an interdependence between metaphysical questioning and ethics is denied, then ethics is the other which, by its absence, constitutes the essence of metaphysics. Life is taken for granted and wholly subordinated to the ramifications of reasoning; life becomes the unaddressed condition of possibility for philosophical enquiry. Life, when subordinated to reason, becomes technical and monstrous. In this context, the only way in which life can make itself felt is as death; and if individuals fail to construct a relation to their own individual deaths, then there is an ever widening opening for the development of the kind of man-made mass death to which Wyschogrod, in her study *Spirit in Ashes: Hegel, Heidegger and Man-made Mass Death*, draws attention.[24] The denial of any interdependence between ethics and metaphysics is taken to its limit in the actualising of metaphysics as technology, in which human responsibility is elided to the utmost degree in favour of a logic of technical development. This erasure of human responsibility in all its deficiency, however, is still a question of responsibility. There is still in this erasure a question of ethics at work and there is still a question about the flourishing of human beings. 'I was only following orders' is still an ethical stance, although evidently a deficient one. Once an interdependence between metaphysics and ethics is accepted, then ethics becomes a way of developing an understanding of multiplicity and alterability, by contrast with metaphysics as the site for the construction of singleness and fixity. Ethics becomes the other of metaphysics and thus definitively disrupts metaphysics. Ethics as the other of metaphysics is then not a single other, mutually interdependent with and definitively distinguishable from metaphysics. It is an other which disrupts and displaces all such stable opposition.

An ethical questioning is distinct from a metaphysical one, in eliciting not a single answer but multiple responses. Ethical questioning is essentially relational, making reference back to the questioner as well as to the process of questioning. The identity of the questioner is in question in ethical questioning. This, however, is also true of the fundamental ontology set out in *Being and Time*; and it is to this theme in *Being and Time* that I shall work back in the course of this book. Ethical questioning is concerned with the processes at work within questioning itself. It is concerned as much with its own conditions of possibility as with providing analysis of any preselected problem. Ethical questioning works backwards, analytically, to reveal its own conditions of possibility. Metaphysical questioning, by contrast, is concerned with producing a result, with an end posited as independent of the process of enquiry. Thus metaphysical enquiry has the form of *poiesis*, leaving the identity of the questioner unquestioned; by contrast, ethical enquiry has the form of *praxis*, transforming the identity of the enquirer. If completable, metaphysical questioning would result in a simple, transparent, perlucid structure, graspable in its entirety. This is the *Durchsichtigkeit* of Heidegger's *Being and Time*. Appearances to the contrary, this result cannot be attained, since the appearance of perlucid simplicity is achieved at the cost of denying and concealing the ethical conditions of possibility for there being enquiry at all. These ethical conditions of possibility demonstrate themselves in *Being and Time* as the irreducible ambiguity, facticity and fallenness of *Dasein*. The reduction of ethics in metaphysical systems is demonstrated in the irresponsibility characteristic of technical systems and in the ethical failings of Heidegger's preoccupation in the 1930s with constructing a history of metaphysics while affirming the Nazi state.

RETRIEVING PHILOSOPHY

In *Being and Time* (1927), both the terms 'ethics' and 'metaphysics' appear in inverted commas. While 'metaphysics' loses its inverted commas in the inaugural lecture, 'What is metaphysics?', (1929),[25] 'ethics' does not get put in question in this way.[26] My claim is that this bracketing of ethics reveals all the more powerfully the relation between philosophy, metaphysics and ethics. The epigraph for this chapter is taken from the lecture, 'What is metaphysics?' It is Heidegger's translation of a section from Plato's dialogue, the *Phaedrus* (279a), which might more usually be rendered as: 'for by nature, friend, the human spirit exists within philosophising'. It makes a connection between human being and the occurrence of philosophy. Between this inaugural lecture and the late lecture 'The end of philosophy and the task of thinking' (1964),[27] Heidegger changes his view of the state of philosophy, from affirming an interdependence with human being to declaring that its possibilities have been exhausted. Heidegger states in that later lecture: 'Philosophy is metaphysics', and questions: 'What does it mean that philosophy in the present age has entered its final stage?' There is a shift here from the earlier questioning of metaphysics, in order to retrieve the philosophical tradition in a new beginning, to exploring a 'task for thinking', an *Aufgabe*, which is the giving up (*aufgeben*) of metaphysics. However, Heidegger recognises that if this thinking is predicated on an overcoming (*Überwindung*) of metaphysics, then metaphysics has not yet been surrendered. This overcoming of metaphysics seems to be proposed from a stance outside metaphysics, but such a stance presupposes the coherence of metaphysics, outside of which it supposedly lies. Thus Heidegger thinks instead in terms of recovering from metaphysics (*Verwindung*). He writes in the slightly earlier 1962 paper 'On Time and Being': 'To think being without beings means: to think being without regard to metaphysics. Yet a regard to metaphysics still prevails even in the intention to overcome metaphysics. Therefore our task is to cease all overcoming, and leave metaphysics to itself.'

In this study, I defend Heidegger's earlier view of philosophy against the later one by disputing his identification of philosophy with metaphysics. Instead, I identify a repressed ethical dimension in Heidegger's enquiries and indeed in all metaphysical construction. This opens up a gap between what for Heidegger appears to be one and the same event: the recovery from, or overcoming of, metaphysics and the ending of philosophy. For my reading of Heidegger, the critique of humanism and the related discussion of anthropology are central. This brings my enquiry into close proximity with that of Michel Haar in his study *Martin Heidegger et l'essence de l'homme* (1990).[28] However, the relation between ethics and metaphysics in Heidegger's thinking is not explicitly an issue for Haar, who is more concerned with Heidegger's questioning of what it is to be human. Haar points out that Heidegger, in the introduction to the text 'What is metaphysics?' added in 1949, links a transformation of metaphysics with a change in the essence of what it is to be human:

> So long as human beings remain the *animal rationale*, they are the *animal metaphysicum*. So long as human beings understand themselves as the rational creature, metaphysics, in accordance with Kant's observation, belongs to the nature of human beings [*zur Natur des Menschen*]. However, a thinking which could go back into the ground of metaphysics would bring with it a change in the essence of human beings [*Wandel des Wesens des Menschen*], with which change a transformation of metaphysics would commence. (*WM*: 363)

The important shift here is from writing in terms of a fixed metaphysical '*Natur des Menschen*' to writing in terms of what I would term a mobile, negotiable, ethical '*Wesen des Menschen*'. The metaphysical animal has a fixed nature, whereas the human nature to come would be mobile, a developing process. In this same lecture, Heidegger also remarks: 'Metaphysics remains the first element of philosophy. It does not arrive at the first element of thinking. Metaphysics is overcome in the thinking of the truth of being' (*WM*: 363). I dispute this insistence that metaphysics is the first element of philosophy, and I dispute this diagnosis of a shift from philosophy to thinking. If the first element of philosophy is taken to be a relation between ethics and metaphysics, then Heidegger's thesis about the end of philosophy is disrupted, in favour of the thought that the transformation of metaphysics and of what it is to be human leads into a retrieval of ethics.

For Heidegger, philosophy has come to an end with the fracturing of the tradition, grounded in classical Athens, in which it took shape. Metaphysics has reached the last form in a sequence starting with Greek thinking; it has become homeless and is being disseminated throughout the world. It has lost its ethical ground in the projects of European peoples. The constructs resulting from metaphysical enquiry have become detached from the tradition out of which they emerged and are being disseminated throughout the world through the spread of technical relations which makes real in the world a metaphysical erasure of difference between abstract possibility and reality. The powers accumulated through metaphysical questioning and through scientific developments are no longer the prerogative of a particular segment of the human race; they no longer take place within territorial or sectarian lines of demarcation. The completion of metaphysics and the end of philosophy occur in the form of a relation to the world in which ethical specificity has been abolished. The history of metaphysics then contains an implicit ethical commitment to a Euro-Christian will to superiority. With the universalisation of the scope of technology, there ceases to be any such differentiating effect in the will to power contained in the elaboration of technology. Euro-Christian superiority is abolished and this will to power loses its ground and becomes nihilistic. For Heidegger, the last form of metaphysics is Nietzsche's inversion of the Platonic privilege of a domain of ideas over a domain of the senses. This view of Nietzsche is developed in the Nietzsche lectures given between 1936 and 1942, first published in part in the *Nietzsche* volumes of 1961, and then in the complete works.[29] The 1951–2 lectures *What is Called Thinking?*[30] continue the analysis by developing a relation between Nietzsche and Parmenides, marking a connection between a beginning and an end of the philosophical tradition.

For Heidegger, Nietzsche is a metaphysician since, in the notions of will to power and eternal return, Nietzsche, in Heidegger's view, proposes a theory of truth and of identity. Nietzsche is the last metaphysician, since the valorising of a domain of the senses over any domain of ideas leads into the abolition of the difference between ideas and sensations which takes place in technical relations. *Being and Time* is strongly marked by a reading of Nietzsche. Heidegger subsequently uses Nietzsche's own most distinctive thoughts to reveal the limitations of Nietzsche's critiques of metaphysics and of nihilism, but his readings of Nietzsche in the 1930s and 40s also constitute a response to the failure to complete the enquiry projected in *Being and Time*. In the lectures on Nietzsche, Heidegger imitates Nietzsche's brief account of how the 'true world' became a fable, reducing the history of metaphysics to a series of gnomic words for being. Heidegger thus reveals a process at work in that history, which cannot be taken up into that history, a process which he calls the history, destiny or sendings of being. This permits an understanding of technology as also a sending of being, in which the question of being is displaced by the question, what is it to be human?, and the significance of this second question, as still a question of being, is in turn erased by the presumption that it permits of a generalising answer. In between *Being and Time* and these lectures on Nietzsche, there lies the notorious *Rektoratsrede* of 1933,[31] in which Heidegger endorses Nazism and, in vulgar Nietzschean style, affirms the will to essence of the German university. There are thus at least three phases in Heidegger's response to Nietzsche. However, my concern is not with charting these shifts in Heidegger's readings of Nietzsche but with Heidegger's use of these readings in diagnosing the fate of philosophy in the age of technology.

Heidegger's essay 'Overcoming metaphysics', 'Überwindung der Metaphysik', (1954),[32] arises out of this protracted encounter with Nietzsche's thought. Heidegger identifies technicality, *Technik*, as 'equivalent to the concept of metaphysics completing itself, (*das Wort hier identisch gesetzt mit dem Begriff der sich vollendenden Metaphysik*)', (*VA*: 95). It is important that metaphysics be understood not as an event in accordance with the wishes of human beings, but as self-completing. This completion is an event which takes place above and beyond the control of human beings. It is the event through which philosophy ceases to be a human construct and becomes an objectively functioning system in the world. It ceases to be a practice specific to Europeans and becomes a form of life in which all human beings find themselves involved through the impact that technology has on world ecology. For Heidegger, technical relations are the culmination of the history of philosophy, for they make actual the abstract relations which in metaphysical enquiry are only hypothesised. In technical relations, the distinction between sensations and ideas is erased. Metaphysical system becomes actuality in the permeation of the world by technical relations and by the technological possibilities on which those relations are based. Technical relations erode the difference between abstract structures and everyday life, between formal processes and substantive relations. The everyday thus becomes metaphysical; and metaphysics becomes everyday. The completion of metaphysics in technology is the actualisation, not the abolition of metaphysics: 'metaphysics is now for the first time beginning its unconditional rule in beings themselves, and rules as being in the form of what is real, in the form of objects, lacking a conception of truth' (*VA*: 67). The actualisation of metaphysics in technology leads to the loss of a gap between theory and practice; between theory and what there is. This erases the site at which theories of truth are constructed. There is no third place from which the relation between theory and what there is might be viewed and in which the accuracy of the accounts given of that actuality might be assessed. In the era of technology, the human stance is subordinated to one within a system, such that truth becomes at best a procedural, recursively defined notion. Heidegger claims that in this age of completed metaphysics philosophy becomes anthropology, a theory of what it is to be human: 'Philosophy in the age of completed metaphysics is anthropology' (*VA*: 82). Instead of a theory of truth and of reality, there is a theory of the human stance from which in other circumstances theories of truth and reality might have been developed.

Reality becomes the set of actual and possible technical relations. This claim is developed in the 'Letter on humanism' (1947) and in the 1938 paper 'The age of the world picture' first published in *Holzwege* (1950), but written in 1938.[33]

Heidegger's work, with its emphasis on the predominance of technical relations, reveals an ethical crisis, since actualising metaphysics in technical relations makes these relations the ethical substance of human existence. Heidegger seems to assume that with the withdrawal of being both ethical reflection and moral theory become impossible. Moral theory becomes impossible with the withdrawal of being, since that withdrawal takes with it the possibility of constructing theories of truth, of identity, of individuation and of individuality, which are needed if there is to be a theory of individual agency and responsibility as a condition of possibility for moral judgement. Furthermore, the withdrawal of being leads to a forgetting of being and to the loss of a sense of there being anything other than a domain of facts. However, this withdrawal and forgetting can reveal that human beings and no one else have responsibility for whether or not there is responsible activity in the world. Thus the withdrawal and forgetting of being, while undermining thinking about individuality and about truth, can also reveal the urgency of a revival of ethical reflection. For Heidegger, the end of philosophy fractures the tradition through which such an ethical system might be transmitted. This fracturing of tradition leads him to affirm a vision of a future radically cut loose from both past and present. It leads him to his endorsement of Nazism in the *Rektoratsrede* of 1933, which has an anticipatory structure, privileging a vision of the future over any sense of continuities drawn from an understanding of the past:

> The beginning still is. It does not lie behind us, as something that was long ago, but stands before us. As what is greatest the beginning has passed in advance beyond all that is to come and thus also beyond us. The beginning has invaded our future. There it awaits us, a distant command bidding us catch up with its greatness. (*SB*: 473)

This anticipation is marked by a forgetting of the irreducible claim to recognition of the stranger, which would disrupt any such claim about the greatness of 'our' future.

In the name of some underdefined ideal, an arbitrary set of relations is to be imposed on the present, justified by reference to a version of the past, in order to bring about some supposedly desired future. Politics thus becomes a substitute for an ethical system based in custom and community, conjuring up instead a notion of community out of a vision of some fantastical future. It is a form of ethics in which identity and truth are imposed, rather than permitted to emerge out of human lived relations. This politics is grounded in a metaphysical will to truth and identity, in the absence of any spontaneously generated conceptions of truth and identity. However, in the discussion of Oedipus, in the slightly later *Introduction to Metaphysics*, Heidegger reverses this order. The situation of Oedipus is fateful since it lies outside and in advance of political order, revealing how that order comes into existence. Thus, here there is an ethical relation in advance of setting out any political or metaphysical order and identity. An ethical relation without the order and identity established in community is necessarily destructive; as is an ethics grounded in a pre-given order and identity. In these lectures, Heidegger writes of the *polis* as: 'the there, wherein and as which historical being there [*Dasein*] is. The *polis* is the historical place, the there in which, out of which, for which history happens' (*EM*: 152–3). By suspending the question of ethics, Heidegger opens up the possibility of rethinking the relations between ethics, politics and metaphysics. In this study, I explore Heidegger's suspension of the question of ethics, merely indicating here the implications for thinking about politics. In the space opened up by this questioning it might be possible, in opposition to a grounding of ethics in politics, and of politics in metaphysics, to reverse the order and reveal a grounding for metaphysics in politics, deriving a theory of truth from a theory of a common good; and to ground politics in ethics, deriving a theory of the common good from a theory of human flourishing. This may be the retrieval of Aristotle's thought which Heidegger seeks, but fails to achieve, in *Being and Time*.

I suggest that the ethical crisis marked out by Heidegger's work does not signal an end of philosophy; it signals a shift in the internal dynamic of philosophy. Instead of focusing on a supposed completion of the possibilities of metaphysics, I propose to identify a shift within philosophy, in the relation between metaphysics and ethics. It becomes possible to see this relation as central to philosophy; to see metaphysics and ethics as equally balanced forces in a continuous conflict; and to assert that it is a metaphysical reading of the tradition which insists on endings and completions whereas an ethical reading puts the emphasis on new beginnings and openings. My argument is that Heidegger's thought of a turning and of a new beginning requires both a metaphysical reading of completion and an ethical reading of opening. For the purposes of this discussion, then, ethics is to be distinguished from moral reflection. Unlike moral reflection, ethical enquiry does not presume a universal scope and a focus on the activities of individual human agents. Moral reflection culminates in the abstract moral thinking of Kantian practical philosophy, with its emphasis on universal principles and on constructing criteria for judgement. It connects up to discussions of the legality of law and theories of sovereignty. Ethics, by contrast, is concerned with the formation of individual human beings as the individuals they are, with a connection back to Aristotle's analyses of character formation. Ethical reflection is distinct from moral reflection to the extent that it permits a logic of singularity to work in the formation of principles of action and habits of living. In response to challenge, various kinds of justification may then be offered, of which the moral, universalising move is one; the appeal to tradition another; an appeal to difference a third; and yet another an appeal to expedience. There is also a distinction to be made between an everyday notion of ethical reflection, concerned with what to do next, and a transcendental ethics, concerned with the conditions of possibility for any reflection whatsoever. The question of ethics, while making it possible to pose questions about a relation to an other as similar to self and as different, to pose questions about the nature of value, about the nature of the good life, about principles of judgement and the derivation of moral imperatives, is not reducible to all or any of these. It is the question of the place of ethics in philosophy and the place of abstract reflection in human living.

Ethical enquiry unlike metaphysical enquiry puts in question the humanity at the site at which philosophy emerges. Thus Heidegger's enquiries are for me ethical in the sense that they put this humanity in question. They are meta-ethical in revealing this difference between the ethical and the metaphysical modes of enquiry. I identify metaphysical questioning as concerned with a 'what' of enquiry and ethical questioning as concerned with a 'how'. I take these two to be interdependent, but to be subject to forms of pressure leading to the elimination of one or other dimension. Thus a pure metaphysics seeks to deny that its producer is human, with a particular history; and it seeks to erase any question of the preconditions for enquiry. Metaphysical enquiry represses specificity and conditionality, and its emblem is the *causa sua*, the self-causing cause. Pure ethical enquiry, by contrast, represses generality: indeed it is characterised by silence, for entry into language requires the surrender of the specific. Its emblem is the silence of Abraham, as characterised in *Fear and Trembling*.[34] This silence resonates in the writings of Hölderlin and Nietzsche and constitutes their importance for Heidegger. My reading of Heidegger explores an interdependence between these two stances, the attempt to elide all location in metaphysics and the equally impossible attempt to affirm location in ethics. Neither, taken on its own, is possible, for once a gap has opened up between location and a moment of affirmation, then that location is no longer, if it ever was, secure.

There is a connection here to the inarticulacies of the Heideggerian thematics of the uncanny, homelessness and dwelling. These, roughly speaking, pick out the points at which the irrepressible ethical dimension of enquiry burst through in Heidegger's early, middle and postwar thinking. The notion of the uncanny as an ungrounding homelessness, *Unheimlichkeit*, occurs in *Being and Time*. It results from the experience of anxiety opening out of the encounter with the limits of existence, and introduces the themes of care, meaninglessness and death. This existential reading of the uncanny reinstalls a sense of belonging through the thematics of listening for and responding to the call of being, which turns into the moment of self-constitution. This is discussed in Chapter 6. In the *Introduction to Metaphysics*, this ungroundedness and homelessness is explicitly connected up to a moment of violence and destruction, in a pre-political form of existence given the name 'Oedipus'. This is discussed in Chapter 5. Thus in 1935, the destructive moment of the fracturing of tradition is no longer given the positive role of releasing the repressed and forgotten elements of the philosophical tradition. This destructive moment becomes a constitutive feature of *Dasein*, marking the dangers of an unrestricted quest for self-constitution. Confronting this moment of ungroundedness and homelessness, confronting this potential for a violent, destructive dispersion of the self is the condition for reformulating a relation to ethics. In the postwar writings, Heidegger develops a notion of dwelling through which he seeks to break out of the rigidities imposed on the modern world by technical relations. Heidegger develops the notion of an *Aufenthalt*, a habitation, in which living might become possible. This is juxtaposed in the 'Letter on humanism' to the homelessness which is becoming world destiny. It is developed in some of the papers in *Vorträge und Aufsätze* (1954) into the notion of acquiescence named in the title of the late lecture *Gelassenheit*. This homelessness is the generalisation of nihilism and this connection is discussed in Chapter 3. Heidegger's attempt to read Hölderlin as offering a sense of homecoming is discussed in Chapter 4. These three eruptions of the notion of homelessness mark the unresolved status of the question of ethics in Heidegger's writings.

Heidegger does not ask the question 'what is ethics?' alongside his question 'what is metaphysics?' in 1929. In his paper *Identity and Difference* (1957),[35] discussed in the next chapter, he denies that the questioning of technology is a question of ethics. However, he does raise the question of ethics in the 'Letter on humanism'. He discusses the Heraclitean phrase '*ethos anthropoi daimon*', 'the ethos of human beings is destiny' or 'character is destiny', and concludes:

> If then, in accordance with the basic meaning of the word *ethos*, the name 'ethics' says that it considers the true habitation of human beings [*Aufenthalt des Menschen*], then that thinking which thinks the truth of being as the primary element of human beings, as something which exists, is already an originary ethics. This thinking, then, is not first of all ethics, because it is ontology. (*WM*: 353)

The puzzle is why Heidegger presumes that ontology is not ethics. While Heideggerian ontology is a form of thinking which takes place in advance of a division within philosophy into metaphysics and ethics, there is a tendency for this ontology to be reduced to metaphysics, through the tendency to elide the question 'what is it to be human?' In the terms already set up, there is a tendency for location to be elided and for the double questioning of 'what?' and 'how?' to be reduced to the single question: 'what is there?' In the inaugural lecture 'What is metaphysics?' (1929), the focus for attention is no longer the question of being, but instead the question, taken over from Leibniz, 'why is there something rather than nothing?' This shift of focus represses the ethical dimension of the concern, but it is a repression which culminates in 1938 in the analysis of technical relations as the current mode of arrival of being. In this most extreme form of the forgetting of being, philosophy is reduced to anthropology. The analysis thus reveals a new, if inadequate, form of ethics: the transformation of what it is to be human in response to technical relations. In this way an initial repression of ethics gives way to the revealing of a new, if inadequate, form of ethics: the subordination of human beings to the requirements of technology.

In his lectures on Leibniz, *The Metaphysical Foundations of Logic* (1928), which are contemporaneous with the inaugural lecture, Heidegger also raises the question of ethics. In these lectures Heidegger juxtaposes ethics and metaphysics on two occasions.[36] On the first occasion, he states: 'The understanding of being forms the basic problem of metaphysics as such' (*MFL*: 136); and he then elaborates:

> The understanding of being is to be brought to light by way of *Dasein's* mode of being, which is primarily existence. The constitution of *Dasein's* being is such that the intrinsic possibility of the understanding of being, which belongs essentially to *Dasein*, becomes demonstrable. The issue is therefore neither one of anthropology nor of ethics but of this being in its being as such and thus one of a preparatory analysis concerning it; the metaphysics of *Dasein* itself is not yet the central focus.

This first reference to ethics invokes a restricted notion of ethics, subordinated to metaphysical or ontological enquiry. This is not the unrestricted notion of ethics towards which I see Heidegger's enquiries tending. The second reference to ethics in the 1928 lectures occurs in an explanation of the relation between ontological enquiry and factical existence, through the introduction of the term 'metontology', transformational ontology. On this second occasion, the phrase in question runs: 'And here also, in the domain of metontological-existential questioning, is the domain of the metaphysics of existence (here the question of an ethics may properly be raised for the first time)' (*MFL*: 157). Thus the metaphysics of existence, as a relation between the generality of ontological enquiry and the specificity of ontical analysis, makes ethical questioning possible. However, Heidegger does not pursue the question of ethics in this context. In *The Metaphysical Foundations of Logic*, Heidegger refers to a *metabole* or *Umschlag*, as the occasion for the transformation of ontology into metontology, without fully explaining what this turnabout might be. In the later writings he invokes a *Kehre* which he failed to perform in *Being and Time*. He writes of this in the 'Letter on humanism':

> An adequate following through of this other thinking, which leaves subjectivity, is all the same made more difficult since, when publishing *Being and Time*, a the third section of the first part, 'Time and Being' was held back (see *SZ*, p. 39.) Here the whole turns itself around. The section in question was held back because the thinking failed to come to language in an adequate speaking of this turn and could not be accomplished with the language of metaphysics. (*WM*: 325)

I suggest it is this turn which Heidegger is trying to invoke through the use of the terms '*Umschlag*', 'metabole' and 'metontology'. Since Heidegger does not develop the term 'metontology' in these lectures and does not use it on any other occasion known to me, I deduce that he was not satisfied with it. Thus in addressing the meaning of the turn, I prefer, in place of this curious relation between fundamental ontology and metontology, to return to the juxtaposition of the terms 'metaphysics' and 'ethics'. Fundamental ontology as an analysis of *Dasein*, offers an account of the site at which being reveals itself. It also invokes the experience of actually existing finite beings. While *Dasein* is the site at which being reveals itself, the site at which *Dasein* reveals itself is human being, individual and collective. Fundamental ontology is thus both ontological, concerned with the general conditions of possibility for existence, and ontical, concerned with the actual existence of human beings. I suggest that the relation between ontology and the ontical marks the relation in Heidegger's thinking between metaphysics and ethics.

In *Being and Time*, Heidegger attempts to reveal a reversal at work, in the relation between *Dasein* and *Sein*. While *Dasein* is what is initially given, he seeks to reveal how *Sein* is nevertheless always already given in advance as that which makes possible the givenness of *Dasein* and the emergence of entities as entities. The problem is that *Dasein* is not fully given; thus *Sein* cannot be shown to be given in advance. Heidegger cannot complete the movement from *Dasein* to *Sein*, so he cannot trace out a process in reverse, starting out from *Sein*. *Dasein* is given in part in the relation of the enquirer to their own determinate existence; and this in turn is revealed by a relation to the individual's death. This relation to one's own death as a limit on the free play of possibility becomes a condition of possibility for the sense of being breaking through into the context of finitude. Thus the relation which was to be produced in the course of the analysis between *Dasein* and *Sein* turns out to be always given in advance, as a condition of possibility for the enquiry itself. A pre-ontological understanding is given to *Dasein* in advance of any systematic thinking. The end of enquiry is thus given before it begins. This for Heidegger is not a vicious but a hermeneutical circle. However, he has enormous difficulty in showing just how the reversal turns this hermeneutical circle from a methodological device into a substantive analysis of the relation in question: hence the incompleteness of *Being and Time*.

At a certain point in the enquiry in *Being and Time*, in a section withheld, or indeed never written, metaphysics converts into ethics; generalising, dislocated analysis reverts into ethical, self-related questioning. Abstract ontological enquiry becomes demonstrably inseparable from the existential commitments of ontical actuality. The question of being reveals and is revealed by the *ethos* of *Dasein*. The converse is shown in the later analyses of technical relations: ethical self-related questioning becomes general and dislocated. It is for this reason that I read Heidegger's texts in inverse chronological order, to work back from a conversion of the lived relations of human beings into rigid structures, into technical relations, back to a conversion of metaphysics into ethics, into fundamental ontology. Heidegger cannot explicitly state these reversals because of the nature of his conception of ethics and because of the problematic status of ethics in the modern context, for which the distinction between metaphysics and ethics is not secure. In the modern context, in place of community-specific conceptions of ethics, ethics has become detached from both religious and political grounding. General answers with universal scope are given to the question 'what is it to be human?' The generalisation of the answers given and the universalisation of the scope of the question evacuate the content of ethics and erase the difference between ethics and metaphysics. Ethics ceases to be a domain for negotiating specific experiences of silence and with the unnameable; it ceases to provide an unacknowledged ground for metaphysical enquiry. This erasure of the difference between ethics and metaphysics is a final move in a cumulative forgetting of being. Metaphysics and ethics become indistinguishable in their simultaneous erasure of the question 'what is it to be human?', and their conversion of human being into the empty ground for the elaboration of the technical transformation of the world. I read Heidegger's texts as revealing this process at work, although he cannot name it as such, since he works with a restricted conception of ethics as concerned only with the relation of human being to being human, instead of the unrestricted notion, needed for identifying these developments for what they are. The unrestricted conception of ethics needed is concerned not just with the relation of human beings to being human but with a relation to difference, to otherness and to being in general. Heidegger, in revealing the universalisation of ethics at work in the globalisation of technology, fails to make clear that this universalised ethics is still only the restricted ethics in which the forgetting of being is erased.

The generalisation and universalisation of ethics threatens to result in a reduction of the question 'what is it to be human?' to a metaphysical fixity, with an abstract definition of what it is to be human taking priority over a lived negotiation with being human. The fixity is more dangerous than other metaphysical fixities, since in the name of ethical differences people are massacred, distinct groups subjected to genocide. Ethics ceases to be a set of questions about what it takes for human beings to flourish, an issue for individuals to confront within whatever specific context of existence. Ethics becomes a set of issues for which there is offered a global, indeed a final, solution in all its horror. This is the culmination of a historical tendency whereby human beings cease to belong to discrete, marked groups and become, like the entities postulated in Greek philosophy, of a single nature, determined in relation to the current sending of being, as technology. This can lead to death for those who are not useful in relation to the needs generated by technical relations and technical processes. The actualising of metaphysics in technology reduces the question of ethics to a question about the nature of human beings in terms of usefulness and productiveness, a question which received a certain kind of answer in the death camps.

Ethical enquiry thus becomes a universalising discourse, in terms of all human beings; conversely, the actualising of metaphysics in technical relations disconnects metaphysics from the non-human domain of eternity, thus restricting metaphysics to human contexts. Thus ethics, by expansion, and metaphysics, by restriction, acquire the same scope. However, metaphysical structures, as technical relations, have become not just an abstract system of concepts, like Leibniz's *Monadology*, but a lived human context. Thus metaphysics, on its completion as technical relations, becomes the place of residence of human beings. It is an inhabited, altering system of relations; it has become ethical. All the same, there is a metaphysical reduction at play in Heidegger's declaration that

only metaphysics is being actualised in technical relations. To avoid such reduction he must also indicate the reification of ethics. This reification generates
a mass-produced form of living, which elides the singularity indispensable for a
fully ethical discourse in which human beings construct a relation to themselves,
to their limits and thereby to others. However, while these relations may be erased
at the level of theory, they still take place at the everyday level. The everyday is
thus both the actualising of metaphysics as technical relations and the ongoing
ethical practices of human self-relation, through which we adapt to these new
conditions. Therefore, viewed as a theoretical structure, technical relations may
be the actualising of metaphysics, but as a lived experience they are a reification
of ethics. To take only the theoretical view is to re-enact the metaphysical
reduction against which Heidegger warns; it conceals the precondition for there
being such a theoretical view: that there be a stance from which analysis is
conducted and from which a choice of a kind is made about what view to take. It
conceals the fact that for good or ill technical relations constitute the main human
habitat. Thus human beings are provided with a kind of habitat, but one which
takes human beings away from their proper point of return: a relation to being, a
location within ontological difference and a relation to identity.

The actualising of metaphysics in technical relations is marked by a dearth of
substantive ethical thinking. For all the proliferation of medical ethics, business
ethics and the ethics of investment, what marks contemporary human life is an
absence in place of a sense of what human living is about. For Heidegger, the
question of ethics much mooted in current work would be a sign of the absence
of ethical thinking, not a sign of return. For Heidegger, a question of ethics can
be posed only in relation to a new principle of order, a new *dike*, in response to a
renewed sending of being, the *Seinsgeschick*, or destiny of being, which is both a
sending of entities and a withdrawal of being. Through this, human beings might
be brought back into relation with the basic constituents of order and disorder.
However, for Heidegger the epoch of technical relations is the epoch in which, in
the presentation of technical relations as all there is, being has withdrawn itself to
the utmost degree, taking with it the possibility of setting out any such new
ordering and any sense of individuation or agency. Human beings cannot construct an ethics in these conditions because there is no way of asking the question
'what is it to be human?' The technological age brings with it a breakdown of the
everyday, traditional ethics of community and a breakdown of the discrete
groupings within which everyday ethics can flourish. The question 'what is it to
be human?' ceases to have a specific location within community and tradition. It
ceases to be a problem for individual groups and communities to work out in
practice. Ethics becomes a general, not a specific form of enquiry, concerned not
with particular kinds of human beings, but with human being in general. This
generality disconnects ethics from actual existence.

In order for technical relations to predominate in the contemporary world,
human beings turn themselves into the kind of creature which can adapt to the
dictates of technical relations. Thus, whatever kind of change in what it is to be

human Heidegger might have anticipated or hoped for, what is actually taking place is this process of self-accommodation. In being taken for granted, this new form of humanity becomes a given rather than a process in the development of which individual human beings play a part and to which we can construct a relation. It becomes a fixed nature rather than a developing process for which individuals can take some responsibility. This reduction of process to fixity and the elision of all sense of responsibility is a reduction of ethics to metaphysics. What is in fact a process of self-transformation is represented as a non-negotiable fact, concealing the evidence of a capacity to respond to circumstances. This conceals the human capacity to respond to and conform to what there is. This generalisation and reduction of the question 'what is it to be human?' plays a fateful role in the Nazi approach to marked groups: the disabled, socialist, gay, Romany and Jewish. It is a generalisation which Heidegger disputes in his critique of philosophical anthropology, *Kant and the Problem of Metaphysics*,[37] published in 1929, four years before the Nazi upsurge. He pursues this critique in the questioning of anthropology and of humanism, which are discussed in Chapters 3 and 4. The actualising of metaphysics as technical relations, like the Nazi upsurge, reveals a problem for conceptions of agency, which can no longer be thought in terms of individuals.

The refusal of these gestures of completion is then to insist that the question 'what is it to be human?' is not susceptible to generalised answers; that the answer to such a question, in so far as there is one, is an experience, not a definition; that what it is to be human is itself not fixed; it is in process of transformation, as much under the influence of these new technical relations as, at any other point in human history, it has been influenced by political context and theological belief. There is still a task for self-transformation to be thought through, but not in the name of either theology or technology. The Nietzschean theme of self-overcoming is also insufficient since individuals are unable to transcend their context for such self-overcoming to be fully conceivable, let alone achievable. The image of *Übermensch* cannot provide a response to the problems posed in a context structured through complex, transcontinental technical relations. Heidegger's conception of *Dasein*, located existence, as both individual and collective reveals this constraint on Nietzschean self-overcoming: the problem of historical constraints which cannot be transformed and overcome at the level of an individually articulated will to power. However, against Heidegger and now in favour of Nietzsche, Nietzsche insistently thematises a relation of human being to itself, whereas there is a troubling displacement in Heidegger's thinking. The self-overcoming of human being promised in the structure of *Dasein* in *Being and Time* becomes the overcoming of metaphysics, as though the overcoming of metaphysics could offer what the *Übermensch* could not: a breakthrough to another beginning. The death of the individual, made central in *Being and Time*, is similarly metamorphosed into the end of philosophy. These moves block the revelation in *Being and Time* of the importance of death, as revealing finitude, not eternity, as the basic mode of temporality. They make it difficult to see in *Being and Time* a critique of Nietzsche's thematics of *Übermensch* and of will to power, without which the Nietzsche lectures of 1936–42 seem one-sided. Both Nietzschean will to power and Heideggerian *Dasein* are moves in a process of displacing a bifurcated view of human beings as the living creature with reason. It is this split which makes human being a metaphysical creature, for whom the duality in conceptions of what it is to be human, as both living and reasoning, is displaced by an elision of the living aspect in favour of the reasoning aspect. Nietzsche reaffirms the aspect of life, through his themes of will to power and eternal return. Heidegger affirms the aspect of death.

In *Being and Time*, Heidegger suggests that retrieving the dimension of life requires a retrieval of a sense of mortality, without which there is no limit to technocratic interference with natural processes. Both Heidegger and Nietzsche are concerned to counteract the subordination of life to abstract reason and the concomitant loss of any sense of what it is to be human. However, this duality can also be overcome through an implementation of technology, erasing the difference by destroying both. Heidegger seeks to reveal the duality and then to transform its overcoming into a positive rather than a nihilistic force. In *Was heißt Deuken?* (1954), Heidegger summarises some of his views on Nietzsche and articulates the question of a split in human being:

> Through this split human beings are prevented from becoming unified in their essence and from becoming free for that which is called the real. Therefore above all this belongs to Nietzsche's way of thinking: to go out beyond the kind of humanity which has occurred up until now, which has not yet attained a stability of essence, to go out into a complete setting out of that full process of essencing which has so far taken place. The thinking of Nietzsche does not at base seek to upset anything, but sets about this retrieval of what has taken place up until now. (*WHD*: 66)

This, I suggest, is also, or perhaps only, a description of Heidegger's work; and in the next two chapters I shall pursue the manner in which Heidegger reads the texts of other philosophers in order to develop his own thinking. Heidegger's analysis centres during the 1930s on a logic of metaphysical construction, culminating, as he sees it, in Nietzschean will to power. Far from being irrelevant to the problems of *Being and Time*, however, these enquiries turn to a more detailed engagement with the philosophical tradition in order to reveal the conditions specific to the context in which the analysis of *Dasein* was broken off.

The actualisation of metaphysics in technical relations has three distinctive features. One is the deepening split between subjective and objective processes. Through the loss of connection and interaction between the two, they become mirror images of each other, reducing human beings to an objective function within technical relations and transforming technical relations into quasi-purposive structures. The second is the detachment of constructive energy from any human emotion, releasing dangerous destructive powers. The third is the systematic way in which what there is can be taken up into technological relations.

There is a vanishing residual domain within which to take up a stance of critique against these processes. In the language of the paper from the 1930s 'The origin of the work of art',[38] the gap between world and earth is vanishing. The principal characteristic of the overcoming of metaphysics in technology is the closure of the gap between what there is and how it comes to be like that, the erasure of ontological difference. This erasure makes it impossible to see what there is as resulting from a complex process in which human beings play some part. Another way of expressing this process is to point out an erasure of the difference between ethics and metaphysics. Heidegger identifies technical relations as foreclosing the question of there being a horizon within which human beings and entities are to be found. That horizon, however, is not a metaphysical structure. It is sent by being, but it comes into view for human beings only if human beings respond to it. Thus a relation to a horizon is an ethical relation; and an erasure of ethics is evident in the erasure of the sense of a horizon within which human beings and entities can be revealed to each other. What there is becomes simply the elaboration of technical systems, with a systematic blocking of access to the question 'how does it come to be like this, and not otherwise?' The horizon within which entities present themselves is obscured, and being, that through which the horizon itself is given, is forgotten, blocking the question 'what is it to be human?'

Heidegger's main claim is that in philosophical enquiry there is a forgetting of the primary issue for philosophy. Heidegger calls this primary issue the question of being, *die Seinsfrage*; and he calls its forgetting *Seinsvergessenheit*, the forgetting of being. He claims that this forgetting has entered an extreme phase in the emergence of technical relations as the primary relation in which human beings and entities are to be found. The dominance of technical relations makes the forgetting of being itself unidentifiable. The task for thinking is to uncover the forgetting of being and to retrieve the question of being. This recovery and retrieval presupposes a critique of metaphysical construction, which sets about providing an answer to a question about the nature of entities, *das Sein des Seienden*, providing answers to the questions 'what is there?' and 'what is truth?', while failing to address the puzzle of there being anything at all. The critique of metaphysics does not lead to an erasure of metaphysics; it specifies the limits within which metaphysics make sense. These limits constitute the horizon of enquiry within which metaphysical construction takes place. The possibility of there being a further question, beyond those addressed in metaphysical enquiry, which both makes the enquiry possible and is erased in the process of enquiry, is itself erased in the modern context, for which a question which cannot be directly answered is defined as nonsensical. This is the basis for the extremity of the forgetting of being in the present epoch. The elimination of unanswerable questions and of ambiguity is a central task for positivism and for philosophy in the age of technology.

Thus, in the age of technical relations, the difference between the question about the nature of entities and the question of being is difficult to mark because the question of being is declared meaningless; and correlatively Heidegger's questioning of nothingness is ridiculed. The presumption that Heidegger's question is meaningless is backed up by reference to his insistence on a central role for violent reading and ambiguity in philosophy. In a letter to William Richardson, in response to the proposed title of his book, 'The way from phenomenology to thinking being', subsequently changed to *Heidegger: Through Phenomenology to Thought* (1963), Heidegger wrote:

> The title is just, if the name 'thinking being', *Seinsdenken*, is drawn from the ambiguity according to which it names both the thinking of metaphysics – the thinking about the being of entities, *das Sein des Seienden*, and also the questioning of being in the sense of a thinking about being as such (the openness of being).[39]

Thus, to write about the question of being it becomes necessary to make productive use of ambiguity. I take this theme of productive ambiguity to be central to developing an understanding of Heidegger's claims concerning the end of philosophy and the completion of metaphysics. This ambiguity, *Zweideutigkeit*, connects up to the duplicity, *Zwietracht*, doubling, *Zwiefalt*, and conversation, *Zwiesprache*, between poet and philosopher, which Heidegger discusses primarily in relation to Hölderlin.[40] This I discuss in Chapter 4. This ambiguity is grounded in the notion of the 'between' structure of human existence: between birth and death in *Being and Time*; between earth and world in the 1935–6 essay 'The origin of the work of art'; between earth and sky and between mortality and divinity in the readings of Sophocles and of Hölderlin.[41]

Two central themes for Heidegger's thought then are the destruction of tradition and the violence of interpretation. One effect of Heidegger's insistence on retrieving a forgetting of being in the philosophical tradition is to reconnect present modes of thinking to the histories from which they have emerged. Paradoxically, Heidegger's thinking also plays a role in cutting philosophy and thinking loose from the tradition from which it has emerged, in his insistence on reading that tradition as completed. That reading of completion depends on his highly controversial manner of reading the texts of the tradition, in which respect and fidelity to the author's meaning are displaced by a violent rending of the text to reveal hidden layers of significance. Heidegger reads against the grain of the text to reveal an 'unthought' concealed from its author. He accepts that this level was not recognised by, and may not even be acceptable to, the supposed author of the text. In his paper 'Overcoming metaphysics' (1954), he invokes his reading of Kant in *Kant and the Problem of Metaphysics* (1929):

> In the first instance, the overcoming of metaphysics can only be represented out of metaphysics itself more or less in the manner of an exaggeration. In this way, the discussion of a metaphysics of metaphysics touched on in the writing *Kant and the Problem of Metaphysics* is justified, in so far as it sought to interpret Kant's thought in this context, although the thought itself still remains within the simple critique of rational metaphysics. Thereby more is

attributed to Kant's thought than he himself sought to think within the bounds of his philosophy. (*VA*: 75)

Heidegger also reads his own writings in this way; and I am proposing a reading of Heidegger of this kind. This then provides some kind of justification for reading Heidegger's writings to reveal a revival of ethics at work in the announcement of an end of philosophy in the completion of metaphysics.

Chapter 2

Reason, grounds, technology

It is superficial to claim that contemporary human beings have become the slaves of machines and apparatuses. It is one thing to demonstrate this, quite another to think through how far human beings in this epoch are not only subordinated to technical relations but how far human beings must correspond to the developmental processes of technical relations [*dem Wesen der Technik*]; and how far there are announced in this correspondence [*Entsprechung*] more original possibilities for a free determinate existence of human beings [*eines freien Daseins des Menschen*]. (*SG*: 41)

The epigraph to this chapter is taken from the recently translated lectures *The Principle of Reason* (1957).[1] The question posed here by Heidegger is whether human beings can go beyond simply adapting to the demands of technical relations, and reach out towards these 'more original possibilities for a free determinate existence of human beings'. These lectures provide the third of Heidegger's responses to the philosophy of Leibniz and they in part presume knowledge of those previous responses. These previous discussions of Leibniz are to be found in the lectures on *The Metaphysical Foundations of Logic*,[2] contemporaneous with the publication of *Being and Time*, and in the essay *The Essence of Reasons* (*Vom Wesen des Grundes*),[3] first published in 1929, to which Heidegger refers in the course of *The Principle of Reason*. Leibniz is also placed in the history of metaphysics, as a history of words for being, developed in the notes for the Nietzsche lectures. There is both a continuation of discussion in these returns to the work of Leibniz and a significant shifting of themes. As Lilly points out in his editorial note to the English edition of the lectures, one of the most significant additions is the discussion in the context of Leibniz's work of the term *Geschick*, translated variously as destiny, sending or sometimes as mittence. The term is taken over from *Being and Time*, but acquires new implications as a result of its use in the term *Seinsgeschick*.

In the *Metaphysical Foundations of Logic*, Heidegger performs a part of the critical dismantling of the philosophical tradition announced but not performed in *Being and Time*. The task is to show how the enquiry signalled under the term '*logos*' becomes blocked by the structures imposed by metaphysical preoccupations. This process Heidegger finds at work in Leibniz's attempt to construct a doctrine of judgement. For Heidegger, the replacement of a meditation on the possibility of creating meaning in language by a rigid doctrine of judgement is a stage in the forgetting of being and in the oblivion of that forgetting. Heidegger quite explicitly addresses the theological commitments within which Leibniz's philosophy functions, quoting in his opening pages the observation: '*cum Deus calculat et cogitationem exercet, fit mundus*, when God makes calculations and develops thought, he creates the world' (*MFL*: 28). Heidegger links Leibniz's concerns and concepts back into the neo-scholastic tradition of philosophy in which Leibniz trained and shows the grounding of both the scholastic tradition and of Leibniz's philosophy in Aristotle's enquiries. This insistence that modern philosophy is not independent of the philosophical tradition is a central feature of Heidegger's view of philosophy as a single tradition, starting with the Greeks and coming to an end in the present day. The lectures culminate in an attempt to retrieve the fundamental ontology of *Being and Time* briefly discussed in the previous chapter. They reveal the pattern of converting an encounter with the thought of the other into an attempt to retrieve his own broken-off thinking process, which is recurrent in his work. In the essay on *The Essence of Reasons*, Heidegger elaborates on the significance for phenomenology of his analyses of the world, commenced in *Being and Time*. It was at this time that Husserl suggested Heidegger and he collaborate on an article on Phenomenology for the *Encyclopaedia Britannica*. Heidegger's comments on the draft revealed to Husserl the extent of the disagreements between them. In the essay, the main focus for concern is Leibniz's question: why is there something rather than nothing? The conception of nothingness moves to the centre of concern, seeming to elide the concern with time with which the analysis of 'world' is juxtaposed in *Being and Time*. The question concerning nothingness marks a shift from the question of *Being and Time* concerning the forgetting of being. It is the question made central by the turn to the questioning of metaphysics, marked by the inaugural lecture 'What is metaphysics?' These shifts mark the beginning of the enquiry about the nature of nihilism leading into the discussion of Nietzsche as the completer of metaphysics and into the extended interrogation of the restrictions imposed on thought and language by adopting a metaphysical framework of enquiry.

The main transition at work in Heidegger's reading of Leibniz is the emergence of the view that doctrines of judgement must be replaced by thinking about the essence of language, *das Wesen der Sprache*, as a dynamic process in which human beings are caught up. Heidegger opens out the relation between human beings and technology by reversing the relation between language and human being, showing the priority of language to human beings. What Heidegger comes to see in the course of the 1930s is that the world in which we live increasingly takes on the shape of rigid technical relations, which develop according to their own logic, not in response to human need and initiative. There is then a shift in the kinds of historical events which can take place and in the kinds of historical narratives which can be constructed. Both become detached from human living, since technical relations and their consequences appear given, not invented. Thus the world as technical relations, far from seeming like a projection of human activity, appears as a given matter of fact. Human beings cease to see their role in the transformation of the world into technical relations. We cannot see the interplay between ourselves and being as responsible for holding technical relations in place. The question of technology preoccupies Heidegger from the mid-1930s onwards, culminating in the famous paper 'The question of technology', published in the collection *Vorträge und Aufsätze* (1954). It is already marked in the lecture from 1938, 'The age of the world picture':[4]

> One of the essential phenomena of the modern age is its science. A phenomenon of no less importance is machine technology. However we must not misinterpret that technology as the mere application of modern mathematical physical science to praxis. Machine technology is itself an autonomous transformation of praxis, a type of transformation in which praxis first demands the employment of mathematical physical science. Machine technology remains up to now the most visible outgrowth of the essence of modern technology, which is identical with the essence of modern metaphysics. (*QT*: 116)

In the lectures *The Principle of Reason* Heidegger shows how the evolution of philosophy out of its Greek beginnings into the formal systems of the nineteenth and twentieth centuries has contributed to the emergence of technology as the system of relations constituting the world in which human beings currently are to be found. Leibniz's philosophy becomes for Heidegger a site at which a process transforming abstract thinking into the material relations of technology can be revealed.

In my reading of these lectures, I propose to trace out a double questioning and a doubling by Heidegger of Leibniz's enquiries. The doubling of Leibniz's enquiries takes place in Heidegger's insistence on a dual reading of the Leibnizian phrase '*nihil est sine ratione*'. This can be read as denying the possibility of there being something for which no ground or cause can be given. This is the meaning Heidegger supposes Leibniz to give it. It can also be read as affirming a nothingness in excess of the domain of reasons, causes and grounds, and in excess of the domain of entities for which the Leibnizian principle holds good. The former reading Heidegger calls the principle of reason, as a translation of Leibniz's *principium rationis*. Heidegger calls the second reading a principle of being, *Satz vom Sein*. As Lilly points out there is an important shift within this notion of principle or sentence, *Satz*, between *Satz* as *Prinzip*, the Latin term for a principle, and *Satz* as proposition or more simply as sentence. The former reading can be understood simply as a principle, or axiom, within a logical system, whereas the latter reading can be understood as implying a pronouncement made by being. The double questioning at work is the shift from discussing Leibniz's philosophy to discussing the destiny of philosophy as a whole in relation to the sendings of being and in relation to the emergence of technical relations as the predominant context in which human beings live. This doubling is shadowed by a further doubling in Heidegger's presentation and interpretation of problems posed by his own previous enquiries. These doublings are marked in the form of the publication itself, since it consists of the entire sequence of thirteen lectures delivered between 1955 and 1956, which are then supplemented by the single lecture given in May 1956, in which the focus for attention shifts significantly. The difference of focus between the one-off lecture and the thirteen-lecture cycle is underlined by a shift of focus, halfway through the thirteen-lecture cycle, from discussing Leibniz to considering the history of philosophy in the modern period in more general terms. There is a tension throughout between celebrating and developing a new form of thinking on one side and, on the other, diagnosing an end of philosophy and the contribution to that end made by Leibniz's principle of sufficient reason. This tension demonstrates itself in shifts of approach in Heidegger's observations concerning the function of language within and beyond philosophical enquiry, his presentation of his differences with Hegel, his presentation of the operations of *Seinsgeschichte*, his assessment of the role of science in the completing of philosophy and his invocation of its inception at the time of the Greeks. These will be located in relation to each other and to the text, before turning to the reading of Leibniz.

The one-off lecture is less equivocally engaged in a reflection on current circumstances. It subordinates the account of the development of philosophy from its inception among the Greeks to an analysis of the current conditions and of the role of human beings in them. It locates a connection between measurement, reason and what it is to be human by making central a reading of the bifurcated definition of human beings: man is a rational animal, *homo est animal rationale*:

> To all this which is worthy of thought belongs the simple matter of fact, which has perhaps drawn nearer to us. We can name it when we say: being is experienced as ground/reason. Ground is interpreted as *ratio*, as calculability [*Rechenschaft*]. In accordance with this, human beings are the *animal rationale*, the creature which has the capacity for calculating and which gives summing-ups.

Heidegger then adds: 'This thinking has as the modern European mode brought the world into this current age of the world, the atomic age' (*SG*: 210), and he asks: 'Does this determination, human beings as a rational animal, exhaust the essence of human beings? Is this the last word which can be said of being: being becomes ground?' This question is also touched on in the cycle of lectures, but without the same sharpness of focus. Heidegger asks whether it is possible to develop another kind of thinking alongside the calculative thinking that prepares the way for the atomic age and responds:

> That is the question. It is for thinking the question of the world. With an answer to it, there is a decision about what becomes of the earth and what becomes of the determinate being of human beings [*das Dasein des Menschen*] on this earth. (*SG*: 211)

There is then a tension throughout these lectures between a focus on constructing a history of being and its cumulative erasure in the history of philosophy; and a focus on identifying the specificity of the current circumstances and the challenges they pose to human beings. The former puts emphasis on identifying a sequence of metaphysical constructs. I suggest that the latter puts emphasis on an ethical problem. The cycle of lectures privileges the former over the latter, emphasising the end of philosophy and completion of metaphysics as a basis from which to construct such a history of philosophy, on the basis of a history of sendings of being.

This chapter will show how that same end and completion can be interpreted as making possible a renewal of ethics, a renewal of a questioning of what it is to be human and of what the future may hold for human beings. This chapter explores the tension between these two concerns by working back from a recognition that there are three different endings for the lectures, responding to a triple meaning in Leibniz's principle of sufficient reason: Leibniz's meaning; the direct critique of technology as the upshot of this claim that there is an account to be offered for every state of affairs; and the indirect claim that metaphysics as technology is not a complete account of what there is because alongside that which can be rationally grounded there is also that which simply is. Heidegger's reading leaves Leibniz's meaning on one side. This is not an interpretation of the work of a philosopher, designed to present that work in its full power. Heidegger is preoccupied by the difference between the direct and the indirect claims. This is captured by Heidegger's insistence on calling the direct claim a 'principle of reason' and the indirect claim a 'sentence of being'. Heidegger's reading of Leibniz here is undoubtedly forceful, since Leibniz would not himself have identified a second principle about being as concealed within the principle of sufficient reason. Nor does the principle of sufficient reason for Leibniz have a place within the kind of history of philosophy that Heidegger seeks to construct, as an account of the increasingly successful elision from philosophical enquiry of its central theme: the question of what and how there is what there is. This is not a faithful reading of Leibniz. If such infidelity is thought to be unethical, then it becomes clear that in the reading of the texts of others there are ethical issues in play which need interrogation. In the next section, I make use of insights from the 1957 essay *Identity and Difference*,[5] to bring out the ethical issues at work in *The Principle of Reason*.

THE QUESTION OF TECHNOLOGY

In his lecture *Identity and Difference*, given a year later, on 27 June 1957, Heidegger emphatically rejects the view that he is constructing an ethics of technology. He opens the theme out by identifying as mistaken the view that technology is simply a dimension of human activity, insisting that there are wider contexts in which the development of technology must be located:

the above-mentioned totality of the world of technology is interpreted in advance in terms of human beings, as a being of human making. Technology conceived in the broadest sense and in its manifold manifestations is taken for the plan which human beings project, the plan which compels human beings to decide whether they will become the servant of the plan or will remain the master. By this conception of the totality of the technological world, we reduce everything down to human beings. (*ID*: 34)

He then continues that this reduction of everything to the domain of the human leads at best to the construction of an ethics:

we at best come to the point of calling for an ethics of the technological world. Caught up in this conception we confirm our own opinion that technology is of human making alone. We fail to hear the claim of Being [*Anspruch des Seins*] which speaks in the essence of technology [*Wesen der Technik*]. (*ID*: 34)

This quotation is very revealing for it shows that ethical enquiry for Heidegger is concerned solely with what is human. A distinction between ethics, as concerned exclusively with what it is to be human, and metaphysics, as concerned with everything else, is at work here. Since one of the main aims of this study is to show that Heidegger disrupts such a distinction, this might seem surprising. However, it is a sign of the powerful hold the distinction has, that it can occur even in texts where it is also being disrupted. It is possible for the distinction to be both affirmed and disrupted in the same text. In place of this notion of ethics as concerned with what it is to be human, corresponding to a notion of metaphysics as concerned with the non-human nature of things, I suggest an alternative distinction: that ethics is concerned with responsiveness, and metaphysics with monological construction.

In these lectures on Leibniz, Heidegger is discussing the contribution he supposes the principle of sufficient reason to have made in the emergence of technical relations. In the course of this discussion, there is a cumulative disruption of taking for granted an understanding of what it is to be human, of technical relations and of the relation between them. The relation between these two questions, 'what is it to be human?' and 'what is technology?', forms an approach to Heidegger's claim in *The Principle of Reason* – a claim he developed in 'On the essence of language', published in *Unterwegs zur Sprache* (1959)[6] – that it is language that speaks, not human beings. Heidegger makes the claim concerning the priority of language to human beings towards the end of the lecture cycle, with an implicit reference back to a remark in *The Letter on Humanism* about how language can be thought of as the house of being:

If we restrict ourselves to occidental language and acknowledge this restriction as a boundary from the beginning, then we may say: our language speaks historically. Given that with the indication that language is the house of being, something true might be being said, then this historical speaking of a language is itself sent and structured through the perennial sending of being. For thinking which starts out from the essence of language, this means that it is language that talks, not human beings. Human beings speak only in as much as they respond to language as *Geschick*. (*SG*: 161)

I suggest that this claim about the priority of language underpins Heidegger's self-identification as not engaged in ethical thinking, for Heidegger seems to suppose that if human beings are set in relation to forces above and beyond our control, if human beings are not simply related to some project of self-realisation, then the bounds of ethics have been overstepped. If language is beyond human control in this way, this takes the relation between human beings and language out of the domain of ethics. However, it is also possible to claim that if language can be thought of as the house of being, then the relation between human beings and language can be seen as an ethical concern, since language provides a form of life. The refusal to consider the relation between human beings and language as ethical and as alterable makes it possible for the move into analysing language to repeat the metaphysical reductions of the history of philosophy, without even recognising or indeed vehemently denying that a metaphysical reduction is taking place. I propose that this claim about the priority of language is a rewriting of the relation of priority between being and *Dasein*, and can be read as elaborating how the processes of being, the *Seinsgeschick*, can be thought to be in advance of human existence, activity and speech, but nevertheless to require human existence, activity and speech in order to be made evident.

In the lecture *Identity and Difference* Heidegger also sets out a distance between his own and Hegel's views on the relation between current thinking, history and the history of philosophy.[7] He affirms his own account of a step back into the history of philosophy, rather than inheriting, as did Hegel, a cumulatively produced truth. However, Heidegger seems to retain a Kantian identification of ethics with abstract moral theory, rather than following up the return to Aristotle and the doubling movement in ethical thinking set in play by Hegel's distinction between abstract morality, *Moralität*, and the ethics of actual, lived conditions, *Sittlichkeit*. Heidegger's view that his is not an ethical enquiry results in part from taking over from the tradition a misleading contrast between ethics and metaphysics and between ethics, as concerned solely with what it is to be human, and morality, as referring beyond the domain of the human to some transcendent value beyond the domain of entities. This contrast is found in very marked form in Hegel's writings, and while Heidegger disputes Hegel's view of the relation between history and philosophy, he seems to take over Hegel's restricted view of ethics. Hegel of course seeks to overcome the difference between ethics, as the practices of actually existing human beings, and morality, as absolute standard, in his theory of spirit. Only if ethics is delimited to being solely about human beings is it impossible for ethics also to address forces which go beyond human scope. My suggestion is that it is a mistake to distinguish between metaphysics and ethics on the basis of the extension of their domains of concern. The distinction is to be made not in terms of scope of concern but in terms of manner of approach to analysis. Thus this chapter frames Heidegger's claim concerning language to show that without an enmeshing of human relations and identity in, among other relations, pre-existing language structures there would be no ethical issues. Thus the claim about the priority of language over its speakers is not a barrier to locating an ethical moment in Heidegger's thinking, but on the contrary one point of entry of ethics into his thought. It is a restricted version of ethics which cannot accommodate the priority of language over speakers. Once ethics is identified as a process of negotiating with heteronomy, there is no need to draw distinctions between the domains of ethical and other forms of enquiry so rigidly. I suggest that Heidegger's work shows that ethics can be understood as such a process of negotiation. The next move then is to lay out the failure to challenge Hegel's view of the relation between metaphysics and ethics.

Heidegger's step back from involvement in present processes is set out as necessary in order to unravel the effects of the history of philosophy and to distance the effects of releasing in the world the results of science in the form of technical relations. The step back from involvement reveals a moment of transition and a duality in time: time as an ongoing process in which we are caught up and time as moment of recognition and commemoration. He asks whether the question of being has been touched on in the historical orderings of Hegel's dialectical processes and responds that his own thought of the step back is a thought of abrupt discontinuity, not of cumulative processes:

> But being gives itself even here only in that manner in which it has made way for itself for Hegel's thought. That means, the way in which being gives itself is determined each time out of the way in which it makes way for itself. This manner is, however, one which is sent, which is each time the stamping of an epoch, which for us comes forward only if we are open to it in its own way of having been. We get into the proximity of what has been sent only through the abruptness of the moment of recognition and commemoration [*die Jähe des Augenblickes eines Andenkens*]. (*ID*: 135)

This contrasts with Hegel's presumption that the task is to affirm and continue a sequential development. For Hegel, scientific enquiry is subordinated to and in line with the overarching processes mapped out by philosophical analyses of spirit and of reason. There is no final tension between philosophy and science. For Heidegger, much more than for Hegel, the relation between philosophical enquiry and the emergence of the new scientific disciplines is a problem relation. He analyses philosophical enquiry as producing the categorial shifts required for scientific procedures to be coherent, but he also sees issues of philosophical importance becoming obscured by the issues prioritised in scientific enquiry. Despite this disagreement with Hegel, however, Heidegger seems to retain Hegel's distinction between metaphysics and ethics, between metaphysics as the major task of philosophy and ethics in a subsidiary role. In *The Principle of Reason*, Heidegger re-establishes a distance to Hegel evident in *Being and Time*, but eroded in the appreciative treatment Heidegger gives of Hegel's *Phenomenology of Spirit* in his lectures on Hegel from the early 1930s, especially of Hegel's conception of experience, *Erfahrung*, as process, developed in the introduction to the *Phenomenology*.[8] Heidegger's engagement with Leibniz brings to the fore not the questions of experience, history and of thinking as process, but questions of system and the construction of artificial grounds in place of a taken-for-granted, given groundedness. By affirming a connection between Leibniz and Hegel, Heidegger re-establishes a distance between himself and Hegel.

In the lectures on *The Principle of Reason*, Heidegger explicitly criticises the Hegelian view of history as a process realising abstract ideas in material reality. In the context of a discussion of the status of the temporal and non-temporal, he criticises the presumption that it is possible to give a determinate definition of key terms in philosophy by reference to an unchanging, transcendent essence determining meaning:

> Such a presupposition would take it on itself to be able to grasp all determinations of the essence of being and reason with equal weight and equal form, and this in a representation which hovers above time. What occurs in time would then be understood as the each time limited actualisation of the supertemporal content of the given definition. People try to give out such actualisations of values and ideas as the very marks of history. (*SG*: 159)

Already in *Being and Time* Heidegger criticises what he takes to be Hegel's view of logical form becoming temporal by falling into history. Heidegger rejects the Platonic view that there are ideas in advance of historical and temporal instances. Heidegger remarks that this view has a long history, but that it does not itself emerge out of an understanding and sympathy for history. It is rather prompted by a literal-minded response to a Platonic distinction between material instance and ideal form:

> The representation of history as the realisation of ideas has its own long-standing history. Indeed this named representation of history is almost ineliminable. If we reflect on it then it becomes clear to the glance which has not already been taken up into it that representing the realisation in time of trans-temporal ideas and values does not emerge out of a process of history. In this common representation of history, the Platonistic, note not Plato's, distinction between a world as a sensible alterable one and a super-sensible unchanging domain is carried over without thought and reflection into what at first looks like the course of human affairs and sufferings, and as such a self-directing sequence of occurrences is invoked as history. (*SG*: 159)

Heidegger's problems with this view are threefold. He disputes the understanding of Plato at work in it; he disputes the picture of history as simply the activities of human beings, since he supposes there are superhuman forces at work in history; and he therefore disputes the attempt to understand history as a self-contained process with a single continuous development.

In the preceding lecture 11, Heidegger sets out his alternate view of the history of philosophy as resulting from there being a series of distinct illuminations of being:

> Previously as later on being illuminates itself although in different ways: in the character of a shining forth, of a remaining appearance, or presence, of an over against and away from [*Gegenüber und Entgegen*]. The introduction of these moments remains merely an enumerating indication far removed from any insight into each epoch as a full sending of being and insight into the mode in which epochs each time spring up like buds. (*SG*: 154)

He goes on to observe that there is no simple continuity between epochs and that they do not constitute a cumulative process of transmission. There is a transmission from one epoch to the next, but the new formation emerges from a hidden and unidentifiable source, unlike the emergence of the next stage in a dialectical process, which can be seen as grounded in the forces already in play in the preceding formation.

> Epochs never permit themselves to be deduced from each other and certainly do not set up a course of a process which runs through them. Certainly there is a transmission from epoch to epoch but it does not run between epochs like a bond which connects them. The transmission comes each time out of what is hidden in destiny. (*SG*: 154)

Heidegger's history of being, as a process emerging out of unexaminable and repressed elements within what takes place, is akin to Hegel's view of history as in part consisting in processes not open to human inspection. It is, however, wholly opposed to the role of reason in Hegel's account and opposed to the transhuman standpoint from which a rationality coextensive with the Hegelian system itself is supposed to be identifiable. There is a parallel between Heidegger's questioning of history and his questioning of the adequacy of ethics as a means for reflecting on what it is to be human. In each case Heidegger identifies the analysis as set up in such a way as to cut it off from what Heidegger supposes to be its primary inscrutable source: the history of being. Heidegger claims that the version of history in dispute is held in place by the operations of another set of forces, to which he seeks to draw attention:

> This representation of history and its obdurate claim is itself determined through the sending of being, and that means through the domination of metaphysical thinking. Certainly this exclusive representation of history as the temporal realisation of a transtemporality makes more difficult any attempt to see the uniqueness that conceals itself in a puzzling constancy which gathers together and breaks through every so often in a genuine sending of fate [*des eigentlich Geschicklichen*]. (*SG*: 160)

Thus, for Heidegger, moments of discontinuity are more instructive about what there is than periods in which nothing much changes. At such moments, what comes to the fore are long-hidden forces, which most of the time remain concealed.

Heidegger calls attention to a final complete concealment of the operations of his *Seinsgeschichte* in German idealism:

> When the last trace of the concealment of being disappears, namely in the absolute self-consciousness of absolute spirit in the metaphysics of German idealism, the revealing of entities with respect to their being, that is metaphysics, is completed and philosophy comes to an end. (*SG*: 14)

In Heidegger's view this concealment contributes to the emergence of the science needed to make technical relations possible and is a condition for the adoption and spread of those technical relations in the world as inhabited by human beings.

In these lectures, Heidegger gives a sketch of a reading of Kant as one of the great figures in the history of philosophy. As with the reading of Leibniz, Heidegger identifies in Kant's work a powerful ambiguity and elision of difference between two contrasting meanings of a single term. In his reading of Leibniz, Heidegger emphasises the ambiguities in the principle of sufficient reason, within the term *Grund*. In the case of Kant it is the conception of reason itself suspended between the terms *Vernunft* and *Grund*, that is suggested to be importantly double in meaning:

> At the risk of appearing to exaggerate, we may even say, if modern thought did not speak of the *ratio* in translation in the double sense of both reason and ground, then there would not be Kant's critique of pure reason as the delimitation of the conditions of possibility of objects of experience. (*SG*: 164)

This question of translation in connection to ambiguity is key to Heidegger's thinking about transitions from epoch to epoch, as a remark made shortly before the one quoted above indicates: 'A genuine translation corresponds every time in an epoch of the sending of being to the manner in which a language speaks the sending of being' (*SG*: 164). It is the entwinement of language with the sending of being that gives language priority over human beings and places human beings in a position of subordination to language. The priority of language to human beings is the priority of being to human beings. The theme of ambiguity is addressed at several levels in the course of *The Principle of Reason*. The lectures have a specific form, suitable to the mode of oral address, not to the processes of reading; there is much recapitulation which subtly transforms the relation between the themes already raised. There is a marked forwards and backwards movement between themes, which disrupts any sense of there being a single line of argument. However, the productive ambiguities of spoken form become elusive once transposed into written text. There is ambiguity also at the level of the themes addressed. In the lectures, alongside the interrogation of the forgetting, oblivion and withdrawal of being, there are juxtaposed three major themes for Heidegger's later thought: human beings, technical relations and a correspondence between them. This correspondence is, according to Heidegger, the result of a play of forces above and beyond either human beings or technical relations which has a significant impact on both. This play of forces he calls *Seinsgeschichte* and *Seinsgeschick*, the history and destiny, or sending, of being. Through the operations of this ambiguity, the principle of sufficient reason, as supposedly announced by Leibniz, is gradually displaced into an account of the task and history of philosophy. This account feeds directly into Heidegger's claim about philosophy having come to an end and metaphysics having been completed in the work of Hegel and Nietzsche and then overcome through the spread of technical relations in the human world.

The ambiguity works on several levels. There is first this displacement of the discussion from interpreting Leibniz's texts to formulating independent theses about the status and nature of philosophy. Then there are the divergent meanings Heidegger excavates out of the principle itself, stated as '*nihil est sine ratione*', and translated as '*Nichts ist ohne Grund*' – nothing is without reason. There is the insistence that the principle forms a central feature of philosophical enquiry and yet comes late on the scene, inaugurating a new departure which changes the status of philosophy. There is finally the ambiguous status attributed to philosophy, as up until now always regenerated in the same form and yet in the present epoch completed and transcended. In these lectures Heidegger sets out a connection between, on one side, a complex philosophical argument and interpretation of texts, concerning the evolution of philosophy and the role of a search for foundations within philosophical argument, and on the other, a loss of sense of orientation in the modern epoch, in a dispersal brought about by technical relations and by a detachment from locality. The claim is put at its most striking at the end of the fourth lecture:

> We can say that the more decisively the hunt for control of these gigantic energies is set up through which human need for energy should be served for all time, all the more lacking is the capacity of human beings, in the domain of what is most important, to build and live [*bauen und wohnen*]. It is a puzzling interplay between the claim for a making available of reasons and grounds [*Zustellung des Grundes*] and the withdrawal of groundedness and rootedness [*Entzug des Bodens*]. (*SG*: 60)

There is a startling jump here from the very material notions of building and living and a highly abstract level of analysis and argumentation. There is a startling connection between the attempt in philosophy to produce reasons and grounds and an everyday experience of disorientation. This abolition of a taken-for-granted groundedness through an insistence on presenting grounds and reasons is a version of the process discussed in *Being and Time* in terms of an everyday taken-for-granted sense of fit between self and context and its erosion through a break in its orderliness and the onset of analysis. In that analysis recurrent attempts are made to reconstruct an irretrievable orderliness in a domain which no longer functions smoothly. In *The Principle of Reason* Heidegger similarly links developments at a very abstract level of philosophical argument to the most material of all processes, the textures of actual daily life, as influenced by the new technical relations introduced in the course of the past two hundred years. Perhaps most startling of all here is the assumption, presented almost without argument, that it makes sense to think in terms of such a connection between the highly abstract, non-physical level of philosophical reasoning and the level at which technical relations constrain and impinge on human lives. Hegelian philosophy leads to the thought that any such connection must be highly mediated, not simply set up as a juxtaposition. The starkness of the juxtaposition set out by Heidegger suggests the working of forces beyond human understanding.

In the single lecture, presented in May 1956, Heidegger brutally summarises his argument. He refers back to his claim that the principle of sufficient reason is basic to the history of philosophy and to the developments currently affecting human existence, even though it only emerges on the scene after two and a half thousand years:

> For during the long incubation time of the principle of sufficient reason, the word for being as ground or reason has been being delivered to occidental human beings. Without this delivery there would not be a thinking in the form of philosophy. Without philosophy there would not be occidental European science, no setting loose of atomic energy. However, the address [*Zuspruch*] in the word for being as reason or ground remains without a sound in contrast to the amplification of the principle in the ever more noisy and thoroughly alarming power of its claim [*Anspruch*]. (*SG*: 209)

Here is a fine example of Heidegger seeking to draw attention to hidden processes at work, through the lexical proximity of the words he uses to distinguish between the two elements which he argues are mistakenly taken to be one and the same. The *Anspruch* of technology, its pretension, claim or challenge, takes precedence over the fact that this challenge is presented to human beings, who have some option about how they respond. This repressed dimension in the relation between technical relations and human beings is captured by the term *Zuspruch*. The proximity of the words hides the fact that there are two very different processes at work here: an extension of technical relations and the fact that those relations have come available. The principle of sufficient reason supports the claims of technological control while the significance of *Grund*, reason, ground or cause, as a word for being goes missing.

In the lecture cycle, Heidegger identifies a danger at work in failing to recognise that human beings are not simply at the service of technology. He seeks to establish this by questioning the significance of the present age being called the atomic age:

> What does it mean then that an epoch of world history should be stamped by atomic energy and its letting loose? It means nothing less than this: that the atomic age is dominated by the violence of the pretension [*Gewalt des Anspruches*] that threatens to overpower us through the principle of a sufficient reason and ground being that which must be produced. (*SG*: 200)

The danger is summed up in the preceding sentence, in which Heidegger insists that materialism, while privileging matter over other dimensions of reality, is not itself material but a conceptual, intellectual construct: 'materialism is the most threatening form of intellectual construct since we overlook ourselves most easily and longer in the entanglements of its capacity for violation [*Gewaltsamkeit*]' (*SG*: 200). As a result of concealing the constructed, non-material nature of materialism, the fact that human beings play a role in its dissemination and in its having an influence over human lives is concealed. It becomes a superhuman coercive force, subordinating human beings within given non-negotiable structures. Conversely, what is forgotten in relation to technology is that a series of human actions and decisions, admittedly undertaken without full foresight of all possible consequences, contributes to the danger. The warning seems to be that it would be a mistake to think that more planning, calculation and activity will necessarily bring a remedy for current problems, since they too will have consequences above and beyond the supposed agents' control. This connects to themes in the 'Letter on humanism' about the failure to think about the conditions of possibility for there being action at all: that there be an address to human beings opening up a possibility for action.

Heidegger seeks to develop a different kind of thinking which does not order phenomena into a single system and which makes possible this other form of reflection. This alternative form of thinking he calls a thinking which assigns meaning, *ein besinnendes Denken*, and he contrasts it to metaphysical, calculating thinking, *ein metaphysisches, rechnendes Denken*. Through this alternate form of thinking he seeks to demonstrate a closer connection between thinking and poetry, *Denken* and *Dichten*, than between thinking and calculation. This is the theme that emerges in Heidegger's writings throughout the 1930s in parallel to his work on a history of words of being and in part resulting from his critique of the role assigned in philosophical enquiry to logical construction. Heidegger's insistence on a close connection between philosophical, abstract construction and actually existing relations in the world disrupts the more usual conception of a clear-cut separation and opposition between the two domains. He claims that this clear-cut separation is eroded in the spread of technical relations. The relation between the level of abstract philosophical argument and the material relations in which human beings currently exist is a version of the relation between the non-physical and the physical, the non-sensible and the sensible which has a long history in philosophical enquiry. It plays a role in the construal of history as a process taking place in the course of time, transposing super-sensible, non-temporal, non-material ideas into sensible, material form. The disruption of these oppositions in technology forms part of Heidegger's claim that philosophy has come to an end, for he supposes that they are a condition for there being philosophical enquiry. These oppositions are mediated in theories of art, which Heidegger puts in question in his critique of aesthetics. The displacement of discussion of this relation into aesthetics and into theories of history conceals its centrality to philosophy and to its history.

There is a division of labour between the subdisciplines of philosophy which Heidegger systematically challenges. Heidegger puts another interpretation on this relation between the sensible and the super-sensible, as that which must be set up if philosophical enquiry is to be possible at all. He shows that it is not a simple matter of fact about what there is that there should be such a distinction between a physical, sensible, material domain and a non-physical, super-sensible, non-material domain. He shows that it is a fact about how human beings are inclined to think. Heidegger remarks in the course of the sixth lecture:

> The representation of a transference (*Übertragen*) and of metaphor rests on a distinction if not separation between the sensible and the non-sensible as two independently constituted domains. The setting up of the division between the sensible and the non-sensible, the physical and the non-physical is a basic thrust of that which is called metaphysics and remains a standard for European thinking. (*SG* : 88–9)

He goes on: 'With the insight that this named distinction between the sensible and the non-sensible is inadequate, metaphysics loses its status as a form of thought providing a standard' (*SG*: 89). The term here is '*maßgebend*' which could perhaps also be translated as providing measure and, to write metaphorically, gravity. The next paragraph continues:

> With the insight into the delimitation of metaphysics, the representation which provides a measure for 'metaphor' also becomes invalid. It gives a measure for our representation of the essence of language. For this reason metaphor serves as a much used aid in the interpretation of works of poetry and of artistic developments overall. There is metaphor only within metaphysics. (*SG*: 89)

Heidegger's distinction between *Dichten* and *Poesie* mirrors the distinction between thought and metaphysics: the one does and the other does not cut loose from the determinations set in play by a distinction between literal and metaphorical language use, between metaphysics and ethics, between metaphysics and metaphor. This remark is noted by Derrida in the course of his rethinking of his relation to Heidegger in 'White mythologies'.[9] The aim here is not to pursue Derrida's reading but to link this critique of a distinction between the sensible and the non-sensible, between metaphor and metaphysics, to the connection between thought and poetry which Heidegger is developing from the mid-1930s on. In conclusion to these lectures, Heidegger hypothesises about the possibility of setting up some other standard, some other measure, *Maßgabe*, for providing human beings with a sense of location, in opposition to and replacing this distinction between the physical and the non-physical. In what seems like a reference back to *Being and Time* Heidegger remarks: 'Death is the as yet unthought measure of measurelessness, that is the highest game in which human beings are brought on earth, the game on which human being is conditional' (*SG*: 187). Here there is a reference to the game, which is located by Heidegger in these lectures once in terms of the relation between time and space and once in terms of his reading of Heraclitus. I suggest it is more productive to rewrite this notion of death as a retrieval, not of the Heraclitean play of forces, but of ethics.

Heidegger suggests that metaphysics no longer provides a measure for what is real and that metaphor no longer provides a significant level of analysis for reading poetry. The question is why there should be these 'no longers'. The answer for Heidegger has something to do with the spread of technical relations in the domain of human experience and its effects on what it is to be human and on how human beings are inclined to think, or rather not to think. What Heidegger diagnoses as the completion of philosophy is in part the result of the success of the sciences in making available accounts of what there is through which effective intervention in processes in the world is made possible. It is, however, only if philosophy is taken to be solely concerned with producing accounts of what there is that these scientific successes can be thought to have this effect on philosophical enquiry. There is in this a concealment of the impact of these technical relations on the world and on the possibilities for being human. There is a failure to recognise that the implications of technology pose questions which cannot be solved simply in terms of technology. As Heidegger puts it in the closing section of his paper 'The question of technology' (1951):[10]

> because the essence of technology is nothing technological, essential reflection upon technology and decisive confrontation with it must happen in a realm that is on the one hand akin to technology and on the other fundamentally different from it. (*VA*: 39, *QT*: 35)

The essence of technology is thus ambiguous, in ways which connect to an ambiguity diagnosed by Heidegger as central to philosophical enquiry. The claim about the ambiguity of technology runs: 'The essence of technology is in an elevated sense ambiguous. Such ambiguity points to the mystery of all revelation: i.e. of truth' (*QT*: 33). In 'The question of technology', Heidegger discusses the oddness of there being so little reflection on the impact of the spread of technical relations in our world. This failure to reflect marks an ethical crisis, which Heidegger, as a result of his preoccupation with reading and transmitting the philosophical tradition, cannot identify as such.

What Heidegger calls the end of philosophy in the completion of metaphysics is here interpreted as the emergence of an ethical challenge to the domination of philosophy by metaphysical concerns, which presume that specifying the nature of entities is the primary aim of philosophical enquiry. This challenge prompts a recognition of the priority of a question about the location from which that specification takes place. Instead of Heidegger's emphasis on a cumulative but hidden logic of development, in which even the traces of a history of being disappear, the lectures in *The Principle of Reason* can be read as locating a tension between that emphasis and an attempt to identify the consequences for the essence of what it is to be human resulting from this disappearance and the consequent uninhibited spread of technical relations in our world. One such consequence is that it becomes unclear what the essence of human beings is.

Heidegger suggests that this essence is changing in response to the spread of technical relations and that perhaps it has always been in process of change. This is an important culmination of his questioning of a static conception of essences throughout the 1930s which he supposes is handed on in the Latin-based tradition of philosophical enquiry. Heidegger's inability to identify in the completion of metaphysics a release of ethics from subordination to metaphysics blunts his analysis and leads him to conclude these lectures with an unhelpful return to an origin of philosophy, interpreting the thought of Heraclitus as prior to that origin.

In the final, thirteenth lecture, Heidegger rehearses the results of his reading of Heraclitus in order to reveal a change in the conception of reason in the European tradition, traceable through the transmission of *logos* as *ratio*, and of *ratio* as reason and ground:

> For '*ratio*' is within the history of thinking for its part a translational word and that means one which transmits. Just as these basic words of modern thinking, reason and ground, transmit a divided *ratio*, so in the Roman word *ratio* there speaks a Greek word, which is called *logos*. (*SG*: 177)

The shift to discussing Heraclitus moves the discussion back to a point in the history of thinking before the emergence of philosophy, in Plato's conversion of truth as revelation into truth as correctness, before the separation of abstraction from experience. However, the shift distracts attention from the fact that this separation has to be continually re-enacted for philosophy to continue to take place. The point which therefore goes missing is that in the modern world the re-enactment of a separation between abstraction and experience no longer takes place in the same way, because of changes in the structure of everyday experience brought about by technical relations. The image borrowed from Heraclitus of the world as a game or a play of forces blocks off rather than encourages further thought along the lines developed in the lectures up to that point. The final sentences of the lecture are:

> Nothing is without reason. Being and ground: the same. Being as grounding has no ground and plays as the absence of ground of this play, as destiny plays being and ground to us. The question remains: if we and how we can play within this, hearing the principles of this play leading us into that play. (*SG*: 188)

Who this 'we' might be, however, is left unclear, and instead of clarifying this, there is simply a reiteration of the main claims of the lectures, that at a certain point in the history of being, being and ground become constructed as equivalent terms, with the result that the role of being as an absent and unrepresentable ground, as an abyss in the chain of reasons, which is required for that chain of reasons to function, is concealed. This concealment of being as the absent ground makes it possible, according to Heidegger, for Kant and Hegel to develop the thought of absolute self-consciousness and thus finally to erase the traces in the tradition of the concealment of being, thus contributing to the triumph of technology in the world. Instead of this, it is more instructive to show how the technical relations permeating our world make a negotiation between abstractness and experience a constant feature of experience. It is no longer a problem reserved for discussion by an intellectual elite. It is more instructive to see the spread of technical relations in the world as precisely this disappearance of the gap between abstractness and experience, eroding the place in which philosophy used to take place. The spread of technical relations in the world is the spread of abstractness in experience. There is here not just a completion of metaphysics but a transformation of ethics.

In the twelfth lecture, Heidegger gives a concluding sentence that focuses not on an abstract 'play' of forces and an abstract 'we' enmeshed in those forces, but on the need to look carefully at the specific relations pertaining in the present:

> What is needed is a readiness to look at our atomic age in order to see that, if, according to Nietzsche's claim, God is dead, the world of measurement remains and puts human beings everywhere in its measurement, in so far as it mismeasures everything in accordance with the *principium rationis* (principle of reason). (*SG*: 170)

The claim is that the principle of reason imposes a distortion and reduction on more complex phenomena. This measurement, *Rechenschaft*, is an ambiguous term, since it is both an active assigning of measure and definitive summing up beyond negotiation. The former, in which human beings play an active role, goes missing, and what takes over in place of a world ordered in accordance with a conception of judgement is a world ordered in terms of a definitive set of measurements and calculations:

> In the institutional practice of measurement, *Rechenschaft*, there comes to view how it comes about that something is how it is. *Ratio* means measuring, but measuring has two meanings. Measuring means first of all measurement as an activity; it also means what that activity results in, that which has been measured, the laid-out measurement, the institution of measuring [*die vorgestellte Rechnung, die Rechenschaft*]. (*SG*: 168)

In this lecture Heidegger introduces the play of forces which in the next lecture is discussed in relation to Heraclitus. Here it has a quite different inflection. It is introduced in the context of a distinction between the destiny of being, which underpins the history of philosophy, and fatalism:

> The destiny of being is a claim on, address [*Zuspruch*] and claim to, pretension [*Anspruch*], as a claim or fate, out of which all human language speaks. Claim [*Spruch*] is in Latin *fatum*. But this *fatum* as the claim of being in the sense of a self-withdrawing destiny is not fatalistic, simply for the reason that it cannot be. (*SG*: 158)

He goes on: 'Why not? Because being, in so far as it sends itself, brings the freeness of the play of space and time [*des Zeit-Spiel-Raumes*] and with that frees human beings first of all in the freeness of the possibilities of essence which are on each occasion sent.' Thus there is a process of freeing in advance of any individual, human claim on freedom. Even without remarking that these possibilities are not given in advance in a fixed essence, but are themselves modulations of essence, the claim locates a concern with the way in which what it is to be human is itself in question and in process of change. The aim of the interpretation here is to undermine Heidegger's resistance to calling this an ethical issue. While these changes are not simply willed by human beings, and have sources in non-human forces, this cannot without argument be taken as sufficient ground for denying them to be ethical issues.

RETRIEVING *BEING AND TIME*

The exposition in *The Principle of Reason* refers back in various ways to Heidegger's much earlier work, to *Being and Time* (1927) as well as to the essay *The Essence of Reasons* (*Vom Wesen des Grundes*, 1929), and there is a parallel between the ways in which Heidegger rereads Leibniz and rereads his own texts to impose and extract meanings that are far from self-evident in them. He retrieves these previous discussions in the sixth lecture in the cycle by drawing attention to a danger in the interpretative move made there:

> The completion of the insight that the principle of sufficient reason does not make a statement immediately about grounds or reason but about entities is a dangerous step. It leads into a critical zone of thinking. Because our thinking, even when it is well practised, often remains unassisted at decisive points, and we need some additional assistance. (*SG*: 84)

He goes on:

> This is true of my treatise 'On the emergence/essence of groundings/reason', which first appeared as a contribution to the *Festschrift* for Edmund Husserl in 1929. The constructions remain correct, but all the same they lead into error. First with respect to the possible course which the principle of sufficient reason offers for the particular question about the essence of reason; and second and most of all with respect to that meditation with which all thinking is lit up and in the service of which the named treatise sought to locate itself. (*SG*: 84)

What is not clear is whether the essay itself leads into error, or whether it opens up a line of enquiry which can lead to error. Heidegger claims that the positive assertions in it remain correct but that if taken on their own they will lead into error.

It would appear that Heidegger thinks that the essay construes the principle of sufficient reason one-sidedly, from the stance of the metaphysical question about entities taken as a whole, to the exclusion of an adequate reflection on the question of being. Heidegger goes on to claim that the key error is the failure to see what is closest of all, as a result of attempting to establish too quickly some basis for enquiry:

> It is clear that we see a matter of fact and have it lying clearly in front of our eyes. All the same, we do not notice in what is lying there what lies closest of all. The danger that thinking fails to notice itself is often increased when thinking presses on too quickly towards false groundedness. Such a pressure can in connection to locating the principle of reason work especially unfortunately. (*SG*: 85)

What lies closest of all, and is according to Heidegger therefore neglected as something requiring reflection, is thinking itself. Here there is a connection back to his lectures from 1951–52, *Was heißt Denken?* (1954), which are concerned with the problem of a failure to think about the importance of thoughtfulness. These lectures can then be seen to fill out another dimension of the enquiry which he suggests was foreshortened in the earlier essay on *The Essence of Reasons*.

In a later passage in the cycle of lectures in *The Principle of Reason*, Heidegger refers back to *Being and Time* in somewhat similar terms. The remark about *Being and Time* mentions interpretations of that text given by, among others, Nicolai Hartman:

> In the language of the treatise *Being and Time*, which is still clumsy and provisional, the claim is: the basic pull of the determinate existence, which is human being, is determined through an understanding of being. Understanding being here never means that human beings possess as subjects a subjective representation of being and that this, being, is merely a representation. (*SG*: 146)

Having put to one side this possible misunderstanding, Heidegger continues:

> Understanding being means that human beings, in their essence, stand in the opening of the projection of being and set out this intended understanding. Through this experience and thought through understanding of being, the representation of human beings as subject is put to one side, to speak with Hegel.

On the next page he goes on to show how this putting to one side of the conception of human beings as subjects disrupts the definition of human beings as rational animals. Heidegger starts by claiming that the history of thought is not just a history of random changes of opinion:

> The history of thought is definitely different from the history of changing opinions and teachings of philosophy. The history of thinking is the sending of the essence of human being along with and out of the sending of being. The essence of what it is to be human is sent along with the destiny, which makes it possible to bring entities in their being into language. (*SG*: 147)

The key element here is that Heidegger supposes that the being of entities changes and that therefore there is something different to be brought into language at different epochs; something different to which human beings are also responding in their own being as well as something different for human beings to attempt to bring into language:

> At bottom, this claim is nothing other than an interpretation of the old determination of the essence of what it is to be human from the standpoint of the question of being: *homo est animal rationale*; human beings are the living animal gifted with reason [*der Mensch ist das mit Vernunft begabte Lebewesen*].

With this interpretation, he transforms the more usual understanding of human beings as autonomous controllers of their activities and destinies.

There is also a connection to the claim in the introduction to *Being and Time* that the main question prompting its writing is a puzzle about there being many meanings of the word 'being'. In these later lectures Heidegger makes two observations about multiple meanings. In the concluding pages, he writes:

> This correspondence, however, is the genuine manner [*eigentliche Weise*] according to which human beings belong to the opening of being. The multiplicity of the meanings of a word emerges not first of all from the fact that human beings, in speaking and writing, mean different things at different times. The multiplicity of these meanings is always an historical one. It arises from the fact that in speaking we are each time differently set out and claimed by the sending of the being of the being of entities. (*SG*: 161)

Thus the multiplicity of the meanings of being, a central problem for discussion in *Being and Time*, is here set out as resulting from shifts in the sending of being, which is prior to the unrolling of history as occurrences in human lives. The other remark about multiplicity occurs much earlier in the lecture cycle:

> For the three titles, the Greek word *azioma*, the Latin word *principium* and the German word *Grundsatz* speak from very different domains of representation. Behind this appearance of a harmless multiplicity of meanings hides the basic pull of the history of occidental thought: the history, which is not past [*vergangenes*], but a sending which is preserving and determining [*währendes und bestimmendes*] us today as never before. (*SG*: 40)

This distinction between the past as past, *vergangenes*, and the past as that which is still operating and constraining current activity, *währendes*, is highly significant for Heidegger. It connects back to the distinction between *Vergangenheit* and *Gewesenes*, closed and open past, noted in the previous chapter and back to the distinction, in *Being and Time*, between completed tradition, *Tradition*, and active handing on, *Überlieferung*.

In his discussion of Leibniz, Heidegger takes fragments from published texts and puts emphasis on remarks from letters. This leads to the accusation of distortion by reading fragments out of context and taking parts of sentences torn out of the context formed by sentence and treatise. Heidegger gives himself leave to do this by claiming that there are processes at work in philosophical texts above and beyond the control of authors. He writes in conclusion to the ninth lecture about the relation between Kant's three critiques: 'Kant himself tried over and over again to make visible through a more obvious architectonic the inner unity which he certainly saw. In this Kant knew more than he was able to present through the architectonic of his works' *(SG*: 128). This remark brings to a conclusion a series of reflections on the greater difficulty of reading and interpreting the texts of Kant and Leibniz compared with reading Greek texts:

> Although the thought of Leibniz and Kant is according to historically reckoned temporal distance much closer to us than the thought of the Greeks, it is much less easy to gain access to modern thought in its basic tendencies since the writings and works of modern thinkers are differently constructed, more complex and shot through by the inheritance (*Überlieferung*) and, above all, set up in a dispute with Christianity. (*SG*: 123)

Heidegger is about to address himself to the relation between reason and limit in the thought of Kant; and, almost in the manner of Socrates and his daimon, he invokes a guiding thought:

> We will take to heart the following guiding thought: the greater the thought of a thinker, which in no way is covered by the range and number of their writings, so much the richer is the unthought at work in this thought, that is that which first and only through this thought emerges as the not yet thought. (*SG*: 123–4)

This 'not yet' provides a link back to the discussion of time and *Dasein* in *Being and Time*. It is this unthought in Leibniz's work and indeed in the history of philosophy which Heidegger seeks to reveal through his violent readings. I suggest that there is also an unthought in Heidegger's thought to be revealed: its relation to ethics and the relation between his silence about ethics and his loquacity about metaphysics. This 'not yet' links into the developments which Heidegger supposes are to come, precipitated through the ever extending impact of technical relations in the world and on human relations in that world. It also gives a clue that Heidegger cannot suppose himself to be able to exhaust the meanings at work in another's or indeed his own text. The unthought at work in the thought of a thinker is that which makes their own self-interpretation only one among many possible readings and interpretations, displacing the authority of the speaker and thinker over the value and meaning of their writings, remarks and thoughts. In a further clarification of his relation to others, there is this remark about the status of Aristotle's *Metaphysics*: 'The understanding of others becomes a misunderstanding first of all there where it pretends itself to be the only possible truth and at the same time therefore falls below the level of that which is to be understood' (*SG*: 136). This observation must apply to Heidegger's readings as well, which are therefore not to be understood as claiming to be the only ones possible. The relation of partial self-understanding contained in the thought of the unthought of great thinkers must also be taken to hold for Heidegger.

In the opening lecture, Heidegger locates as a puzzle the lateness in the history of philosophy of the emergence of a questioning of the principle of sufficient reason: 'But the principle of sufficient reason, this issue which lies so close: lying so close that this abbreviated version of the principle for so long could not be thought. Why has it not bothered us even though it spreads all around?' The answer to this question is: 'Answer: because our relation to that which lies closest is since forever dull and blunted. For the path to the nearest is for us human beings at every time the longest and therefore the most difficult' (*SG*: 16). Here is the problem about the inaccessibility to human beings of what lies closest to them, which is central to *Being and Time*. Later on in the lecture cycle, Heidegger reverts to his diagnosis from the early 1950s in *Was heißt Denken?* that this unquestioned proximity is thought itself. Here, what is unthought is the unquestioned reliance on the principle of sufficient reason in philosophy and in thinking more generally. In these earlier lectures on thinking, Heidegger addresses the failure to think about thinking in order to reveal what is overlooked in the development of modern technology. He summarises the thought towards the end of the lectures:

> If the Greek thought of *einai*, what there is, as the being of entities, in the sense of the presence and with that of the objectivity of objectively given relations, were not dominant, then not only would airplane motors not function; they would not even exist. If the being of entities were not revealed as the presence of what is present, then electrical nuclear energy would never have emerged and would not be able to place human beings in the technically determined work which permeates everywhere. So a lot hangs on whether we hear what this title word of occidental European thinking, this *eon,* says or not, for it provides the measure of what there is. (*WHD*: 142)

The lectures in *The Principle of Reason* explore and develop this observation from these earlier lectures.

It is plausible to read both the question of thinking and the question of sufficient reason as versions and rewritings of the forgotten question of being which Heidegger poses in *Being and Time* as the great unaddressed question of the history of philosophy. I suggest that there is a fourth element in this unaddressed proximity to be added in. What lies closest of all to us is ourselves and the failure to pose questions about what it is to be human. This failure conceals the fact that what it is to be human is different in different epochs, depending on the structural conditions constraining what possibilities present themselves to human beings. These two themes, the concealment of what is closest and the non-givenness of what it is to be human, recur throughout Heidegger's thinking and can already be found in *Being and Time*. In the opening passages of *The Principle of Reason*, Heidegger observes that atomic physics both presupposes and generates a shift in the manner of representation among human beings. He makes the claim in two stages, first setting out the characteristic of modern scientific enquiry, which represents itself as having direct access to its objects:

Even there where the sciences draw their customary relation to their object into scientific methodological reflection, that relation to the object is represented as something immediately given. This holds even for that domain in which the relation of the knowing subject to the object really has changed in essential ways, as in modern atomic physics. (*SG*: 19)

He then continues: 'It is only touched on in passing that a change in the relation to objects is prepared in modern atomic physics, which in the course of this passage through modern technical relations has changed human modes of representation as a whole' (*SG*: 19). These changes in human modes of representation match changes in the objective circumstances in which human beings find themselves, both of which, taken together, constitute new possibilities and new challenges to which human beings, by failing even to identify what is going on, make themselves unable to respond. These changes in modes of representation and changes in context are indications that there is also a change at work in human being itself.

In the second lecture, Heidegger retrieves from the first lecture the claim about the status of the principle of sufficient reason as a principle basic to philosophical enquiry. He draws attention to a threat posed to a productiveness in language by a process of reduction at work in the overextension of the rigorous language use characteristic of technical interaction and control. He first notes the productive translation of Latin terms into German in the course of the eighteenth century:

The translation of the Latin term *principium* through the newly formed word '*Grundsatz*' [basic principle] occurs first at the beginning of the eighteenth century in our use of language; which appears only as an inconspicuous incident in the history of language. Similarly, the to us customary terms, for example '*Absicht*' [intent] for *intentio*, '*Ausdruck*' [expression] for *expressio*, '*Gegenstand*' [object] for *objectio*, were first formed in the eighteenth century. Who would dispute that these German words are already fully developed terms? (*SG*: 32)

He then continues:

Today nothing is developing any more. Why? Because the possibilities for a thoughtful conversation are absent, because instead our speaking is directed into electronic thought and calculation machines, a process which will lead in modern technical relations and science to completely new modes of procedure and to consequences which are not anticipated. These will in all likelihood bring thought, as a process of giving meaning, into something without use and therefore make it redundant. (*SG*: 32–3)

This remark about productive language use is then the basis on which Heidegger goes on to explore a double reading of the principle 'nothing is without reason', giving it different stresses in enunciation. It can be read as claiming that every entity has a cause or reason that explains how it has come to be: 'Every entity has a cause [*Jedes Seiendes hat einen Grund*]'. There is another reading which suggests that the principle itself has no grounds:

> We stand before two possibilities, which both stimulate our thinking in equal measure. Either the principle of sufficient reason is the one principle, altogether the one thing, which is not affected by what the principle states: everything which is in any way has necessarily a ground. In this case it would be the greatest puzzle, that exactly the principle of reason and it alone falls outside its own realm of validation; the principle of sufficient reason would then remain without a ground.

Heidegger then adds: 'Or the principle of sufficient reason has a ground and necessarily so. However, in this case, this ground could not be a ground like any other' (*SG*: 27). This leads to a recognition that there are three different levels of reflection at work here: one concerned with beings as entities, another concerned with the being of these beings, and a third concerned with being as such. These distinctions retrieve the ontological difference between beings as entities and being as such. This difference is referred to again later, in lecture ten, as the hidden theme connecting up three very different ways of responding to the gap which opens up between the two readings of the principle of sufficient reason. These three different ways are Kantian transcendentalism, Nietzschean transition and Heidegger's preferred leap, the *Sprung*, which transforms thinking: 'The transcendental, the transition and the leap are certainly not identical but they are similar in so far as they belong together with the distinction between being and entities' (*SG*: 134). There are here distinct levels of reflection, and for Heidegger the move from one to another is simply a leap, not a continuous process of transition. Any attempt to reduce the sharpness of the distinction between levels simply results in an erosion of difference and a reduction of meaning.

In the third lecture, Heidegger warns against the dangers of an erosion and reduction of meaning at work in technical relations. One such change which he analyses is the transition from an analysis of basic principles of thought to the construction of axiomatic systems. These he identifies as designed to exclude or contain contradiction, in a way attempted by Hegel in his dialectical logic, but with much less economy of thought and therefore less successfully from the point of view of releasing energy for the further development of theory. There is a transition from principles as starting points for thought, which may be brought into question in the course of argumentation in the manner characteristic of Socratic dialogue, to presuppositions, which can be taken as foundational for the development of theory and forgotten about in the course of developing that theory. In this third lecture, Heidegger observes:

> Basic principles make it clear already in their name that the domain of order, which, according to the usual understanding, is the concern of axioms and principles, is a domain of sentences or propositions. Simply from this understanding of axioms as propositional there has developed in recent times the

representation of axioms according to which the role of axioms is to make secure, as suppositions and determinations, the construction of a system of propositions without contradiction. (*SG*: 40–1)

Heidegger then remarks that these axioms are determined in advance of any determination with respect to a domain of objects. They are metatheoretical, adopted by convention, not in response to any evidence about a domain of objects. Thus they can be used to construct domains of objects in ways not yet to be anticipated:

The axiomatic character of axioms consists exclusively in this role of excluding contradiction and securing against it. What an axiom might express, taken on its own, remains without objectively determinable meaning. The axiomatic form of scientific thought which is in this sense without a domain of objects is today confronted by unforeseeable [*unabsehbaren*] possibilities. (*SG*: 41)

The point of this recurrent term '*unabsehbar*', unforeseeable, is that there is no human intention determining how the meaning and construction of these systems will proceed but a logic internal to those systems themselves.

Technical construction has a dynamic over and above the intentions of the individual human beings engaged in that construction. This is the basis on which scientific research is prized: that it leads to breakthroughs of knowledge concerning, for example, genetic structure, making possible a range of interventions in human physiology undreamt of in previous epochs and not anticipated by the researchers. This disrupts any attempt to ground a theory of meaning for scientific language in speakers' meanings, since that meaning develops above and beyond individual human control and intent. In the modern context technical innovations make available forms of action which systematically change human relations to what it is to be human. Heidegger remarks on the effects on human thinking:

This axiomatic thinking is already changing human thinking, in ways which we do not remark and whose impact we do not see through. Human thought accommodates itself to the processes at work in modern technical relations [*Wesen der modernen Technik*]. Whoever reflects on this process will immediately recognise that the often heard talk about the mastering of technical relations by human beings emerges from a mode of representation which functions only on the very edges of what there actually is. (*SG*: 41)

At this point Heidegger makes the remark quoted at the beginning of this chapter about the superficiality of simply remarking that human beings are not masters but slaves of technical relations. A further two inadequate responses are identified in the following paragraph:

It would also be shortsighted and legitimate at the same time if we wanted to judge modern axiomatic thought negatively. It would be a childish and comforting representation, were we to think that this modern thinking lets itself bend back into the great free origining of Greek thought. The only fruitful way leads through this modern axiomatic representation and through its hidden grounds.

For Heidegger, simply rejecting modern technology is as unsatisfactory as any celebration of it as a realisation of a project of enquiry launched by the early Greek thinkers. His wish to contest the construal of modern science as a realisation of the aims of Greek thinkers explains his insistence on returning to those thinkers to dispute current understandings of them. Heidegger does not seek to reject technical relations but to challenge the failure to think thoroughly about their impact. Here is a remark from *Identity and Difference* about the dangers of only half thinking about this impact:

> So long as a reflection on the world of the atomic age in the full seriousness of taking responsibility only goes so far as to propose a peaceful use of atomic energy, and there comforts itself in its aims, thus long thinking remains standing at the halfway mark. Through this half measure, the technical world is extended and made more certain in its metaphysical domination. (*ID*: 105)

The insistence on using nuclear energy only for peaceful use, while a useful half measure in terms of social responsibility, is philosophically inadequate because it does not begin to address the effects of this form of energy and its preconditions on the structures of human experience. In this lecture Heidegger repeats the point that a simple rejection of the technical world is not an answer either: 'However, we cannot simply reject today's technical world as the work of the devil, nor could we destroy it, granted that it does not destroy itself.' What is needed is thought about its impact, and recognition that its impact is much more widespread and deep than is usually recognised.

The third lecture of *The Principle of Reason* concludes by locating a connection between scientific research and the principle of sufficient reason as the stimulus to such research with the following amazing question: 'How should we represent this: the university is founded on the principle of sufficient reason? Dare we make such a claim?' (*SG*: 49). Heidegger seems to be pointing out that universities are full of people deeply committed to the progress of science and the accumulation of scientific knowledge as the most worthwhile human activity. He leaves it to the listener or reader to consider what the effects of this might be, on universities and on the rest of the world, in terms of developing a critical understanding of the relation between human beings and the results of scientific discovery. This concluding remark distracts attention, however, from another process at work in this third lecture, which is the rewriting of Leibniz's principle of sufficient reason not just in the two ways pointed out in the second lecture, but also as a principle of the producibility of reasons, *principium reddendae rationis*, and as the highest or basic principle. It is on this basis that it can be thought of as a founding principle, as Heidegger puts it: 'The principle of sufficient reason is therefore for Leibniz a basic principle of the producibility of reasons' (*SG*: 45).

There are then two rewritings of the principle of sufficient reason, with, first, the principle of reason or grounds stating that all entities have preconditions and the principle concerning being, that there is something which is not an entity, which does not have preconditions. There is then also a rewriting of the first version, as both the principle that these preconditions can be stated and the claim that this principle is basic. Thus from setting up an initial splitting in the meaning of the principle of reason, Heidegger generates a multiplicity of readings which cannot be simultaneously asserted.

It is in the fourth lecture that Heidegger identifies the principle, in its ambiguity, as determining the epoch in which we live. He opens up the focus for attention even more, moving from a connection between scientific research and the foundation of modern secularised universities to a connection between the current historical epoch and the development of nuclear power. He asks: what does it mean that human beings have chosen to name the epoch in which they live after a form of supposedly natural energy?

> human beings have come so far that they have named this epoch, in which their historical determinacy is entering, after the atomic energy which has become amenable to production. We are, so it is said, in the atomic age [*Atomzeitalter*]. (*SG*: 57)

At this point he introduces the theme of strangeness, homelessness and uncanniness (*Unheimlichkeit*) which haunts the Western tradition, from Homer's *Odyssey* to Freud's psychoanalysis. He writes of an unsettlement hidden in the naming of this age:

> We do not need to see through what this means. Who indeed would suppose themselves able to achieve this perspicuity? Here today we can only achieve something else: each can go some way in following up the meanings [*nachsinnen*] of the unsettlement [*das Unheimliche*] which is hidden in the apparently harmless naming of this age. Human beings determine the epoch of their historical determinacy out of the pressure and provision of natural energy. (*SG*: 57)

And he emphasises: 'The determinate existence of human beings is stamped by the atom. [*Das Dasein des Menschen – geprägt durch das Atom.*]' What is remarkable here is that an historical epoch is named after a source of supposedly natural energy. This disrupts the relation between history and nature which is set out in distinctions between the natural sciences and the humanities. Heidegger argues, uncontroversially, that the nuclear age is possible only on the basis of nuclear physics and the discovery of elementary particles. More controversially, he goes on to suggest that without the principle of sufficient reason, as developed by Leibniz, but implicit in the philosophical tradition from its inception, the search to eliminate contradictions in theory and observation would never have been pursued with such effect as to produce the necessary science. He claims: 'We are who we are today only in so far as the enormously powerful claim of the producibility of reasons functions through us [*Wir sind nur die heutigen, die wir sind, insofern uns der großmächtige Anspruch der Zustellung des Grundes durchmachtet*]' (*SG*: 60). At this point he sets up two forces in opposition to each other: a sense of everyday groundedness and the drive to find contradictionless grounds for systematic theory through the application of the principle of sufficient reason. He opposes the abstract *Grund* of theoretical construction to an experience of everyday groundedness as *Bodenständigkeit*, autochthony or standing one's ground. He identifies the search for reasons as directly undermining the sense of everyday groundedness.

Heidegger identifies the principle of sufficient reason as operating in an uncanny, *unheimisch*, fashion:

> The nuclear age is special as a planetary epoch of human beings in so far as the power of this enormously powerful principle, the principle of the giveability of reasons (*principium reddendae rationis*) develops, indeed is let loose in an unsettling [*unheimliche*] manner in the domain which provides measure for the determinate existence of human beings [*des Daseins des Menschen*].

He goes on:

> It is to be thought in word and matter that the unique letting loose of the claim of presenting and providing reasons threatens everything which is settled [*alles Heimische*] for human beings and robs them of every ground and basis for having a sense of groundedness, robs them of that from which for a long time has grown every great epoch of humanity, every intellectual activity, opening up of worlds, every stamping of a human image [*Menschengestalt*]. (*SG*: 60)

He then remarks how few people seem to be aware of this as an issue, and here recurs the theme that the most obvious is the least thought about, raised, as noted, in the first lecture in relation to the principle of sufficient reason itself, but also applicable here in the context of the naming of the current historical epoch. In conclusion to this lecture he says: 'It is important to notice in what region we find ourselves, when we think about the principle of sufficient reason reflectively' (*SG*: 61). With this clue, Heidegger proceeds in the next lecture to consider the effect of this principle on conceptions of objectivity. He makes connections between atomic energy, nuclear science and a particular kind of objectivity in the following way: 'The reason whose production is required accomplishes at the same time what it is to be adequate as a ground, that is to suffice as fully given. For what? In order to place an object firmly in its place' (*SG*: 64). Heidegger goes on to point out that in fact in nuclear physics there are no objects any more, at least in the Newtonian sense: 'Rigorously thinking, we cannot really any more, as will be shown, speak of objects. We already move in a world, if we look carefully, in which objects, as things which stand over against, no longer occur.' He suggests that there is a connection here to the non-representational character of modern art:

That in this age art becomes objectless shows its historical proportionality and this above all, if the art without objects itself grasps that its production can no longer be a form of activity but something for which there is still lacking an adequate word. That there are artistic exhibitions of the modern kind has more to do with the power of the principle of sufficient reason and of the pro-ducibility of grounds than we for the most part recognise. (*SG*: 66)

The insight here is the following: neither the principle of sufficient reason nor modern art has anything much to do with entities any more, at least not with entities as given in advance of the activities of artistic production and scientific enquiry. Both are now concerned with producing entities, not with observing and reproducing objects presumed to be already in existence.

Heidegger identifies a significant difference between the existence of a rose and the existence of states of affairs for which reasons are sought. This introduces a distinction between self-generating processes of growth with an internal given dynamic and processes of production which are set in motion from outside the process itself. He states: 'The rose stands here openly as an example for every-thing which blooms, for everything which grows, for every growth. In this domain according to the word of the poet, the principle of sufficient reason is not valid' (*SG*: 69). The poet referred to is Angelus Silesius. He continues:

Botany will, on the contrary, give us with ease a chain of causes and conditions for the growth of growing things. But we do not need to trouble science for the proof that the growth of things which grow, against the saying of Angelus Silesius, has its why, that is its necessary grounds. For the necessity of the reasons for this growth and blooming everyday experience speaks out.

This everyday experience does not assist human beings in understanding them-selves: 'Human beings in contrast to the rose live variously so, hiding from themselves how their world works, what it holds and expects of them' (*SG*: 72). The principle of sufficient reason holds for roses when viewed from a human perspective, but not for roses taken for their own sake: 'What then is the status of the *principium reddendae rationis*? It is valid of the rose but not for the rose; of the rose in so far as it is an object for our representation; not for the rose in so far as this stands in itself and is simply a rose' (*SG*: 75). Thus two domains of entities open up: those taken as objects of human experience, for which a giving of reasons is required, and those taken for themselves, for which such reasons are redundant. This is a contrast between the domain of enquiry, constructed by human beings, and an everyday world in which what there is can be taken for granted. By failing to consider the difference between these domains, the differ-ence between technical relations and everyday relations is elided. Furthermore, the role of human beings in bringing technical relations into existence is elided as well. It appears as though technical relations have an independent and autono-mous existence and their development can come to evolve as though there were some inexorable logic at work. While technical processes take on the appearance of self-generating processes, human beings are placed in relations above and beyond our control.

In the seventh lecture Heidegger summarises this chain of reasoning in the following way: 'nature becomes an object and indeed a representation which lays out and secures its processes as a fixed set-up and can be counted on [*berechenbaren Bestand*]' (*SG*: 100). This reduction of nature, first to an object for human beings, a *Gegenstand*, of which it is possible to produce representations, *Vorstellungen*, and then to a fixed standing reserve, *Bestand*, conceals that there is a stance from which that reduction is taking place: the stance of human interaction with nature. This concealment in turn conceals the fact that how human beings conceive of nature plays a role in determining how human beings conceive of themselves. Thus the effects of changes in conceptions of nature on conceptions of what it is to be human drop out of view. Heidegger does not pursue this thought at this point, but turns instead to summarise his conclusions concerning Leibniz. It becomes very obvious that this is not a faithful reading of Leibniz's texts, but a construction of them for the purposes of developing his own questioning of the nature of grounds and reasons. In conclusion to the seventh lecture Heidegger provides his five observations concerning the ambiguity of the principle of sufficient reason as both a principle concerning grounds or reasons and a principle concerning being:

The recapitulation of the five main theses named:
1: the incubation time of the principle of reason;
2: the presentation of the principle of reason as a highest basic principle;
3: the claim of the principle of sufficient reason as the most powerful principle which determines our historical epoch;
4: ground as a questionable in order to [*warum*] and as a taken-for-granted while, as long as [*weil*];
5: the change in the way of stressing the principle of reason. (*SG*: 103)

However, Heidegger is not just summarising his own thoughts on Leibniz. He also gives the appearance of giving a definitive reading of Leibniz's importance, as the theorist who produced the explicit statement of this principle. The problem with this is that there are other ways of construing Leibniz's importance, in terms of Leibniz's own philosophical aims and interests. This summary subordinates those interests to Heidegger's own preoccupations.

This is a reading of Leibniz in the context of an overarching analysis of the history of philosophy as culminating in the current condition of human beings. This condition is identified by Heidegger as crucially related to the spread of those technical relations, which Heidegger sees as facilitated by the principle of sufficient reason. This set of presumptions results in a highly selective version of Leibniz's thought. I suggest that this reveals a moment of ethical choice in approaches to reading the text of the other, where fidelity is just one in a number of options. There is one kind of reading that Heidegger is clearly not engaged in: reconstructing the concerns of authors themselves in the development of their thought. This kind of reading studies letters and contemporary discussions of authors' works to discover what considerations might be in operation in any move from one manner of exposition and enquiry to another. This can be called an historicising approach. Heidegger by contrast tends to cite letters and extracts from authors' works in order to explain how he, Heidegger, has come to the view of that author which he is putting forward. There is a second form of reading which attempts to discover a single coherent system in an author's writing and thinking, which attempts to discover, for example, the underarticulated basic system holding the enquiries in Kant's three critiques in relation to each other. This prefers Kantianism to Kant's own thought and sometimes leads simply to a rejection of large parts of what an author wrote on the ground that it is not compatible with some identified overarching main theme of the work. This form of reading can be called, in line with Heidegger's own usage, a metaphysical reading. It seeks to reveal a system of coherent thought at work in the writings. There is finally what I am calling an ethical reading, which openly prioritises the relations of the current interpreter to his or her own present circumstances and preoccupations concerning the future. This prioritises these concerns over the concern both with historical accuracy and with producing an account that puts emphasis on coherence and consistency of exposition. This ethical reading addresses current and future conditions, rather than accepting without question either the value of faithfulness to authors' intentions or the value of coherent, complete interpretation.

The lecture form of Heidegger's discussion of Leibniz permits Heidegger to hold together aims which threaten at several points to diverge and certainly make it difficult to give a straightforward exposition of what is being discussed. My suggestion is that Heidegger's *Principle of Reason* vacillates between a metaphysical and an ethical reading of Leibniz, at some points appearing to state a definitive truth about Leibniz's work and at others providing an ethical reading by taking themes perhaps at most suggested by Leibniz, in order to make possible a response to present conditions and contemporary issues. The thirteen-lecture cycle, especially the first seven lectures, read as a sequence, takes the form of a definitive reading, which the last six lectures and the appended single lecture then subvert. The single lecture has much more the form of a questioning of philosophy from the point of view of current concerns. Were it more obvious that no such definitive reading is possible, and that indeed Heidegger himself rejects such definitive reading, then it would be more obvious what Heidegger is doing: using Leibniz to open out the kind of thinking which Heidegger supposes needed in the present age. The central theses are that only for human beings is there an ambiguity in the principle of sufficient reason and that this principle emerges as a principle at a particular juncture in the development of knowledge, making technical innovation possible. This reveals that the question of technology requires a questioning of what it is to be human, which is taken up in the next two chapters.

Chapter 3

Humanism and homelessness

Homelessness becomes world destiny. *(WM*: 336)

In this chapter I continue discussing an interdependence between two of Heidegger's major concerns, the question of being and a question about what it is to be human. This interdependence is made evident in two letters he wrote after the defeat of Nazism. The first letter was written in 1955 in reply to his old friend, Ernst Jünger.[1] It was at first called 'Over the line' ('Über die Linie'), but was published in 1956 as *Zur Seinsfrage*.[2] Since it presents an extended discussion of nihilism, I shall refer to it as 'the letter on nihilism'. The second is Heidegger's letter to Jean Beaufret from 1946, known as the 'Letter on humanism', responding to Beaufret's queries concerning Heidegger's relation to Sartre's existentialism. Both are published in German in *Wegmarken* (1967, 1978), the collection of Heidegger's writings from 1919 to 1961. The epigraph to this chapter is taken from the 'Letter on humanism'. In it, there is an implied reading of Sartre's texts; in the letter to Jünger, the implied philosophical other is, emphatically, Nietzsche. Nevertheless, in these letters, by contrast to the analysis in the lectures discussed in the previous chapter, Heidegger develops his own thinking more directly, as though having a living interlocutor permitted a greater freedom of thought.

While one letter has humanism and the other nihilism as its theme, they both share a discussion of a transition from philosophy to thinking and of the implications of this for language. The 'Letter on humanism' contains the remark about breaking off the project in *Being and Time* because of a failure to find a form of language for articulating a turn from *Dasein* to *Sein*. The letter to Jünger concludes by moving rapidly from an invocation of Hölderlin through a reference to Nietzsche's breakdown to an even more remarkable quotation from Goethe concerning the use of language. While the references to Heidegger's own earlier work in the 'Letter on humanism' are primarily to *Being and Time*, in the letter to Jünger there are also references to the 1929 lecture 'What is metaphysics?' I shall discuss these two letters in reverse chronological order, developing the question of nihilism first. This permits my discussion of humanism to be informed by the question of nihilism. If justification for this inversion is needed, it is perhaps relevant to point out that the lectures on Nietzsche given between 1936 and 1944 are an extended engagement with the question of nihilism, such that the only slightly later 'Letter on humanism' can be supposed to emerge out of that questioning. The letter on nihilism responds to Jünger's reflections on nihilism. Heidegger asserts: 'The essence of nihilism, which completes itself in the dominance of the will to will, rests on the forgetting of being' (*WM*: 416). The letter links nihilism to the forgetting of being and to the overcoming of that forgetting in a 'recovery' (*Verwindung*) from metaphysics. Thus the question of metaphysics, discussed by Heidegger in relation to Nietzsche during the war years, here turns into the question of the completion and overcoming of nihilism.

Heidegger writes of the overcoming of nihilism: 'such overcoming, however, occurs in the space of a recovery from metaphysics [*solche Überwindung aber geschieht im Raume der Verwindung der Metaphysik*]' (*WM*: 410). And he explains: 'The recovery from metaphysics is a recovery from the forgetting of being. This recovery turns towards the essence of metaphysics. [*Die Verwindung der Metaphysik ist Verwindung der Seinsvergessenheit. Die Verwindung wendet sich dem Wesen der Metaphysik zu.*]' This recovery from the forgetting of being, however, does not lie simply at the behest of human beings. It depends on a turn in being itself. Heidegger remarks that this recovery appears at first sight like an overcoming (*Überwindung*) but that in fact: 'in this recovery there returns the abiding truth of metaphysics which only appears discardable. Its true appropriable essence returns as its own' (*WM*: 410). He elaborates:

> Here there is something else going on than a mere restoration of metaphysics. Furthermore, there cannot be a restoration which simply takes up what has been passed down, as someone gathers the apples which have fallen off a tree. Every restoration is an interpretation of metaphysics. Whoever today believes themselves able to see through metaphysical questioning as a whole in its specificity and history and supposes to be able to follow it should consider, since he likes to feel so superior as he moves in these clear bright regions, from where the light comes for this clear vision. (*WM*: 410)

Here Heidegger obliquely invokes the processes of *Seinsgeschick*, which either do or do not permit a vision of what there is and of how it occurs to appear as such. The recovery from metaphysics is a process grounded in a recovery from the forgetting of being, which is accomplished not by human being but by being itself.

The key sentence here is: 'Every restoration is an interpretation of metaphysics.' Even though the recovery from metaphysics requires a sending of being, it also requires that there be an instance of *Dasein*, constructing a thrown, partial understanding and interpretation of that sending. In this letter, Heidegger's discussion of language centres on questions about a relation between the language of metaphysics and the attempt to think through the implications of a completion or recovery from metaphysics. The language used to declare a transition out of metaphysics can itself be firmly placed within metaphysics, retaining metaphysical patterns of thought. Thus, despite the declaration, the thinking remains metaphysical; and a failure to think about the role of language can block the attempt to think through to an overcoming of nihilism in a recovery from metaphysics. Language for Heidegger is not entirely within the control of human beings. There are in it forces above and beyond human control. In order to go beyond nihilism it is necessary to recognise these forces in language and permit them to come into play in the way language is used in the production of meaning. The relation between the question of being and the question of what it is to be human emerges in this question of language. In the age of technology, the question of being becomes even more inaccessible for human beings, because the demands made on language for the expression of technical relations restrict its expressive capacities. There is a reduction of the powers of language in the contemporary epoch, which is one aspect of the withdrawal of being and of the abandonment of entities and of human being by being, *Seinsverlassenheit*.

This *Seinsverlassenheit*, literally being 'left behind by being' or, more usually, the withdrawal of being, makes itself evident in the extreme matter-of-factness of the way in which what there is presents itself to us in the present epoch. This matter-of-factness is protected from question by the extremity of the withdrawal of being. Heidegger draws attention to the fact that this very matter-of-factness is all the same conditional on being taking this form of withdrawal. The withdrawal is evident in one-dimensional understandings of the term 'transcendence' which emphasise a movement from immanence to transcendence, but have no room for a move from transcendence to immanence. There is in the term a conceptual-isation of the move from entities to being, but no recognition of the correlative move from being to entities. The discussion of transcendence in this letter links back to the discussion of being in *Being and Time* as the *transcendens schlechthin*, the transcendent without qualification. In this later discussion, Heidegger declares transcendence, *Transzendenz*, along with value, *Wert*, and *Gestalt*, to be basic metaphysical concepts, which assist in blocking the development of non-metaphysical forms of language and thinking. Through this analysis Heidegger retrieves the thought of *Being and Time* from the restrictions imposed on it by using such limiting language. The discussion of transcendence also links into Heidegger's insistence on distinguishing between human being, the mortals and a sense for divinity. This connects with Heidegger's critique of the use of human cognitive faculties as a foundation in the epistemologies of Descartes and Kant. The three main themes for discussion in this chapter are language, transcendence and a connection between being and being human.

In this letter to Jünger, the emphasis is on deepening the analysis provided by Jünger, by revealing a further level of meaning at work undetected by Jünger. This is a case study of Heidegger's method of reading into the text of another a level of meaning that is not evident to the writer in writing. Towards the end of his letter, Heidegger claims: 'What is this letter trying to do? It is trying to bring the title 'Over the line' to a higher multiplicity of meanings . . .' (*WM*: 418). According to Heidegger, what is preventing Jünger from reaching this higher multiplicity of meanings is a residue of metaphysical thinking in the use of traditional categories which are locked into metaphysical structures. Crudely, metaphysical structure reduces multiple meaning to univocal, single meaning. Heidegger suggests that Jünger's thought is struggling to break the constraints of this metaphysical language, much as he claims that his own thinking in *Being and Time* was restricted by the inflexibility of the language within which he was then working. Heidegger thus gives a diagnosis relevant to his own work as a response to the work of the other. This I suggest is a recurrent pattern in his responses to others, which is particularly evident in these two letters: the response to the other assists him to analyse problems in his own thinking. Heidegger's letter to Jünger also suggests how Heidegger might have responded to objections on behalf of, for example, Leibniz. Heidegger is quite clear that he is reading into Jünger's writings a level which he supposes Jünger himself to be unable to express. The challenge to metaphysical language permeates the letter.

The letter opens with a distinction between Jünger's requirement to cross the line (*trans lineam*) out of nihilism and Heidegger's own reflection on the line (*de linea*). The change in preposition, from *trans* to *de*, suggests that it is as much a problem of interpreting and understanding what this line might be as one of taking up some active attitude towards it. Heidegger introduces the line under discussion:

> The zero line has its zone as a meridian. The domain of completed nihilism forms the boundary between two eras. The line designating it is the critical line. By means of it is decided whether the movement of nihilism ends in negative nothingness or whether it is the transition to the region of 'a new turning of being' [*einer neuen Zuwendung des Seins*]. The movement of nihilism must accordingly be intended of itself for diverse possibilities and according to its essence have a number of meanings. (*WM*: 380)

By considering various meanings of this line, distinctions between possible meanings of nihilism can begin to emerge. Thus it is possible to distinguish between negative nihilism, which simply results in a negation of existing value, and affirmative nihilism, which negates that value because that value is valueless, thus clearing the way to another beginning. Jünger is very much concerned to make such a new beginning possible. Heidegger points out that, in Jünger's case, the language in play on this side of a transition is the same as that in use on the other side of a transition:

> However, this attempt to have a discussion by letter with you, to say a bit about the line, meets with a particular difficulty. The reason for that lies in the fact that in the 'beyond' of 'on the line', that is in the space this side and that side of the line, you speak the same language. It seems that the position of nihilism has been given up, but its language remains. (*WM*: 388)

The implication is clear: in order for nihilism to be overcome it is necessary to find a different language from the language of nihilism, which for Heidegger, because of its function in eliding the question of being, is the language of metaphysics. For a transition out of nihilism to take place it is not a question of moving from one locality to another, but of transforming the locality in which we already find ourselves, transforming our stance with respect to that locality. Heidegger clearly supposes that this transformation takes place through attaining a different relation to language. In conjunction with the language of a 'restoration of metaphysics', this refusal of the image of crossing over out of nihilism subverts the interpretation of Heidegger as crossing over out of, or going beyond metaphysics.

Heidegger seeks to make himself and his readers capable of occupying the site or locality (*Ortschaft*) at which we find ourselves in a different way, such that the alternative to the language of metaphysics and its nihilistic implications becomes available. The loss of a sense for a different way of occupying this site connects with the theme of homelessness in the 'Letter on humanism'. The theme of homelessness is introduced in the letter on nihilism through a reference to Nietzsche's remark from *Will to Power*, which Heidegger cites as 'The Plan, *WW xv*, p. 141', to the effect that nihilism is the strangest of all guests. Heidegger explains that nihilism is the strangest of all guests because it reveals that there is no longer a home for anyone:

> Nihilism is the 'strangest' [*unheimlichsten*] of all guests because it is as the unconditional will to will complete homelessness [*Heimatlosigkeit*]. There is no point in trying to show this guest the door, since this guest has already invisibly gone right through the household. (*WM*: 381)

Nihilism has made itself at home. However, there is a difference between the nihilism discussed by Nietzsche and that discussed by Heidegger. Heidegger states that the nihilism which Nietzsche detects in Europe has become global: 'So what was at first just a European nihilism is now appearing as a planetary phenomenon' (*WM*: 383). It is on this basis that Heidegger can claim that the approaching completion of nihilism is the domain or border between two epochs: 'The domain of completed nihilism sets up a border between two world epochs' (*WM*: 380). Only if the phenomenon is global can it have this epochal status. Nietzsche is important for Heidegger, because he begins to diagnose the dangers and paradoxes of nihilism. However, to understand nihilism, it is no longer sufficient to be a physician of culture: it is now necessary to diagnose not cultures but the whole of human existence. Heidegger's discussion of nihilism continually returns to a reading of Nietzsche, but also continually affirms the need to go beyond the thinking of Nietzsche.

The theme of irrationalism from the 'Letter on humanism' is retrieved:

> Most worthy of thought is the process that binds together rationalism and irrationalism in an exchange out of which they will never again re-emerge and furthermore do not want to emerge. In this way people refuse every possibility according to which a thinking might respond to a command which holds itself outside this either/or of the rational and the irrational. (*WM*: 382)

In this zone between epochs, customary distinctions between what counts as rational and what counts as irrational are disrupted. The theme of reason and rationalisation is a key one for the diagnosis of nihilism. Heidegger remarks:

> Reason and its conceptions are only one kind of thinking and are determined not by themselves but by that which has been called thinking, to think in the manner of *ratio*. That its dominance arises as rationalisation of all categories, as establishing norms, as a levelling in the course of the unfolding of European nihilism, provides food for thought just as do the concomitant attempts at flight into the irrational. (*WM*: 382)

This theme of flight returns in the context of a discussion of nihilism becoming the normal condition in which human beings find themselves. The assertion of the normalisation of nihilism runs:

> On the one hand the movement of nihilism has become ever more obvious in its planetary and corrosive, many-faceted irresistibility. No one of insight would today deny that nihilism in the most various and hidden forms is the normal state [*Normalzustand*] of human beings (see Nietzsche, *Will to Power*, no. 23). (*WM*: 386)

Heidegger then goes on to identify what he takes to be unhelpful responses to this spread of nihilism. There are, first, attempts to revive dead tradition: 'The best evidence of this are the exclusively reactive attempts against nihilism which, instead of entering into a discussion of its essence, strive for a restoration of what has been [*des Bisherigen*]. They seek salvation in flight' (*WM*: 386). There is also the response of metaphysical abstraction, away from current conditions into a timeless eternity. Third, there is the equally metaphysical attempt to renounce metaphysics without adequately carrying out a critique of it and to take refuge in new disciplines with their concealed metaphysical commitments:

> The same flight is also urgent where apparently all metaphysics is abandoned and is replaced by logistics, sociology and psychology. The will to know which breaks forth here and its more tractable total organisation point to an increase of the will to power which is of a different kind from that which Nietzsche designated as active nihilism. (*WM*: 386)

Heidegger thus preserves Nietzsche's distinction between deliberate destruction of value and a destruction of value resulting from attempts to preserve it or, supposedly, enhance the world.

Heidegger adds a cautionary note about supposing that simply because nihilism in its essence is evident, its completion is therefore also in sight:

> With the fulfilment of nihilism there begins only the final phase of nihilism. Its zone, because it is dominated throughout by a normal state and its consolidation, is presumably unusually broad. That is why the zero line, where fulfilment approaches the end, is not yet visible at that end. (*WM*: 387)

For this reason he distances himself from Jünger's language of crossing the line into the new epoch. He suggests that it may be too early to talk in terms of such a transition in this letter, although in his recently published *Vom Ereignis*,[3] written between 1936 and 1938, he is less cautious. Heidegger identifies in Jünger's thinking a retention of Nietzsche's categories, which, according to Heidegger, are both no longer adequate for current conditions and still metaphysical. Heidegger also criticises some readings of Nietzsche as similarly obstructing further thought. He disputes the presumption that the death of God announced by Nietzsche leads to human beings taking the place of that God as the originator of what there is: 'It would be a really crude explanation, were one to say that here in a secularised world human beings take the place of God as the originator of entities. Certainly the essence of what it is to be human is in play here.' He then makes the crucial observation: 'But this essence, to be understood verbally, this *'Dasein'* of human beings (see *Kant and the Problem of Metaphysics*, first edition, 1929, paragraph 43) is not human' (*WM*: 390–1). Thus, just as the essence of technology is not just technological, so the essence of what it is to be human is not just human. This move blocks the attempt to posit human self-awareness in place of God as the ground of reality and source of order in the world. This self-awareness is only a part of what it is to be human.

This makes it possible to claim that an ethics not only need not but indeed cannot be anthropocentric. A discussion of human beings must be at least bipolar, tracing out the place in which human beings might flourish, between the human and the non-human. If the subject of ethics is what it is to be human, and if what it is to be human is in part non-human, then the subject of ethics is not simply centred on humanity. Any ethical relation of the self to itself or to another is thus conditional on a relation to otherness, as the non-human. The crucial problem then becomes: how is this non-human to be understood? Heidegger suggests that this non-human is only too often understood as animality, which he suggests is not an adequate basis on which to characterise otherness.[4] In the modern epoch, however, human beings increasingly characterise themselves in contraposition to technical relations. Here there is a difference to be marked between understanding oneself in terms of technical relations, assuming those technical relations to be only technical, and understanding oneself in that relation, affirming those technical relations to be conditional on a sending and withdrawal of being. In the latter case, setting up technical relations as the other is not so reductive and distorting. It is indeed this attempt which characterises much of Heidegger's later writings.

VARIETIES OF TRANSCENDENCE

Heidegger's questioning of transcendence in this letter reveals why he is increasingly wary of using the language of transcendence in any description of *Dasein*. He traces out some ambiguities in the term 'transcendence':

Transcendence is firstly the relationship between entities and being, starting from the former and going towards the latter. Transcendence is, however, at the same time the relationship leading from changeable entities to being in repose; transcendence, finally, corresponding to the use of the title 'excellency', is that highest being itself which can then also be called being, and from this results a strange mixture with the first meaning mentioned. (*WM*: 391)

One of the hazards of metaphysical thinking is that it cannot identify different elements of a definition as holding good at different times. There is then a tendency to try to show a compatibility between hopelessly heterogeneous elements, as with the first and third meanings of the term 'transcendence' introduced here. In this sketch of an account of transcendence, and of the weaknesses of conceptions associated with it, there is a suggestion of a parallel with the account Heidegger gives of the weakness of construing accounts of human beings on the basis of comparisons with animals. The problem is that human beings and transcendence are being defined more by contrast to what they are not, by contrast to animals and to ordinary entities, than with respect to their own essence, to what they might be. The focus is not on the specificity of being human, with a relation to and an understanding of being. Heidegger thus distinguishes between a metaphysical conception of transcendence as an established philosophical category and his own preferred terms, *Überstieg*, here translated as transition, and *Sprung*, the leap.

He identifies his thinking as in tension with the forces in play in metaphysical language. He sets out a distinction between metaphysical and scientific concepts and seeks to distinguish a third form of language use from both of these uses. Referring once again to Jünger's use of language, he writes:

In your and my case, however, it is a question not even only of concepts of science, but of basic words such as *Gestalt*, dominance, representation, power, will, value, security, of the state of being present [*Anwesen*] and nothingness, which as absence of the state of being present 'negates' without ever destroying it. In so far as nothingness 'negates', it confirms itself rather as a distinct state of being present and veils itself as such. In the basic words named, a kind of language prevails other than scientific propositions. To be sure, metaphysical thinking also knows concepts. These differ, however, from scientific concepts not only in regard to the degree of generality. (*WM*: 396)

The suggestion is that scientific concepts are hypothetical not categorical, and are thus not metaphysical. However, once the question of justification of forms of language use is posed and responded to, then there is a shift from hypothetical to categorical use, and there is a reversion to metaphysics. Heidegger asserts that this difference between metaphysical and scientific concepts is also an issue for Kant in the *Critique of Pure Reason* and goes on to identify both Jünger and himself as making use of a range of terms which have a different status from that of scientific terms:

> metaphysical concepts are in their essence of a different sort in so far as that which they comprehend and the comprehension itself remains the same in some original sense. Therefore, in the realm of the basic words of thinking it is even less a matter of indifference whether they are forgotten or whether one keeps on using them untested and moreover uses them there where we should step out of the zone in which the 'concepts' named by you say what is authoritative, that is the zone of complete nihilism. (*WM*: 396–7)

Metaphysical concepts proffer definitive descriptions of what there is such that there is no gap between what there is and how it is described. This makes it impossible for there to be forces above and beyond human understanding and thus excludes any invocation of being and of the sendings of being, which Heidegger supposes to be crucially and critically forgotten in the European tradition. Heidegger claims that Jünger's thought is expressed in the terms of established philosophical categories and that therefore he cannot think through to the full meaning of its own insights. It is this full meaning which Heidegger seeks to reveal in his letter.

Heidegger puts his thought concerning the relation between thought and language in the form of a string of questions:

> In what language does the basic outline of thinking speak which indicates a crossing of the line? Is the language of the metaphysics of the will to power, of the *Gestalt* and of values to be rescued on the other side, by crossing the critical line? What if the language of metaphysics itself and indeed metaphysics as metaphysics, whether it be that of the living or that of the dead God, forms the barrier which forbids a crossing of the line, that is the overcoming of nihilism? If this is so then surely the crossing of the line would necessarily become a transformation of language and demand a transformed relation to the essence of language? (*WM*: 399)

The metaphysics of the dead God clearly is a reference to Nietzsche. In both kinds of metaphysics, the use of metaphysical language prevents both the completion of metaphysics and an overcoming of nihilism. It obstructs the move into the new form of thinking, of a new and non-metaphysical set of relations between human beings, being and the future. Heidegger makes a question out of his view that the transformation of language is needed for the completion of metaphysics and the overcoming of nihilism, for a transition to a non-metaphysical, non-nihilistic era. This string of questions prompts him to comment: 'I am writing all of this in the form of questions, for as far as I can see, thinking can do no more today than consider without stopping what calls forth these questions' (*WM*: 399). This question form permits Heidegger to avoid the paradoxes of assertion, in which he would appear to have asserted the existence of the form of language which he supposes to be as yet unavailable. The question form evades any straightforward recuperation into the logic of a metaphysics of presence. Heidegger then cites a remark of Jünger's: 'The moment at which the line is crossed brings a new direction of being and with it there begins to shimmer what is real' (*WM*: 400). Heidegger opts to reverse the order here: 'The sentence is easy to read but difficult to think. Above all, I should like to ask whether, on the contrary, it is not rather the new direction of being which first brings the moment for the crossing of the line' (*WM*: 400). He is thus marking the priority of being and of the sendings of being over any results in a process of transition. This priority is elided in metaphysical language.

Heidegger then specifies the condition of human beings in relation to being as that which prompts such a new beginning. It is not a transient condition:

> To be sure, the turning towards and away of being if we pay sufficient attention to them never present themselves just as if they touched human beings only occasionally and momentarily. The essence of human beings rather depends on the fact that it endures and dwells [*währt und wohnt*] for a time in either the turning towards or the turning away. (*WM*: 401)

Thus the process of overcoming will also be one with duration, perhaps longer than a human lifespan. It is characteristic of the present circumstance of a turning away of being that human beings should tend to think in terms only of the short term and in terms of an encounter with themselves, their activities and other entities, leaving out the relation to being and to processes which it is hard to think of as completable. Heidegger remarks a parallel between over- and underestimating both the scope of what it is to be human and the significance of being. He also sets out linkages between the two processes, in a typically convoluted remark, which only just maintains its momentum through the parallel structure of the two main sentences:

> We always say too little of 'being itself' when, in saying 'being', we leave out the being present in the essence of human beings and thereby fail to recognise that this essence itself helps to determine 'being'. We also say too little about human beings if, in saying 'being', not 'being human', we set human beings apart and only then bring that which has been set apart into relation with 'being'. We always say too much, however, if we mean being as the all-encompassing and thereby represent human beings as a special being amongst others (plants, animals) and put both into the relationship; for there already lies in the essence of human beings a relationship to that which, through the relating, determines the relation as 'being'. (*WM*: 401)

Thus human beings are unlike other kinds of entity in that human beings already have a relation to being; they do not acquire that relation for the first time in the attempt to analyse different kinds of being and the relations between them. As a consequence of this special status, only human being can have a relation to nihilism.

The language of transcendence can be taken to pick out the move of a located identity away from and out of its immanent placing. In *Being and Time*, Heidegger uses the language of ecstatic illumination for this, to indicate that there is no question of leaving behind altogether the facticity of the condition in which *Dasein* is for the most part to be found. In contrast to the ecstatic relation between *Dasein* and context, there is also in *Being and Time* the claim concerning being as the transcendent itself:

> Everywhere there is the transition (*Überstieg*) which comes back to being, the '*transcendens schlechthin*' (*Being and Time*, section 7), '*das Sein*' *des Seienden*. Transition is metaphysics itself in which this name does not now mean a doctrine and discipline of philosophy, but this: that there is [*es gibt*] such a transition (*Being and Time*, section 43c) (*WM*: 407)

Here there is a shift from metaphysics as restrictive and reductive to metaphysics as a marker of a transition out of distorted thinking. This is the restoration of metaphysics. It is at this point that Heidegger claims that the overcoming of metaphysics is the overcoming of the forgetting of being, and a restoration of metaphysics. He claims that: 'in the recovery there returns the abiding truth of metaphysics which only appears discardable. Its true appropriable essence returns as its own' (*WM*: 410). Heidegger proposes that in order for this restoration to take place it is necessary for human beings to ask the question 'What is metaphysics?', as he himself did in his inaugural lecture. I am suggesting that this restoration requires also a restoration of ethics and requires that the question be asked: what is ethics? My answer to this question is that ethics is more than simply ethical and more than simply concerned with humanity. The transition of which Heidegger writes is possible only when there has already taken place the Nietzschean descent, the *Abstieg*, out of the rarefied abstractions of metaphysics and nihilism, out of the philosophical categories of which transcendence is one, back into the determinate contexts of human existence. However, Heidegger also identifies Nietzsche as the philosopher of the limit: the thinker in whose thought the forgetting of being is most pronounced. This is implied by the claim that Nietzsche is the last metaphysician.

Heidegger sets out the relation between nothingness, nihilism and the withdrawal of being by setting out a question and then replying:

> Does nothingness vanish with the completion or at least the overcoming of nihilism? Presumably, overcoming is only attained when, instead of the appearance of negative nothingness, the essence of nothingness which was once related to 'being' can arrive and be accepted by us mortals. (*WM*: 404)

If this nothingness of nihilism is disconnected from being, it can only be understood as a negative force. The overcoming of nihilism requires setting nothingness back into relation with being. The first stage is to recognise that this nothingness which finds expression in nihilism is not external to human beings. Nihilism can be overcome if human beings repossess and take responsibility for the nothingness which is set loose through externalising it. Heidegger specifies the relation between the essence of completed nihilism and the completion of metaphysics thus: 'The zone of the critical line as the place of the essence of completed nihilism should then be sought out where the essence of metaphysics develops its utmost possibility and draws itself back together' (*WM*: 408). Heidegger supposes this takes place 'where the will to will sets out and challenges everything present solely in the general and uniform placability of component parts' (*WM*: 408). This challenge occurs in human beings and comes to expression in the life-work of Nietzsche. Nietzschean will to power in combination with the culmination of scientific research in technical relations makes this challenge a reality in the world. To go beyond this completion and to overcome nihilism, it is necessary to return to the occasion for the forgetting of being: the attempt by human beings to construct systematic exhaustive theory. Heidegger expands on the step back or return necessary for an overcoming of nihilism:

> The entry into its essence is the first step by which nihilism is left behind. The path of this entry has the direction and manner of going back. This does not, to be sure, mean a going backward into times lived through in the past in order tentatively to refresh them in an artificial form. The 'back' here designates the direction towards that locality (the forgetting of being) [*jene Ortschaft (die Seinsvergessenheit)*] from which metaphysics obtains and retains its derivation. (*WM*: 416)

This locality of the forgetting of being is human being itself. The need is to step back into the question of what it is to be human. This is the step back of the essay *Identity and Difference* discussed in Chapter 2. It is not a return to a previous historical period, the time of the Greeks or a time before the institutionalising of the Christian Church. It is an everyday occurrence, which is memorialised and concealed in metaphysical construction.

Because human beings have this relation to nihilism, indeed because human beings are implicated in the emergence of nihilism, human beings are necessarily going to be involved in the processes of overcoming nihilism:

> The essence of human beings itself belongs to the essence of nihilism and thereby to the paths of its completion. Human beings are the essence put to use by being to constitute the zone of being and therefore also the zone of nothingness. Human beings do not stand in the zone of critical nothingness. Human beings are this zone, although not simply for their own sake and not of their own accord. (*WM*: 406)

It is for this reason that Heidegger disputes Jünger's claim that the time has come to step beyond nihilism and by implication to step beyond metaphysics. Heidegger, by contrast, is claiming that human beings are the very nihilism and metaphysics which Jünger hopes may be transcended. The mode of life adopted by human beings in the age of technical relations is nihilistic and constitutes the completion of metaphysics. The overcoming of nihilism requires human beings to overcome this nihilistic self-renouncing way of life and to return to human being as potential for change. Heidegger thus seems to be claiming that, despite his enormous efforts, Nietzsche fails to affirm potentiality and is thus incapable of affirmation. Heidegger claims that there is a connection here back to a change in human beings: 'In the zone of the line, nihilism nears its completion. The totality of the 'human resource' can only cross over the line when they step out of the zone of a completed nihilism. Accordingly, a discussion of the line must ask what the fulfilment of nihilism consists in' (*WM*: 387). Heidegger argues that a transformation of human beings into a resource is required for the development of technical relations and for the completion of nihilism:

> Nihilism is completed when it has seized all the component realities and appears everywhere, when nothing can assert itself any longer as an exception in so far as nihilism has become the normal state. However, it is only as this normal state that its completion is realised. The former is a consequence of the latter. (*WM*: 387)

That is, the normalisation of nihilism is a condition for its completion. In this 'normal state' even human beings have been subordinated to the emptying-out processes of nihilism, one sign of which is the decline of language. To go beyond nihilism, this transformation of human beings into a resource must itself be overcome.

Heidegger makes a connection back to the analysis of *Dasein* in *Being and Time*, which is here developed into the thought that human beings are the placeholder for nihilism. This means that human beings are the site for the occurrence of nihilism and that without human beings there would be no nihilism. Heidegger recoups this theme with a reference to *Dasein*: 'The *Dasein des Menschen* is "held within" "this" nothingness, which is quite other to entities. This could be put another way: human beings are the placeholder for nothingness' (*WM*: 412–13). This nothingness, which is quite other to entities, is nothingness only if the role of being in the presencing of entities is not recognised. In the current epoch, the withdrawal of being in its extremity leads to being manifesting only as nothingness. It is human beings who are the placeholders both for being and for nothingness. With the forgetting and abandonment of being, human beings become the placeholders only for nothingness. This is an important claim. What the onset of the completion of nihilism suggests is not that it has suddenly become the case that human beings are the placeholders of nihilism. What has happened is that human beings have changed in their stance towards that nothingness. In becoming a functionary in technical relations, it becomes harder for human beings to recognise a dimension of negativity in themselves and to recognise nothingness as a feature of themselves. The deepening forgetting of being makes this recognition even harder. This failure to recognise nothingness as a feature of the human condition, or in Heidegger's language, a feature of *Dasein*, the site at which the essence of what it is to be human is revealed, is an aspect of the forgetting of being. A disowned nothingness is projected out into the world. Although that world is also a projection of human beings, such that the nothingness in the world is no less a part of what it is to be human than having a world at all, human beings, by dissociation, permit both world and nothingness to gain a force over against them. This leads to a deepening nihilism.

At the end of philosophy, with the completion of metaphysics and of nihilism, nihilism and metaphysics become the unacknowledged ethics in which human beings live in relation to themselves, each other, and to being. This is an ethics not in the sense of a desirable or, indeed, best form of life, most conducive to human self-realisation. It is a form of ethics in the sense of being a way of going on, of constructing an accommodation to existing forces and relations. It is not a critical ethics, since, instead of seeking to transform existing conditions and forces, for example by criticising the language in which they are identified, it takes meaning and language as given, non-negotiable, fixed points of reference. Coming to terms with nihilism and metaphysics is a coming to terms with the essence of what it is to be human: the creation of nihilism, the sense of homelessness and the transient nature of human existence. Rejecting humanism as an answer to what it is to be human permits human beings to ask again what it is to be human and to get back in touch with that element in themselves which generates both nihilism and metaphysics in the attempt to contain that nihilism. In conclusion to this letter to Jünger, Heidegger claims that Nietzsche heard a command that human beings should prepare for world domination. The preparation for world domination entails a conflict, but not one such as world war:

> This is not a war but the *polemos*, which causes gods and human beings, free human beings and the enslaved, first to appear in their essence, and it brings about a setting up of distinct elements out of being. Compared with this, world wars remain mere foreground. They are able to decide less and less, the more technological their armaments become. (*WM*: 418)

Heidegger comments:

> Nietzsche heard this command to reflect on the essence and emergence of this planetary domination. He followed the call to this path of metaphysical thinking which was assigned to him and collapsed on the way. Thus runs the usual historical interpretation. But perhaps he didn't collapse. Perhaps he merely went as far as his thinking could. (*WM*: 418)

Since, in his readings of other philosophers, Heidegger continually addresses his own circumstances, it is not overly fanciful to suppose that in this comment on Nietzsche there is an element of Heidegger coming to terms with the limitations of his own thinking. Far from being an empowerment of human beings, this world domination imposes uniformity on human beings. Heidegger reads this domination as leading to the imposition of a restricted image of what it is to be human and to the imposition of a single relation between human beings and the world. As a result, human beings become more and more alike, since they are determined in their relation to the world they inhabit by this one set of technical relations. This thus appears in turn to confirm humanist generalisations about what it is to be human.

It is the spread of technology that both brings the spread of nihilism and appears to make a certain version of humanism true by making human beings more and more alike and interchangeable. Nevertheless, the actual increase of uniformity among human beings is not proof of the truth of humanism. Rather, it is evidence for the cumulative effects of nihilism. Heidegger's discussion of technology suggests that its domination is one in which human beings too become part of what is dominated, since human beings also become a resource which can be deployed in fulfilment of a technically ordered plan. Thus, as a result of these preparations, human beings can be transformed into a resource to be deployed in the realisation of technically based plans rather than being placed in the multiplicity of relations which pertain when there are distinct forms of human community, with distinct cultural and symbolic systems. Nietzsche could not pursue his thought further because the full implications of industrialisation and the spread of technology were not yet evident. Nihilism was for Nietzsche still a European condition, and not, as it becomes for Heidegger, a global condition. Once a multiplicity of lived relations is replaced by a single relation of domination between human beings and the world, it can easily be reversed, from the domination of the world by human beings to the domination of human beings by the world in which they live. Human beings can think they dominate the world, but if what there is in the world is understood to be fixed and self-determining then human beings have no option but to fit into the relations thus determined.

Heidegger concludes his letter with a reference to the distinction, set out in his discussion of phenomenological method in *Being and Time*, between the 'what' of enquiry and how it is set out. This is the distinction between the form of questioning that is answered by stating an essence and the form of questioning that permits only of provisional answers, suggesting how what there is has come to seem as it seems. 'What this letter is trying to demonstrate may prove all too soon to be inadequate. How it would like, however, to cultivate reflection and discussion, Goethe says in a statement with which I should like to close this letter', and the quotation from Goethe is a surprise:

> if anyone regards words and expressions as sacred testimonials and does not put them, like currency and paper money, into quick, momentary circulation, but wants to see them as exchanged intellectual trade and barter as true equivalents, then there can be no blame for drawing attention to the fact that traditional expressions, at which no one any longer takes offence, nevertheless exert a damaging influence, confuse opinions, distort understanding and give entire fields of subject-matter a false direction. (*WM*: 419)

The mistake, then, is to suppose that language stays fixed and standard in its meaning and is not subject to alteration and erosion. The fixed equivalents of intellectual trade are false, whereas the transient uses of circulation are more in line with the alterable nature of language as process and not as fixity. Such fixity is metaphysical, erasing not only the potential but also the necessity of change in response to changes in the sendings of being. In this letter, then, Heidegger is pointing out that metaphysical language use is one such false direction. He seeks to test out received terms, to reveal a logic at work within them which may be counteractive to the direction of enquiry.

Metaphysics is conditional on a forgetting of being; its completion is conditional on the oblivion of this forgetting. Overcoming metaphysics requires coming to terms with the forgetting of being, which remains concealed within metaphysical construction and within metaphysical language use but which re-emerges with the winding up of metaphysics. This winding up is required if there is to be a return to the point at which being is forgotten. This return is needed in order to retrieve a relation of belonging to being and to overcome the terrors of homelessness and ungroundedness:

> an adequate and preserving reflection succeeds in seeing that metaphysics in accordance with its essence never permits a human living to settle in its own locality, that is in the essence of the forgetting of being. For this reason, thinking and creative language use must return to the point at which in a certain way it has always been and all the same never started building. We can only make ready a living place in that locality by building. (*WM*: 416)

Thinking will reveal to us that we already live in proximity to being and that our home is the site of a chasm between the sendings of being and the entities which are sent. This is the ungroundedness that metaphysical system seeks to cover up by constructing foundations and reasons explaining the appearance of an order in what there is. It is the human relation to ungroundedness which constitutes the specificity of human being in contrast to other kinds of entity. Without an affirmation of that relation to ungroundedness it is impossible to affirm the humanity of human being. Heidegger insists that the construction which is achievable through thinking is not a stable and substantial construction: 'This cannot be the erection of a house of God, nor yet a dwelling-place for mortals. It must be content with setting up a path which leads back into the locality of the overcoming of metaphysics and thereby permits an exploration of the destiny of an overcoming nihilism' (*WM*: 416–17). A house of God might provide a transcendentally grounded reality; a dwelling-place for the mortals might provide a substantive ethics. The proposed path provides a provisional ethics, in line with the open-ended nature of Heidegger's thinking at this stage. The way in which to feel at home is to recognise that being human is being in process, on the way to, but never completely acquiring, an understanding of being: of self, of context and of the forces within which one finds oneself placed. In order to get on the way, the rigidities of metaphysics and humanism have to be challenged, and the nihilistic emptiness which they conceal as substantive theory must be revealed. If nihilism and metaphysics are coextensive with humanism then an overcoming of nihilism and metaphysics is an overcoming of humanism.

WHAT IS HUMANISM?

In the 'Letter on humanism', Heidegger moves on from the theme of humanism to the theme of homelessness, which is taken up again in his late address, *Gelassenheit* (1959).[5] In that address he speaks of the homelessness brought about by the destruction of the Second World War and by the economic necessity to move into the cities away from the land. He goes on to remark that staying on the land also brings with it a form of homelessness:

> Many Germans have lost their homeland, have had to leave their villages and towns, have been driven from their native soil. Countless others whose homeland was saved have yet wandered off. They have been caught up in the turmoil of the big cities and have resettled in the wastelands of industrial districts. They are strangers now to their former homeland. And those who have stayed on in their homeland? Often they are more homeless than those who have been driven from their homeland. (*DT*: 48)

There is in this speech a shocking and resonating silence about Nazism and the genocidal destruction of Jewish communities and homes. Heidegger seems outrageously content to elaborate his own responses to homelessness and fails to think that the history of the persecution of Jews in Europe may be intertwined with a failure in the history of Europe and its philosophy to think through to this homelessness, now understood not as a social or economic condition but as an ontological feature of what it is to be human. Heidegger identifies a failure within the European tradition to address this homelessness in the loss of a relation to being. He does not consider that this failure may lead to a hostile projection not just into the world but onto peoples with specific markings in relation to conceptions of exile and homelessness: gypsies and Jews. There are two possibilities: either this failure to address the German transformation of European anti-Semitism into organised murder blocks Heidegger's capacity to think in terms of a revival of ethics, or his insensitivity to ethical issues grounds both this silence and that failure to make the transition from questioning metaphysics to questioning ethics.

This resonating silence concerning the Holocaust is also evident in the 'Letter on humanism'. Heidegger starts by setting a threefold process in play: restoring thoughtfulness to thought; restoring meaning to language; and thereby cumulatively retrieving a sense of the location in which human beings find themselves, establishing a relation for human beings to themselves in a context greater than their own activity. This process of thinking leads Heidegger to reassess his own work in highly positive terms, but it does not lead him to reassess his involvement with Nazism. The theme of a transformation of philosophy into another kind of thinking is stated at the end of the 'Letter on humanism':

> The thinking which is on its way is no longer philosophy, because it thinks more originally than metaphysics, which term says the same as philosophy. This future thinking can no longer lay aside, as Hegel required, the name 'the

love of wisdom' and become wisdom itself in the image of absolute knowledge. This thinking is the descent into the poverty of a provisional essence.
(*WM*: 360)

The 'Letter on humanism' has two conclusions: one, this one, concerning a
transition from philosophy into another kind of thinking, and another declaring
the coextension of philosophical enquiry as ontology with ethical enquiry. This
descent (*Abstieg*) into provisionality is a return from metaphysical absoluteness
to ethical contingency. This 'provisionality' (*Vorläufigkeit*) retrieves a term from
Being and Time, while the 'descent' is a reference to Nietzsche's Zarathustra,
who descends from his mountain solitude to confront the many-sided ignorance
of modernity. This is one of many points in the course of these letters where there
are marks of Heidegger's extensive readings of Nietzsche in the late 1930s and
the years of the war and of his attempts to make a connection from the analyses
of *Being and Time* into those readings of Nietzsche.

In this letter Heidegger is responding to a series of questions from the
Frenchman, Jean Beaufret, who translated much of Heidegger's writings into
French. These questions are not stated at the outset of the letter but emerge in the
course of it. There are three of them, with an unstated fourth concerning irrationalism. The first is the question of how to give back a meaning to the word
'humanism'. This gives the letter its title. There is, second, a question about
clarifying the relation between ontology and ethics and, third, a question about
how to prevent philosophical enquiry becoming adventurist. The unstated context
is the defeat of Nazism, although, in what is written, Heidegger takes the main
issue to be his relation to Sartrean existentialism. In the letter Heidegger distances
himself from Sartre's thinking and from Sartre's attempted retrieval of Kantian
ethics through the theme of commitment. The 'Letter on humanism' starts dram-
atically with the following claim: 'We are still far from thinking sufficiently
decisively about the essence of action [*Wir bedenken das Wesen des Handelns
noch lange nicht entschieden genug*]' (*WM*: 311). The first paragraph then
proceeds through a dazzling sequence of moves, taking in relations between
being, thought and poetry, and between *techne, poiesis* and *praxis* in early Greek
thinking. It makes reference to the importance of ambiguity and the relation
between being, language and the mode of living of human beings on the way.
This whole first paragraph leads up to the question whether irrationalism is the
upshot of the attempt to bring thinking 'back into its own element' out of a
subordination to bringing about action and effects outside itself. Heidegger asks
in turn: 'Can one really call the attempt to bring thinking back into its element
"irrationalism"?' (*WM*: 313). This is certainly Lukacs's view, although Heidegger
does not here attribute the view to Lukacs.[6] This question is not explicitly posed,
but it puts in question the status of Heidegger's enquiries. Heidegger returns to
this unstated fourth question in his letter to Jünger.

In response to the question of how to give meaning back to the term 'humanism', Heidegger sets out an everyday understanding of action, suggesting by

implication that it is inadequate: 'People think of action as the effecting of an effect [*das Bewirken einer Wirkung*]' (*WM*: 311). Heidegger then adds his preferred inflection: 'But the essence of action is completion. And completion means to bring something into the completeness of its essence, to bring it forward into this, *producere* (lead forward into).' What is completable, he goes on, is what is already in essence there; and what is already there, is being. His thoughts about the completion of metaphysics and of nihilism are thus parallel to this thought: that their essences are already in existence. It merely requires a process of development for that essence to emerge into view. Then a turn takes place from the point of view of everyday experience to that of being, through an insistence on the role of thinking, which links into the discussions of the 1951–52 lectures in *Was heißt Denken?*: 'Thought brings to completion the connection from being to the essence of human beings. Thought does not make and effect this connection. Thought merely offers it up to being as that which is of itself handed over from being' (*WM*: 311). On the surface, this language is mystifying. And indeed Heidegger goes on immediately to make the claim about language being 'the house of being': 'Language is the house of being. Human beings live in the accommodation which it offers' (*WM*: 311). There is then a relation between the withdrawal of being, the impoverishment of language, and the sense of homelessness experienced by human beings. This homelessness can be addressed only by overcoming the forgetting of being, setting up relations between human being and being and between language and being.

In the 'Letter on humanism', Heidegger sets out as central a relation between thinking, human beings and being:

> Thinking acts in so far as it thinks. This action is perhaps the simplest and highest, because it concerns the relation of being to human beings. All activity rests in being and goes in the direction of entities. Though, on the other hand, thinking allows itself to be claimed by being, in order to say the truth of being. Thinking completes this allowing. (*WM*: 311)

For Heidegger, it is because thinking can be affected by being, by forces above and beyond itself, that it has priority. These forces, constituting *Seinsgeschick*, are neither natural nor historical, neither human nor inhuman. They are the forces through which distinctions between history and nature, between the human and the non-human, first emerge. They generate the epochal shifts to which Heidegger seeks to draw attention, which he supposes human beings cannot predict or control, but to which human beings can only respond. Heidegger then appears to disrupt the discussion by asking whether there is a linguistic form in French, equivalent to the ambiguous genitive in German, which permits a simultaneous thinking of the process of exerting influence and of responding to these transnatural forces. He remarks three pages later that this genitive pronounces a dual thought, *ein Zwiefaches* (*WM*: 314). However, this deflection subsequently turns out not to be a digression, for it permits Heidegger to identify a relation to creative language use as critical in the development or failure of a process of thought. He identifies as reductive the imposition on language in European grammar of a distinction between subject and predicate:

> In this the terms 'subject' and 'object' are inadequate titles of metaphysics, which from early on have taken over the image of European logic and grammar. What conceals itself in this process we can today scarcely begin to sense. The freeing of language from grammar in an originating ordering of essences is reserved for thinking and creative language use [*Denken und Dichten*]. (*WM*: 311–12)

This freeing of language is for Heidegger a precondition for human beings to develop a relation to themselves that is not subordinated to the reductive processes of technical control. The suggestion is that language would be less distorting if grammar and logic were not always imposed on it, restricting what can be said and thought. Lifting this restriction would in turn free human beings for possibilities other than those prescribed by technical relations. The basis of Heidegger's self-distancing from Sartrean commitment emerges in the next sentences, where he insists on two levels of engagement: 'Thinking is not simply *l'engagement dans l'action* for and through entities in the sense of an actuality of the present situation. Thinking is *l'engagement* for and through the truth of being, whose history is never past but is always imminent' (*WM*: 312). He continues: 'The history of being carries and determines every condition and situation of human beings' (*WM*: 312). Thus, in order to consider any question about the flourishing and purposes of human beings, it is necessary first to develop a sense for the history of being.

That history, as seen in the previous chapter, is one in which there are sudden and systematic alterations in the relations in which human beings find themselves and relate to themselves. One such change is the emergence of technical relations in their full force. Heidegger suggests that, in order to understand the wide-ranging impact of these forces, it is necessary to recognise technical relations as not just technical relations, but as the latest emanation of being, revealing what there is in the world in a particular, systematic way. Heidegger insists that, in order to understand this form of thinking which responds to being, it is necessary to free ourselves from any technical interpretation of thinking (*der technischen Interpretation des Denkens*). Heidegger traces this thinking back to the time of Plato and Aristotle, and he thus introduces his preoccupation with tracing a history of philosophy as a single history of the reduction of thinking from an autonomous status to a means expediting action: 'Its beginning reaches back to Plato and Aristotle. Thinking there is construed as a *techne*, a process of considering in the service of doing and making. This considering thus is already seen with respect to *praxis* (doing) and *poiesis* (making)' (*WM*: 312). It is the notion of destiny that permits the significance of the beginning of a process to be grasped only at its moment of completion. Heidegger's thinking about the fate of philosophy is thus informed by his retrieval of this notion of destiny in the construction of the history of being as *Seinsgeschick*. In the completion of a process, the significance of its beginning emerges for the first time.

The subordination of thinking to external ends contributes to the forgetting of being and the loss of dimensions beyond those of human activity. It disempowers thinking. The *theoria* of later Greek thinking is for Heidegger already a gesture of reaction to these processes. He describes it as: 'a reactive attempt all the same to save thinking in its autonomy from acting and doing. Since then "philosophy" has been in the constant need to justify its existence with respect to the "sciences".' The determination of knowledge as theoretical is already caught up in the technical interpretation of thought as intended for the pursuit of goals external to itself. Logic, according to Heidegger, becomes a means for attempting to secure this autonomy of thinking from subordination to practical applications. However, these attempts cannot succeed, because the form of thinking handed down in philosophy itself is marked by this negative determination of not being applied. It is for this reason that Heidegger seeks to develop another kind of thinking which he supposes lies outside the philosophical tradition. My interpretation construes this other kind of thinking as the silenced ethical moment in philosophy which is retained but suppressed within the tradition and which can be retrieved at the moment of the completion of metaphysics. Heidegger thus affirms a form of thinking distinct from scientific enquiry and prior to any distinction between a practical application of thought and pure reflection as *theoria*:

> The strength of thinking consists in contrast to the sciences not merely in the artificiality that is technical theoretical exactness of concepts. It rests in speaking remaining purely in the element of being, allowing the simplicity of the many dimensions of being to dominate. (*WM*: 313)

This other form of thinking responds to the ambiguity and multiple dimensions of being, whereas technical, artificially developed languages seek to disambiguate and impose a single coherent structure on what there is. This is the metaphysical impulse, which culminates for Heidegger in the precision of the modern physical sciences. He suggests that this other form of thinking takes place most easily in speaking, in conversation with another. The exactness of scientific enquiry presumably takes place in writing, with no specific addressee. He looks on the use of language in speech as having a beneficial flexibility, although he also remarks the healthy, even healing, compulsion [*heilsamer Zwang*] towards carefully thought-out linguistic expression in writing. This raises the possibility that an ethical openness can be turned into metaphysical closure by putting spoken thought into written form.[7] Conversely, it is only in the written form that the unthought of an enquiry can come to expression.

Heidegger then turns to the question of humanism: 'The question comes from the intent to hold on to the word "humanism". But I ask myself if that is necessary, or is the danger that all names of this kind pose not yet sufficiently obvious?' (*WM*: 313). And he continues, with some pertinence for the production of postmodernist interventions:

> But the market of public opinion always needs something new. And there are always people ready to provide it. Even the terms 'logic', 'ethics', 'physics' first emerge as soon as originating thinking has come to an end. The Greeks thought without such titles. They never called thinking 'philosophy'.

The use of these labels for Heidegger is a sign that thinking has lost its way and has surrendered its autonomy: 'it has become a matter for schools and a matter for culture . . . One no longer thinks but occupies oneself with "philosophy".' With an implicit reference to the discussion in *Being and Time* of the anonymous mode of public opinion, Heidegger remarks that neither the public nor the private space are conducive to thinking, the one dominated by fashion and the other irreversibly marked by a withdrawal from the public space. Heidegger thus construes private existence as an attempt to absent oneself from the half-meanings and distortions of the public domain. The private domain 'reveals against its own will a subordination to the public space. Language comes under the dictatorship of the public space' (*WM*: 315). It is, however, remarkable, given that this was written in 1946, that there is no reference to the Nazi propaganda machine, nor to the place which Heidegger sought within it. A distinction between philosophical concerns and those of thinking emerges in the remark: 'Reflection on the nature of language must reach another level. It cannot any more be mere philosophy of language' (*WM*: 315–16). He claims that this is the point of his reference to language in *Being and Time*: 'For this reason *Being and Time* (section 34) contains a reference to the dimension of emergence in language and touches on the question: in what way of being is language on every occasion language?' Heidegger suggests that language goes through systematic changes as a result of shifts in the relation between language and being, but this relation between being and language remains concealed in the domination of conceptions of subjective control, propagated in the public domain. The presumption that subjective meaning has always been of major significance in the determination of meaning and the development of language conceals the fact that this is not necessarily so. It conceals the possibility of there being thoroughgoing changes in the relation between human beings and the languages we speak, such that speakers' meaning might be a temporary, not a permanent authority in determining meaning.

Heidegger warns against current preoccupations with the corruption of language as another concealment of what is most important about language:

> The widespread and rapidly increasing emptying out of language does not just corrupt aesthetic and moral responsibility in the use of language. It endangers the essence of human beings. And a careful use of language is not enough to prove that we have gone beyond this essential danger, this endangering of essence. It could indeed suggest that we have not yet truly seen the danger and cannot see it, because we have not put ourselves in its view. (*WM*: 316)

Thus the problem posed by this erosion of language is one which may not even have been properly identified yet. The passage continues, reversing the order of the supposed analysis: 'The recently much spoken of, although long overdue, discussion of the decline of language is, however, not the ground but the consequence of the process that has brought language under the domination of the modern metaphysics of subjectivity and drives it out of its own element.' Heidegger claims that the essential element of language, that wherein it grows and is nourished, is its relation to being and its responsiveness to shifts emerging from the *Seinsgeschick*. The concealment of this relation in the forgetting of being leads to the decline of language. This critique of reducing language to a means of pursuing separately determined ends runs parallel to his critique of reducing philosophical enquiry to a quest for explanations and grounds. It connects with the designation in *Being and Time* of the language of the public sphere as *Gerede*, as interminably garrulous.

Heidegger claims that a language which is responsive to being is sparse and interspersed with silence:

> If, however, human beings are to bring themselves once more into proximity with being, then above all human beings must learn to exist in the nameless. They must in the same way learn about being led astray in the public realm and about the powerlessness of the private realm. Human beings must, before they start talking, let themselves be addressed by being, and undergo the risk that through this claim they may have little or seldom anything to say. (*WM*: 316)

The climb down into thought and away from using it to extend technical control in the world is a step away from a world divided up into a public and a private domain, divided into a world of work and a world of domestic life. It breaks away from established forms of communication and may lead, Heidegger suggests, to a form of speechlessness, even madness, not, perhaps, as a result of having nothing to say, but from having no way of saying it. The subsequent remarks about how he simply did not have the language available at the time of writing *Being and Time* to explain the turn from *Dasein* to being and from being and time to time and being confirms this suggestion. Heidegger proposes the promotion of a form of language that is not subordinated to a pre-given set of ends, co-operating with given ways of interacting. Heidegger gives the name '*Dichten*' to this form of language, and he finds it at work in Hölderlin's poetry. Language thus is a medium through which new ways of going on and of interacting come into existence. This form of language as creative of new forms of life is an ethical form of language, by contrast to a metaphysical subordination to already established interpretation and practice. However, just as language may be used for its own sake and not just for the purposes of realising other ends, so philosophical enquiry can be pursued not to expedite the extension of the means of technical intervention in the world, not to provide explanations and grounds for already identified processes, but again for its own sake, bringing into existence new forms of relation between human beings and the play of forces in which human beings find themselves. In this way a Heideggerian restoration of philosophy becomes conceivable.

Heidegger's 'Letter on humanism' suggests that humanism, far from being a celebration and affirmation of what it is to be human, can impose restrictions on human possibility. Heidegger suggests that if human beings, as individuals and in groups, are to flourish, then we must free ourselves from the restrictive presumption that what it is to be human is given in advance of our individual and collective existences. Heidegger links this discussion of humanism to his discussion of care in *Being and Time*:

> What else is care about, if not in connection with bringing human beings back into their essence? What does it mean except that human beings should become human? So indeed a version of humanity is a presumption of this thinking. For this is humanism: making sense and having cares; that human beings should be human and not in-human, which means outside of their essence. And yet, in what does this humanity of human beings consist? It lies in their essence. (*WM*: 317)

Thus Heidegger comes round to claiming that what it is to be human has been concealed as a question by the spread of various versions of humanism, which pretend to provide an answer to the question 'what is it to be human?' but which in fact dogmatically block the question off. He sets up a brief history of humanism and then invokes humanisms in Marx, Christianity, German idealism and Romanticism. He then brings the discussion back to the question of his relation to Sartre's existentialism. Heidegger observes that, for Marx, it is the nature of human beings to be social. By contrast, Christianity, according to Heidegger, defines what it is to be human in opposition to a conception of *deitas*. He remarks of Christianity: 'In this broader sense, Christianity is also a humanism, in so far as its teaching is all about the health of the souls (*salus aeterna*) of human beings, and the history of human beings takes place within the bounds of a history of salvation [*Heilsgeschichte*]' (*WM*: 318). By implication, Heidegger is proposing his own *Seinsgeschichte* as an alternative to such *Heilsgeschichte*, positing a non-human set of forces at work in human destiny, but providing no positive theory about them. As a result of the Christian view about human beings, 'Human beings are not of this world, in so far as the world is thought theoretically with Plato as a temporary passage through to a beyond' (*WM*: 317). It is the Roman contribution to the development of conceptions of humanism with which Heidegger is principally concerned.

Heidegger remarks that the term *humanitas* is a Roman term, developed in the Republic as a means of setting up a contrast with barbarian existence:

> The truly human human being is here the Roman, who applauds Roman *virtus* and is made noble through 'incorporating' the *paideia* of the Greeks. The Greeks are the Greeks of late Greek culture, whose education was acquired in the schools of philosophy. Their education is concerned with *eruditio* and

> *institutio in bonas artes. Paideia* understood in this way is translated as
> '*humanitas*'. (*WM*: 317–18)

Thus Heidegger points out the historical interdependence of the tradition of
teaching philosophy in Greek and Roman society and the development of a
common but distorting view of what it is to be human. Not least of these
distortions is the exclusion of 'the barbarian', and of course women and slaves,
from exposure to the humanities and thus from the possibility of graduating to
full human status. This is not an inclusive conception of what it is to be human.
Heidegger notes that this translation of *paideia* as *humanitas* is to be treated with
caution. As discussed previously, for Heidegger the emergence of significant
ambiguity through translation is a sign of a shift of epoch. In this translation there
is, according to Heidegger, the birth of humanism: 'In Rome we encounter the
first humanism. [*In Rom begegnen wir dem ersten Humanismus.*]' (*WM*: 318).
However, in the context of the exclusive use of the term '*humanitas*' in both
Republican and Imperial Rome, and most of all in the implicit context of the Nazi
Race laws, it is critical to whom this 'we' can be taken to refer. The absence of
clarification is not just careless. It shows a total lack of concern for those
destroyed through the exclusive use of such terms. Heidegger proceeds unabashed,
to detect in the Italian Renaissance an encounter with these half-understood
Greek ideals, modified through the experience of the decline of the Roman
Empire and the spread of Christianity: 'the *homo romanus* of the Renaissance
stands in opposition to a *homo barbarus*. But the in-humanism now is the
supposed barbarism of the Gothic scholasticism of the Middle Ages' (*WM*: 318).
In all versions of humanism Heidegger traces this double marking, of a return to
half-understood Greek ideals and a gesture of setting oneself apart from some
perceived barbarian.

This he supposes to be true of Winckelmann, of Goethe and of Schiller, all
three of whom he sets up in contrast to Hölderlin:

> This shows itself in the humanism of the eighteenth century in Germany,
> which is carried through Winckelmann, Goethe and Schiller. Hölderlin, on the
> other hand, does not belong to 'humanism' because he thinks the destiny of the
> essence of human beings more originally than this 'humanism' is capable of
> doing. (*WM*: 318)

It is then worth asking why, if Goethe is a humanist of this distorting kind,
Heidegger should end his letter to Jünger with a quotation from Goethe rather
than from Hölderlin, whose poem *Bread and Wine* is also cited in the concluding
pages. This German humanism is just one version of a kind of humanism that
emphasises a historical tradition reaching back to the time of the Greeks. Heidegger
introduces another version of humanism, as a conceptual construct, not an interpretation of historical tradition. This construct acquires variant meanings depending
on how the concepts in the construction are determined:

However, if one understands humanism in general to be the attempt to make human beings free for their humanity and therein to find their worth, then humanism is different depending on the conceptions of 'freedom' and 'nature' of human beings. And similarly the ways to achieving this freedom vary. (*WM*: 318)

Thus Heidegger distinguishes between an approach based in a history of ideas and a definitional, conceptual approach to establishing the meaning of 'humanism'. He suggests that freedom and nature in human beings are understood sufficiently variously in different epochs to constitute differences in what it is to be human at those different times. Heidegger also distinguishes between versions of humanism which seek to retrieve some past ideal and those, such as Marxism and Sartre's existentialism, which do not: 'The humanism of Marx needs no return to antiquity, nor does that which Sartre conceives of as existentialism.' While these various humanisms seem very different, Heidegger points out that they have one set of features in common:

> While these kinds of humanism are quite different with respect to their aims and causes, whatever the form of the doctrine may be, the kind and means of their realisation brings them together. For the '*humanitas*' of the *homo humanus* and the 'human' in human being is determined by reference to an already established interpretation of history, of nature, of the world, and of the cause of the world, which means with reference to an interpretation of entities as a whole [*des Seienden im Ganzen*]. (*WM*: 319)

This is a key passage, for two reasons. An interpretation of entities as a whole is for Heidegger always metaphysical. Such an interpretation elides the ontological difference between what there appears to be and the way in which it appears. The attempt to analyse entities as a whole while proclaiming itself a theory of everything fails to address the question how it is possible for there to be anything at all. This conceals the alterability of what there is and conceals the temporary status of that which the metaphysical account takes to be permanent, unchanging reality.

For Heidegger then, these humanisms illegitimately take for granted a fixed meaning of history, nature and the world. Thus, for Heidegger, these humanisms are metaphysical and dogmatic, in asserting but not proving the stability of the meanings of the terms in question. He continues:

> Every humanism is either grounded in metaphysics or makes itself out to be the ground of a metaphysics. Every determination of the essence of human beings which presupposes an interpretation of what there is without posing the question of the truth of being, implicitly or explicitly, is metaphysics. In this and indeed with respect to the manner in which the essence of human beings is determined, there shows up a peculiarity of all metaphysics, that they are 'humanistic'. (*WM*: 319)

Metaphysics presumes an understanding of human being as a stable unchanging structure. In providing such an account, 'every humanism remains metaphysical'. All presume that there is a single answer to the question 'what is it to be human?' There is then a tendency to try to ground the possibility of knowledge as a stable predictable set of relations in the world. This is a metaphysical prejudice. By contrast, supposing that this must be an open question, to be resolved in different ways at different times, and by different individuals, is a non-metaphysical response, in the language of this interpretation, an ethical response to the question. Here, Heidegger puts together a single European history in five stages – Greek origins, Roman culture, Christianity, Marxism, and the present condition – as symptoms of a single trajectory. He claims that every humanism since the Roman version has had a metaphysical understanding of what it is to be human which conceals rather than poses the question as a live issue. The present epoch mirrors those Greek origins in not being so strongly committed to humanism, thus retrieving the possibility of producing a different non-univocal response to the question 'what is it to be human?' Heidegger writes of the Latin metaphysical interpretation of the Greek conception of human beings as creatures possessed of reason:

> The first humanism, that is the Roman one, and all kinds of humanism which since then come down to the present, presuppose a universal '*Wesen*' of human being as self-evident. Human beings are supposed to be the *animal rationale*. This determination is not just a Latin translation of the Greek *zoon logon exon*. It is a metaphysical interpretation. This determination of the essence of human beings is not false, but it is conditional on metaphysics. (*WM*: 319–20)

Thus there is here a crucial role for the interpretation offered of human beings. Such determination of the essence of human beings is false if it is assumed to be unconditional. However, it is the point of metaphysical construction to present itself as unconditional, hence the self-refuting nature of metaphysical construction. The problem is that 'metaphysics posits entities in their being and thinks the being of entities in this way. But it does not think the difference between the two.' Metaphysics elides the difference between human beings in their being and the being of human beings, understood as responsive to processes above and beyond the human domain.

Heidegger then refers to his earlier works, *The Essence of Reasons* and *Kant and the Problem of Metaphysics*, both published in 1929, as though this observation concerning metaphysics clarifies what is under enquiry there. The problem is that 'metaphysics does not think the truth of being itself. Therefore metaphysics never asks in what way human being belongs to the truth of being. Metaphysics has not only never posed this question. The question is to metaphysics as metaphysics inaccessible' (*WM*: 320). Metaphysical enquiry precludes discussion of the conditions under which it becomes itself possible. Metaphysical systems exclude the possibility of fundamental change; they exclude the possibility that the future may be different from the present; they exclude the possibility that present conditions may be radically different from past conditions.

They exclude recognition that there might be elements or forces at work in the world above and beyond the domain theorised by metaphysics, that is above and beyond the domain recognisable to human beings as currently constituted. These forces are therefore ruled out of account, and it becomes impossible to conceive the essence of what it is to be human as in part responsive to such forces, altering in response to changes in them. Heidegger by contrast insists on the priority of being in any questioning of what it is to be human. This remains inaccessible to metaphysical thinking.

Heidegger claims that there is in every metaphysical definition or determination of what it is to be human a hidden revelation of being which is inaccessible to metaphysical enquiry:

> With respect to the determination of human being, however, the *ratio* of the *animale* and the reason of the living creature may be determined as 'capacity for principles' or as a 'capacity for categories', or in another way, everywhere and every time the essence of reason is based in the fact that for every perception of entities in their being, being itself is already illuminated and has occurred in its truth. (*WM*: 320)

Furthermore, for Heidegger humanism assumes a contrastive approach to defining what it is to be human rather than reflecting on being human itself, for its own sake. Heidegger asks: 'Are we really on the right track to the essence of human beings, if and so long as we delimit what it is to be human as a living creature alongside plants and animals and God?' (*WM*: 320). This set of remarks is brought to an end with the statement that the problem of metaphysics is that it offers a form of thinking about what it is to be human by reference to an understanding of what it is to be animal, rather than by thinking in the direction of being human:

> People think in principle continuously of *homo animalis*, even when *anima* is posited as *animus sive mens* and later as subject, person, spirit. Such positing is the mode of metaphysics and through it the essence of human beings is underestimated and is not thought with respect to its derivation [*Herkunft*]. The derivation of this essence remains always also a future of essence for humanity, which is caught up in history. Metaphysics thinks of human beings out of a sense of what it is to be animal, not in the direction of acquiring an understanding of what it is to be human. (*WM*: 320–1)

This leaves out of account the possibility that the historicality of human beings may make the essence of what it is to be human alterable, not fixed, and thus in transition, not definable for all time. It conceals the thought, from *Being and Time*, that the form of existence of human beings is quite different from the modes of existing of other kinds of entity, in that human beings have a relation to their essence and to their identity. For Heidegger, human beings are historical in the sense of being affected by the sendings of being in ways that other animals are not. Thus, while animals may have a natural history, human beings are located within the frameworks set up by the history or sendings of being.

Heidegger claims he is against humanism because humanism does not provide a sufficiently enhanced view of what it is to be human. His own determination of being human is as a placing within a domain opened up by the sending of being, at which that sending can be either affirmed or ignored. He claims that this is not a rejection of the more usual views, but a deeper understanding of them:

> Through its determination of the essence of what it is to be human, the humanistic interpretation of human beings as *animal rationale*, as 'person', as an intellectual-soulful-bodily entity, is not declared false and rejected. Rather, the thought is that the highest humanist determination of the essence of human beings does not capture the full worth of what it is to be human. (*WM*: 327)

The thought is that being against humanism makes it possible to develop a greater respect and understanding for what it is to be human:

> Thus the thought of *Being and Time* is against humanism, but this opposition does not mean that this thinking sets itself up in opposition to being humane and takes the inhumane first, defends inhumanity and takes no interest in the worth of human beings. The thinking in *Being and Time* is against humanism because humanism does not place the *humanitas* of human beings high enough. (*WM*: 327)

Heidegger observes that the question about giving meaning to the term 'humanism' has led to a reconsideration of the question about the essence of human beings:

> Indeed, this thought on its own, which brings us to the insight of the questionability of the essence of humanism, leads us to think more originally about the essence of human beings. With respect to this more essential humanity of the *homo humanus* there emerges the possibility to return to the word 'humanism' an historical meaning which is older than its historically calculated great age. (*WM*: 341)

Here Heidegger is proposing to retrieve the concept of humanism, not to reject it. A number of themes from *Being and Time* are picked up here: the difference between the existence of *Dasein* and the modes of being of other entities, the historicality of *Dasein* and the difference between points of destination and points of origination, between future and past. In the following paragraph, Heidegger recalls from *Being and Time* the language of the *Lichtung* of being, the clearing or lighting up of being, and introduces his rewriting of *Existenz*, a central term in the analysis of *Dasein*, as *Ek-sistenz*:

> This standing in the clearing of being I call the Ek-sistence of human beings. This way of being occurs only to human beings. Ek-sistence understood in this way is not only the basis of the possibility of reason, *ratio*, but this ek-sistence is that in which the essence of human beings preserves the derivation of its determination [*die Herkunft seiner Bestimmung*]. (*WM*: 321)

This provides him with a basis on which to affirm a distance between his own enquiries and those of Sartre. His conclusion with respect to Sartre is succinct:

> Sartre, by contrast, expresses the basic principle of existentialism thus: existence precedes essence. He thereby takes *existentia* and *essentia* in a metaphysical sense, which since Plato has put essence before existence. Sartre turns this assertion round. But such an inversion of a metaphysical assertion is still a metaphysical sentence. (*WM*: 325)

It is the same move as the one he makes with respect to Nietzsche's relation to Plato, and perhaps no more satisfactory.

At this point the focus for discussion shifts from responding to Beaufret's queries concerning Sartre to a diagnosis of what prevented the completion of *Being and Time*. The focus is not on Sartre or on Nietzsche, but on Heidegger's self-interpretation. Heidegger insists that a turn from the analysis of being and time to an analysis of time and being is already in play in *Being and Time*, even though the third section was held back because the appropriate language was not available to express it: 'This turn is not a change of the standpoint of *Being and Time*, but one in which the attempted thinking first achieves the location from which what takes place in *Being and Time* is experienced and in process, out of the basic experience of the forgetting of being' (*WM*: 325). The forgetting of being is thus claimed to be still a key theme. Here again, there is a conjunction of a claim to continuity in Heidegger's emphatic self-interpretation with an overly emphatic reading of the thought of another philosopher, in this case Sartre. The engagement with Sartre has led not to a reading of Sartre but to a gesture of self-affirmation. Heidegger claims with respect to the incompleteness of the enquiry in *Being and Time*:

> As long as philosophy is preoccupied with dismantling the possibility that it arrive at the real task of thinking [*die Sache des Denkens*] about the truth of being, it remains safely beyond the reach of the danger of collapse as a result of the hardness of that task. In this way 'philosophising' about a collapse of thought is divided by a complete gulf from such collapse itself. (*WM*: 340)

In the letter to Jünger, Heidegger reverts to this question of the collapse of thought, which he seems to identify in Nietzsche's work. Again, it is possible that Heidegger is here diagnosing a problem in his own thought.

In the 'Letter on humanism', Heidegger invokes Hölderlin, in order to introduce the notion of a home as a proximity to being which inevitably goes missing with the forgetting of being. He writes: 'This home of historical living is the proximity of being' (*WM*: 335). It is the retrieval of being which is required for a sense of homelessness to be overcome:

> Only in this way out of being can the overcoming of homelessness begin, a homelessness in which not just human beings, but the essence of what it is to be human, have been straying. This homelessness resides in the abandonment

of entities by being and is a sign for the forgetting of being. It is in accordance with this homelessness that the truth of being remains unthought. (*WM*: 335)

The abandonment of entities by being demonstrates itself in the reduction of language to nothing but a medium controlled by human beings and the reduction of theories of what there is to no more than metaphysical systems defining what there is as entirely present to human beings. The overcoming of this homelessness requires a return of being into language and into theories of what there is, such that a context of a non-human otherness can be retrieved. The place (*Ortschaft*) in which human beings find themselves is always where they live, but it is necessary to affirm a non-human dimension to that context if human beings are to live without becoming wholly caught up in whatever theoretical reduction is currently being offered by metaphysical construction. As shown in the previous chapter, Heidegger diagnoses that contemporary reduction as taking the form of technical relations. This is not just a reduction in theoretical terms; all contemporary living is framed by the possibilities offered by those relations. Heidegger proposes that we must affirm a less reduced living-space, a more active dwelling, if there is to be any thinking at all. The difference is between living in pre-given, disowned relations and recognising that, however disowned, such pre-given relations provide a way of being and of constituting a relation to being. On this basis it does not seem so inappropriate to call the preoccupation with dwelling an ethical concern.

My interpretation is that a return of ethics, as the repressed of metaphysics, is required, if an overcoming of homelessness is to be thought in its entirety. Heidegger's remarks in *Gelassenheit*, introduced at the beginning of this section, show that he did not manage to do this. The opening question of the 'Letter on humanism' about what it is to act introduces this thought of the absent sense of groundedness without which activity merely has consequences; it cannot be called action. Heidegger distinguishes between acting in pursuit of already established ends, subordinated to the requirements of technical relations, and seeking to bring about a fulfilment of what it is to be human. This, he suggests, is possible only by affirming a relation to being, to a set of forces above and beyond the domain of human representation. This relation to being provides the sense of having a place in the world, a home, a dwelling place, and it is this sense which is required for a substantive and creative ethical relation to the world to be possible. It seems plausible to suggest that Heidegger's failure to address himself to his own and the collective responsibility for persecuting the Jews restricts his capacity to think in terms of ethics and of an ethical revival as a condition for the retrieval of the question of being. I suggest that it is possible to free Heidegger's project from the limitations he imposed on it and recognise it as the development of a non-anthropocentric ethics.

In this discussion of homelessness, Heidegger makes sympathetic references to Marx's analysis of alienation:

What Marx derived in an essential and significant way from Hegel as the alienation of human beings reaches back in its roots into this homelessness of modern human beings. This is drawn into the image of metaphysics through the destining of being, is made fast through metaphysics and the destiny of being and is covered up as homelessness. (*WM*: 336)

Heidegger contrasts an implicit agreement on the importance of ungroundedness and on the role of theoretical construction, between himself and Marx, to a distance between Marx and both Husserl and, perhaps surprisingly, Sartre:

Because Marx, in so far as he experiences alienation, reaches into an essential dimension of history, the Marxist insight about history is superior to customary history. While Husserl and indeed, as far as I can see, Sartre too fail to recognise the essentiality of the historical in being, neither phenomenology nor existentialism can come into that dimension where there would be a productive conversation with Marxism. (*WM*: 336)

This is a worrying observation, since it is unclear how familiar with the works of Sartre and of Marx Heidegger is, and thus unclear what in their work he is responding to. It should be noted that this was written well before Sartre's work resulting in *The Critique of Dialectical Reason*[8], became known. Heidegger shifts rapidly from this discussion of Sartre to a discussion of Marx. According to Heidegger, Marx's materialism is not simply the view that the basic component of reality is physical. It is rather the view that what there is results from the human capacity to transform materiality:

The essence of materialism hides itself in the essence of technology, about which a great deal is written and not much thought. Technology is in this sense a destiny sent by the destining of being [*ein seinsgeschickliche Geschick*], a destiny from the truth of being, which is peacefully sustained in forgottenness. (*WM*: 337)

Again, this claim to a proximity between his own thought and that of Marx would not be accepted by most Marxists.

Heidegger comments sarcastically on reactions to his various refusals to accept the self-evidence of humanism, of logic, of values, and on reactions to his affirmation of being in the world; and he rejects the equation of references to the death of God with atheism:

What is more 'logical' than to suppose that the denial of humanism is the affirmation of inhumanity? . . . Because in all these cases, there is a speaking out against all those things which humanity holds high and holy, this philosophy is thought to be an irresponsible and destructive 'nihilism'. For what is more 'logical' than to suppose that whoever doubts the self-evident entities and takes the side of the non-existing therefore preaches empty nothingness as the sense of reality? (*WM*: 343)

Heidegger insists on distinguishing between the destruction of ontology announced in *Being and Time* and the nihilism which he analyses in the second letter:

> In *Being and Time* there is somewhere talk of a 'phenomenological destruction'. One supposes, with the help of a much-invoked logic and reason, which itself is not positive, that this is negative and promotes the rejection of reason and deserves therefore to be branded as infamous. People are so full of this 'logic' that everything which is opposed to the usual somnolence of opinion immediately becomes an objectionable opponent. Everything that does not uphold the well-known and loved positive is consigned to the previously prepared grave of the negative which denies everything and therefore ends in nothing and completes nihilism. In this 'logical manner' everything is allowed to decline into a nihilism which has been discovered with the help of logic. (*WM*: 344)

Heidegger seeks to reverse the accusation and show that criticisms of his work are themselves nihilistic and indeed irrational. Heidegger contests the use of logic to construct conclusive formal arguments. He invokes another use of reason to analyse the negativities of the current condition and to come to terms with them. He calls the one-sided endorsement of formal logic, without reflection on the emergence of logic from an historical evolution of thought, irrationalism: 'irrationalism as a renunciation of *ratio* dominates unrecognised and unopposed in the defence of logic which supposes it can do without a reflection on the term *logos* and on the emergence of *ratio* out of *logos*' (*WM*: 345). This irrationalism is the cutting loose of this present formation from the conditions for its emergence, in terms of which it makes sense. He thus addresses the question of a suppressed irrationalism in his own enquiries by reversing the accusation at possible accusers.

Heidegger outlines his opposition to values not as a rejection of value, but as a rejection of the subjectivism that he supposes is necessarily built into the affirmation of any system of values. His opposition to values is based in his sense of the devaluation of value inherent in supposing that there is value only because human beings make evaluations. This claim is critical for his reading of Nietzsche. It is central for his claim that only through a critique of the affirmation of value is it possible to think the essence of nihilism and not just reproduce it. The claim runs:

> All evaluation, even where it evaluates positively, is subjectivising. It does not allow entities to be, but permits entities simply to be as the object of its own evaluating activity. This peculiar effort to prove the objectivity of values does not know what it is doing. For even if one declares 'God' to be the highest value, it is still a diminishing of the essence of God. This thinking in terms of value is the greatest blasphemy. (*WM*: 345–6)

He insists that his claim that human beings are in the world leaves open the question of the nature of God: 'The proposition: the essence of human beings consists in being in the world contains no decision about whether human beings in a theological metaphysical sense are creatures of this world or also creatures of another world' (*WM*: 347). His version of existentialism, he insists, unlike that of Sartre, is not necessarily atheistic: 'With the existential determination of the essence of human beings nothing is yet decided about the existence or non-existence of God; nor indeed about the possibility or impossibility of gods' (*WM*: 347). Indifference to God is for Heidegger a form of nihilism. The question whether God is near or draws away from human beings cannot even be posed if there is no sense of holiness, which can only be located through an awareness of some non-human forces, which Heidegger calls the sending of being. Only in proximity to being can there be a question about God.

Heidegger distinguishes between humanism and thinking about humanity. He insists that thinking about human beings in relation to being is more productive than the dogmatism of humanism. Indeed, 'To think about the truth of being means at the same time: to think about the *humanitas* of *homo humanus*. *Humanitas* can be engaged in the service of the truth of being, but without humanism in the metaphysical sense' (*WM*: 349). Heidegger then poses the key question: 'if *humanitas* is so essential for thinking about being, must ontology not then be completed with an ethics?' (*WM*: 349). Heidegger acknowledges the question:

> Where the essence of human beings is thought essentially out of the question of the truth of being, whereby human beings are not drawn to the centre of entities, the requirement for a binding indication is bound to arise and a requirement for a set of rules which will say how human being, which is experienced as existence in the response to being, should live. (*WM*: 349)

He explains his reluctance to affirm that his ontology is an ethics by explaining the dangers of understanding ethics as a code giving a coherence to populations, rather than as a form of thinking through which human beings can discover for themselves a relation to themselves, to their context and to being. He detects a danger in displacing responsibility for self on to the producers of such codes, a danger which is more pressing when there is confusion about the status of being human:

> The desire for an ethics becomes all the stronger as the open unknowing of human beings increases, no less than a hidden unknowing increases. A connection through ethics is all the more sought after where human beings have been handed over to a mass existence and can be brought to a reliable stability only through a collectivity and order of plans and action which are grounded in technical relations. (*WM*: 349)

Leaving unquestioned those technical relations would make the code not an ethics for human beings in relation to forces above and beyond our control, but a technique for self-aggrandisement. This kind of requirement in Heidegger's view conceals what is really important about ethics and repeats a concealment which he supposes took place with the emergence of the subdisciplines in Greek philosophy.

He makes the following surprising comparison between Sophocles and Aristotle, to Sophocles' advantage, and introduces a remark supposedly made by Heraclitus, through which Heidegger goes on to clarify his views on ethics:

> The tragedies of Sophocles contain, if such a comparison is allowed, a more original expression of the Greek *ethos* than the lectures of Aristotle on 'ethics'. A remark of Heraclitus, which consists in only three words, says it simply, and the essence of *ethos* emerges without mediation into the light. (*WM*: 350)

The remark is '*ethos anthropoi daimon*', for which the usual translation is: 'A human being's character is their destiny.' But Heidegger insists that this is to write in a modern, not in a Greek way. He claims instead that: '*Ethos* means abode, dwelling-place.' He goes on to interpret the dwelling-place of human beings as the proximity of divinity: 'The (familiar [*geheuer*]) habitation of human beings is the opening for the coming near of God (of the unknown, [*Un-geheuer*])' (*WM*: 353). He explains his view of this return of ethics in his thought:

> If then, in accordance with the basic meaning of the word *ethos*, the name 'ethics' says that it considers the true habitation of human beings, then that thinking which thinks the truth of being as the primary element of human beings, as something which exists, is already an originary ethics. This thinking, then, is not first of all ethics, because it is ontology. (*WM*: 353)

Here is where the return of ethics in Heidegger's thought takes place most emphatically, with Heidegger himself claiming that ontology is in this sense an originary ethics. He elaborates by stating:

> Thinking that questions the truth of being and therefore determines the habitation of the essence of human being in derivation from being is neither ethics nor ontology. Hence the question about the relation of each to the other no longer has a basis in this domain. All the same, your question, thought through more originally, has a meaning and an essential weight. (*WM*: 354)

This is the most major modification of the enquiry in *Being and Time*, in suggesting that ontology is as impossible as ethics.

My suggestion is that if ontology is understood as also ethical in intent, then neither term need be rejected. Heidegger continues with a reference to the naming of language as the 'house of being': 'The language of the house of being is no transference of an image from "house" to being, but if we think from the perspective of the essence of being, we will one day be able to think what "house" and "living" are' (*WM*: 355). The transition from merely living to a full dwelling requires an affirmation of a relation to being. This is more important than any construction of rules of conduct and moral laws:

> It is more important than all setting out of rules that human beings find a habitation in the truth of being. Only with this habitation is there a preserving of the experience of retention [*Halt*]. The truth of being donates this retention,

which is the basis for all conduct [*Verhalten*]. 'Retention' means in this language 'shelter' [*Hut*].

Here Heidegger moves from the play on words, *Halt* and *Verhalten*, to *Hut* and *behüten*, 'shelter' and 'to shelter', and on to 'house', *Haus*, and 'housing', *Behausen*:

> Being is the shelter which shelters human beings in their ek-sistent essence, in accordance with its truth, so that the shelter can also house that existence in language. It is for this reason that language is both the house of being and the housing of the essence of human beings [*des Menschenwesens*]. Only if language is the housing of the essence of human beings is it possible for historical humanity and human beings to be not at home in their language, so that language becomes the place for empty human activity. (*WM*: 357)

This dual role for language goes missing through the abandonment of being, and human beings can lose all sense of the subordination to language on which the later papers and the interpretation of Leibniz discussed in the previous chapter insist. The next chapter explores Heidegger's responses to Hölderlin and his hopes of the emergence of a new word for being through poetry. There, Heidegger develops these notions of homecoming and dwelling poetically between mortality and divinity, between earth and sky.

Chapter 4

What is it to be human?

> What is human being? A transition, a direction, a storm that sweeps our planet, the return or revival of the gods? We do not know. But we saw that, in this puzzling essence, philosophy occurs. (*GA* 29/30: 10)

This chapter continues the strategy of working backwards from Heidegger's declaration of an end of philosophy after the defeat of Nazism to reveal key continuities in Heidegger's thinking. It will also confront Heidegger's engagement with Nazism. Heidegger hoped for a revival of philosophy in conjunction with the rise of Hitler, through a uniquely German reception of the Greek origins of European thought and writing. This is the hideous fascistic moment in Heidegger's thinking, in which he does violence to philosophy by seeking to conjoin it with Nazism. It comes clearly to expression in the 1943 lecture 'Heimkunft: An die Verwandten',[1] in which Heidegger anticipates a specifically German future, affirms a sense of belonging as German, and constructs a homecoming as a return to that sense of belonging. This, however, is a violence external to philosophy through which Heidegger sacrifices both philosophy and those designated as non-German in the name of a misguided homecoming. There is another moment of violence in Heidegger's thinking which is not thus extraneous to philosophy. In this chapter and the next I trace the impact of this moment of violence, with a view to assessing not Heidegger's Nazism but his philosophical significance. The moment has three aspects. There is Heidegger's rejection of philosophy in favour of thinking; there is Heidegger's preference for the plays of Sophocles as an authority on ethics over Aristotle's writings; and there is his challenge to the separations within European thought between poetry and thinking, between metaphysics and ethics, between science and art and between freedom and nature. Central to this chapter is the challenge to the distinction between poetry and thinking; the other three distinctions are discussed at greater length in Chapter 5.

In the 1930s the themes of ambiguity and homelessness come into critical conjunction in Heidegger's thinking. These two themes were introduced in the two preceding chapters as the ambiguity of his readings of the texts of others in relation to the ambiguity in the focus of his own enquiries, divided between being and being human; and the relation between humanism, nihilism and homelessness. In this chapter and the next, their conjunction provides a framework for locating both his endorsement of Nazism and his revelation concerning the destructiveness of the human condition in its relation to the overwhelming forces of being. This latter is traced out in Heidegger's responses to Sophocles' *Oedipus* trilogy. This chapter leads into a discussion of that destructiveness in Chapter 5. Here the theme for discussion is ambiguity in relation to the homelessness which Heidegger forecloses into an affirmation of a specifically German destiny in his endorsement of Nazism. This, I suggest, is a moment of dereliction with respect to the forces at work in Heidegger's thinking: the man betrays the thought. In this decade Heidegger came to the view that philosophy has come to an end because it is no longer possible to construct a metaphysical system around a word for being. However, this presumption that philosophy is coextensive with metaphysical construction is open to question; and I suggest that philosophy can also be understood more broadly as reflection on the implications of attempting to construct metaphysical systems, whether successfully or not. Indeed, one of Heidegger's major contributions to contemporary understanding is his suggestion that the spread of technology marks the impossibility of metaphysical construction, while continuing the metaphysical quest for unrestricted scope. There is to me no impropriety in calling this a philosophical insight. There are three major components to Heidegger's work in the 1930s, out of which this diagnosis of an end of philosophy emerges. There is his encounter with Hölderlin;[2] there are his recurrent attempts to construct a history of words for being, which are continually disrupted by the workings of ambiguity; and there is his declaration in the 1938 essay 'The age of the world picture' that metaphysics has been transformed into anthropology, a generalised account of what it is to be human.[3] I shall discuss these in reverse order, leading up to the encounter with Hölderlin and to the abandoning of the hope for the emergence of a word for being out of the meeting between philosopher and poet.

The epigraph to this chapter is taken from the 1929/30 lectures on *The Basic Concepts of Metaphysics: World – Finitude – Solitude*.[4] It brings together the themes of mortality and divinity, which form one half of the postwar fourfold through which Heidegger attempts to develop a post-metaphysical account of the world and of time.[5] Both pairs in the fourfold, earth and sky, mortals and divinities, receive a significant inflection through Heidegger's encounter with Hölderlin. In this encounter the theme of ambiguity, *Zweideutigkeit*, from *Being and Time* is transformed into the theme of the *Zwiesprache*, the dialogue through which access to the thinking of other people, in other epochs, in other modes, becomes possible. This other kind of thinking is set out by Heidegger not as an accomplished fact but as an urgent necessity for the future, to be anticipated. The central concern of this chapter is to consider the temporality and violence implicit in this project of gaining access to otherness. In the 1930s, Heidegger brings together the themes of ambiguity and homelessness introduced in previous chapters with two further themes: violence and the transformation of metaphysics into anthropology. Taken together, these four, violence, homelessness, ambiguity and anthropology, provide a grid for reading Heidegger's writings as revealing the inherently ethical nature of all thinking, language use and philosophical reflection. The four, taken together, reveal how representational thinking elides and conceals this ethical dimension by erasing questions about time and temporality. While the primary effect of Heidegger's thinking is to undermine confidence in the adequacy of representation and representability as the sole resources for thought, a critique of the adequacy of representation also reveals the role of a commitment to representation and representability in eliding the ethical dimension of any thinking whatsoever.

There is a double movement of forgetting, in which the ethical dimension is first obscured and then that obscuring itself is erased. The double movement contains a scarcely detectable temporal dynamic: it conceals the role of forgetting in the deployment of meaning, as an event held in place between forgetting and remembering. This double movement also elides the difference between re-membering, as reminiscence of a completely articulated past occurrence, and remembering as remembrance, which plays a role in constituting that past occur-rence.[6] In representational thinking there is no way of marking a difference between the two kinds of memory, since the puzzle is how there could be access to past events at all, rather than a question about different kinds of event, complete and incomplete. These two kinds of event and two kinds of past have different temporal structures. Through an account of that differential temporality, it becomes possible to place the different kinds of past and different kinds of memory in relation to the different conceptions of time and of events, as complete and incomplete, as closed and as open-ended. Metaphysical construction imposes closure and completion on events and memory. Ethical enquiry opens out the difference between the closed and the open, between the completed and the incomplete, still developing processes, which are the lived relations of human experience. These differences reveal two further themes for discussion: the imposition, through the emphasis on representation, of a one-dimensional account of temporality and a resulting elision of difference between kinds of memory. This chapter introduces Heidegger's critique of anthropology in his 1938 paper 'The age of the world picture' ('Die Zeit des Weltbildes', published in 1950 in *Holzwege*). It then discusses the violence and ambiguity of his interpretative strategies, before turning to the discussion of the temporality of homelessness and homecoming in Hölderlin's poetry.

SOLITARY SPEECH: METAPHYSICS AS ANTHROPOLOGY

The transformation of metaphysics into anthropology is discussed at length in the 1938 paper 'The age of the world picture'; but it is already indicated by a remark from the 1929/30 lectures on *The Basic Concepts of Metaphysics: World – Finitude – Solitude* (1983), in a passage immediately before the passage cited in the epigraph. Heidegger remarks: 'Metaphysics has drawn itself back and is drawing itself into the darkness of the human essence. Our question: what is metaphysics? has changed into the question: what is human being?' (*GA 29/30:*

10). This suggestion is not developed in the 1929/30 lectures, which are taken up with an exploration of the phenomenology of the world and with the attempt to reveal boredom as a basic mood of *Dasein*. Heidegger develops the claim about a relation between metaphysics and anthropology in the 1938 essay. In it there is an ambiguity between anthropology as the last version of metaphysics, with 'man' as the last word for being, and anthropology as a transitional formation, between metaphysics and another kind of thinking, which is to come. This ambiguity is resolved in favour of the latter option in his subsequent thinking. The essay provides a double context for the claim: an interpretation of Descartes as the founder of modern philosophy and a discussion of the emergence of modern science from philosophy. Both themes have a long history in Heidegger's thinking, which cannot be fully traced out here. The paper opens with the following declaration:

> In metaphysics there completes itself a process of giving meaning to the essence of entities and a decision about the essence of truth. Metaphysics grounds an epoch, in that metaphysics gives that epoch a basis for its essential image, through a certain interpretation of entities and a distinctive view of truth. (*HW*: 69)

Metaphysical systems suspend questions about what there is and about truth by appearing to provide answers to these questions. Epochs thus last as long as these questions remain suspended. Anthropology, by contrast, indefinitely postpones the questions about truth and about the nature of entities by relating all such questions back to problems about the status of a subject in relation to its object and in relation to truth. Out of this relation between a subject and its world arise the pseudo-problems of relativism and scepticism; the frame of reference which is thus set up is too impoverished to achieve the reductions of thought achieved in metaphysics.

In this essay, time is already reduced to nothing more than the framing of distinct historical epochs, rendering completely inexplicable how one epoch might be replaced by another. The 'age' (*Zeit*) of the title is nothing but the present epoch; and the 'world picture' displaces and obscures the framing of phenomena through a horizon, which, instead of being conceived of as shifting, is constructed into a rigid definitive account of a fixed 'world'. For the age of the world picture, representation and representability exhaust the possibilities for constructing objects of thought and of reflection. In this context the question 'what is human being?' takes on a special urgency. 'What is human being?' is a key question for Heidegger, not because he supposes himself uniquely equipped to answer it, but because he diagnoses the current age, the age of technology, as providing a significantly different kind of answer to it. Indeed, only in the contemporary age is the attempt made to give to this question a generalised answer with universal application. The problem with such answers is that they restrict our capacity to affirm the diversity of the relations we set up to ourselves, to our self-images, to our stances towards others and to the world in which we find ourselves. The generalised answer makes it appear as though there were one such image and as though those self-images and stances were fixed and given, not chosen and lived. Thus the problem is not one of finding a more adequate answer to the question 'what is it to be human?', but of ceasing to want general answers to it at all. This in turn would permit the question to become a problem encountered by individual human beings in the specific contexts of their own lives. The question would cease to have the status presuming a single, complete, metaphysical answer that blocks the possibility of individual, flexible responses. The metaphysical question distinctive of the current epoch, 'what is it to be human?', does not permit of an answer, since any such answer immediately subverts a central characteristic of that which is being defined: what it is to be human. It denies the self-interpretative capacities of human beings. The unanswerability of the question 'what is it to be human?' marks the unavailability in the modern epoch of a metaphysical specification of being.

The paper opens with a brief summary of the conditions Heidegger sees as required in order for science to flourish. He also discusses the relation between conceptions of nature and of history. He connects positivist history to securing a reified view of the past and suggests that the subordination of nature to scientific protocols is intended to help human beings secure their future, but in fact has the opposite effect. He explains:

> Research ranges over entities, if it can reckon with them in advance [*voraus-berechnen*] in their future unravelling or can sum them up after the event [*nachrechnen*] as something past. Nature and history are set up simultaneously in, respectively, an advance reckoning or a retrospective summing up. Nature and history become the objects of an explanatory representation. This mode counts on [*rechnen auf*] nature and takes history into account [*rechnen mit*]. (*HW*: 80)

History, on this view, is confined to a retrospective summing up of what has happened, cutting off any sense that actions in the past and the present have effects on the future. Scientific enquiry, by contrast, provides hypotheses about how entities will function in the future. By detaching scientific enquiry from its history, the hypothetical status of scientific results is converted into dogmatic truths, in response to the experience of successes in permitting human beings to intervene in their world: to put rockets on the moon; to produce hybrid plant forms; to do brain surgery. The future is turned into a determinist universe that can be predicted and controlled; the past, by contrast, is turned into the domain of freedom, consisting of the results of human activities which are open to interpretation. History becomes a record of those past acts of freedom and becomes a celebration of human freedom. However, this account of history blocks off the thought that there are aspects of the past which remain unknown and unrecognised. The account of science blocks off questioning of the ethical and moral responsibilities of such enquiry with respect to its possible impact on future generations of human beings. There is a strong interdependency between these views of history and of nature.

There is also a connection back to the distinctions made in *Being and Time* between attitudes to both the future and the past. Heidegger distinguishes between an attitude towards the future of expecting relations between human beings and their surroundings to remain stable, *Erwarten*, and a mode of anticipation, *Vorlaufen*, which contains the possibility of drastic changes of framework shifting these relations. This mode of anticipation opens up the possibility of systematic shifts in how what there is appears. This possibility of shifts is subsequently charted through the notion of *Seinsgeschichte*. There are similarly two possible attitudes towards the past. There is the supposition that a single non-contradictory account of past events can be produced in a positivist historiography. There is also the Marxist view of a fundamental conflict between accounts of the past, depending on what vision of the future is adopted. Heidegger, in discussing attitudes to the past in *Being and Time*, does not draw out this parallel, although later remarks in the 'Letter on humanism' about a proximity between his own thought and that of Marx confirm the connection. Instead he identifies a difference between remembering the past and the stance of forgetfulness, linking up not to Marx but to Nietzsche's 'The uses and drawbacks of history for living', which is cited in *Being and Time*.[7]

This distinction between remembering and forgetting with respect to the past opens out distinctions between different kinds of remembering. In addition to the two already identified, reminiscence of a completely articulated past occurrence and remembrance which plays a role in constituting that past occurrence, there is also the mode of recollection, retrieving a knowledge given in its entirety before the beginning of time. Between these three there opens up a series of differences between interpretations of the nature of what there is, the structure of temporality and the relation between the two. Only for remembrance does it make sense to make any strong distinction between expectation and anticipation with respect to the future; and only once these two have been distinguished is it possible to begin to make sense of the significance for Heidegger of the connection between fatality and futurity. Expectation and recollection are potentially obstacles to innovative understandings of the relations between past, present and future and to finding a place within them. They presume continuity and sameness, whereas forgetfulness and anticipation permit change to occur. The future tense is central for Heidegger, since it is with respect to the future that individuals have a destiny and a relation to being. By eliding the difference between past, present and future, this primacy becomes obscure, adding to the forces at work eliding the question of being as an issue for human beings. The two distinctive stances with respect to the past and the future, and with respect to history, recur in the suggested opposition between the metaphysical and ethical stances within philosophy.

In the course of the essay 'The age of the world picture', Heidegger states that a transformation of what it is to be human is one of the changes required for the flourishing of positivist science: 'What is decisive is not that human beings free themselves from previous relations and come to themselves, but that the essence of what it is to be human changes, in so far as human beings become the subject' (*HW*: 81). Heidegger traces this 'becoming the subject' as emerging in Descartes' work: 'The whole of modern metaphysics, including that of Nietzsche, holds itself within the interpretation of entities and of truth set out by Descartes' (*HW*: 80). Heidegger thus agrees with Hegel and with modern analytical philosophy in assigning to Descartes the status of the founder of modern philosophy. The difference between Heidegger's diagnosis and the modern analytical view is that Heidegger diagnoses an end and abandonment of philosophy at work in the emergence of a split between a subjectivism, as a foundation for knowledge, and an objectivism about what there is. Human beings as subjects, becoming the foundation for knowledge, is for Heidegger a mark of the end of philosophy. However, he disrupts the reification of this one vision of what it is to be human by insisting on the alternate visions of being human with which it was at first in competition. The diagnosis of this view of what it is to be human as a trans-formation of a previously existing view subverts its status as a stable, enduring ground for a metaphysical system. At the beginning of the modern period, human beings become the subject and correlatively what there is becomes the object of enquiry, thereby, as far as Heidegger is concerned, making modern science possible and hastening the disintegration of philosophy.

Heidegger claims: 'With Descartes begins the completion of Western meta-physics' (*HW*: 91). He immediately adds: 'However, such a completion is only possible as metaphysics, and thus modern thinking has its own greatness,' and continues:

> With his interpretation of human being as the subject Descartes creates the metaphysical basis for subsequent anthropologies of every mode and tendency. In the emergence of anthropologies Descartes celebrates his greatest triumph. It is through anthropology that there is introduced the transition of meta-physics into the process of the mere stopping and abandonment of all philosophy.

This transition of metaphysics is not a transformation within metaphysics to produce another metaphysical system. It is the end of philosophy, announced more emphatically in the 1964 paper 'The end of philosophy and the task of thinking'. The development of a theory of what it is to be human as the ground for the possibility of there being what there is does not provide an account of what there is as such; it merely posits that it is knowable by human beings. This completion or transition of metaphysics is thus marked by the emergence of an anthropology, in the sense of a theory of human being as a fixed essence grounding the existence of all other entities. This anthropology provides neither a theory of what there is nor an account of truth, which are the two achievements Heidegger ascribes to metaphysical systems. Thus, anthropology is not meta-physics: it is the completion of a process at work in metaphysics of indefinitely postponing questions about truth and about what there is, until some mythical completion of scientific enquiry. This is how Heidegger describes the process:

Making entities into objects for human beings completes itself in a placing before [*Vor-stellen*] which aims at bringing every entity into view in such a way that calculating human beings can be certain of them, and that means have knowledge of them. It then turns into science as systematic investigation only when truth has changed into the certainty of representation. (*HW*: 80)

Thus in the modern epoch, entities become objects for human beings and truth becomes certainty. Philosophy is transposed into an endless observation of entities, in place of offering accounts of what there is. This leads to the elision of any question of being and of any questioning of the way in which what there is results from a process of emergence. Philosophy comes to provide the concepts underpinning an unending programme of scientific research and is then dissolved into the individual empirical sciences. There is no longer a single coherent overview and account of entities as a whole.

Heidegger remarks on the retrieval in Descartes' title: *Meditations on First Philosophy* of Aristotle's title '*prote philosophia*' (*HW*: 80), as that which is subsequently called 'metaphysics'. He states in a long footnote that the transformations of Descartes' basic position in the subsequent writings of Leibniz, of the German idealists and of Nietzsche in no way change that basic position. They are simply variants of a single structure. Thus his reading of Nietzsche, already under way in 1938, can be seen as an attempt to prove that Nietzsche too is putting forward nothing but a further modification within the parameters set up by Descartes, not breaking through to a set of conceptions in which a new epoch, beyond modernity, can be grounded. Heidegger's view is that the humanism and subjectivism implicit in Descartes' philosophy is no longer an adequate grounding for a metaphysical system, but that the attempts made by subsequent German philosophers, including Hegel and Nietzsche, to rescue the paradigm are similarly inadequate. This overarching hypothesis about post-Cartesian philosophy provides the frame for his forceful reading of Nietzsche. In Nietzsche's writings, Heidegger finds a culmination of a process which reduces what there is to nothing more than a projection of what it is to be human. This is Heidegger's understanding of will to power, taken in conjunction with the theses about self-overcoming. Heidegger sees the German tradition of philosophy as offering a series of reinterpretations of Descartes' grounding of entities, grounding what there is in the processes of representation to a subject. Heidegger claims that, with Descartes, human beings become the ground of knowledge. This, for Heidegger, is the significance of the emergence of the concept of the subject in the early modern period.

In the footnote, he adds that this subject is reinterpreted by Leibniz as the monad, by Kant as transcendental imagination, by Fichte as infinite ego, by Hegel as spirit and by Schelling's interpretation of freedom as the necessity of every entity. Oddly, Nietzsche does not figure in the brief list given in this footnote, although earlier in the essay Heidegger claims that Nietzsche's metaphysics is also determined in its structure, if not in content, by the Cartesian move. The last term in this sequence of names for human being as subject, then, is 'will to power'. All of these theories, according to Heidegger, provide an anthropology, a theory of what it is to be human, as a grounding of what there is: 'Human beings become that entity, on which all entities in the mode of their being and truth are grounded' (*HW*: 81). The upshot of human beings acquiring this status of the subject of knowledge is a blocking of the possibility of opening out a question of what it is to be human. Here then is the connection between blocking the question of being and blocking the question: 'what is it to be human?' A series of possible interpretations of being human present themselves, but they prevent rather than encourage thought:

> Only because and in so far as human beings in general and essentially become the subject, must there in consequence be the question: human beings have and want to become a subject as an 'I', which is limited to its arbitrariness and let loose in its individual will, or as a 'we' of society; human beings as individual or as community; as person in society or as mere member of a body; whether as a subject as state and nation and people or as universal humanity of modern human being, which human beings as a modern entity already are. (*HW*: 85)

He continues:

> Only where human being is essentially already subject is there a possibility of sliding into the non-essential mode of subjectivism in the sense of individualism. But also only where human beings remain subjects is there any sense to an explicit struggle against individualism and for community as the target domain for achievement and usefulness. (*HW*: 85)

None of these questions can be addressed; none of them are genuine questions because it has been decided in advance that what it is to be human provides a foundation for knowledge:

> Anthropology is that interpretation of human being which in fact already knows what human beings are and therefore can never ask who we are. For with this question human beings would have to recognise themselves as convulsed and overcome. How could this be suspected in anthropology, when it is merely concerned with a securing after the event of the self-certainty of the subject? (*HW*: 103)

Anthropology is then a general theory of humanity which blocks any opening out in response to the question 'what is it to be human?' Only by coming to terms with the universality of the humanity which is already built into the meanings of the term 'subject' and 'human being' in the modern epoch is it possible for human beings to begin to address questions about who we are as individuals and as groups. These questions remain blocked while the abstract conception of what it is to be human is used to found the rationality of scientific research and technical control in the world.

There is a self-reinforcing process in play. Reducing human beings to subjects, to nothing but the basis on which what there is can be constructed, is interdependent with reducing the world to a fixed image:

> The more inclusively and thoroughly the world is set up as under control and ready for disposal, the more objectively the object appears; the more subjectively, that is the more thoroughly, the subject emerges, all the more thoroughly the engagement with the world and teaching about the world becomes simply a doctrine about what it is to be human, becomes anthropology. (*HW*: 86)

This reduction of the world to a fixed picture is for Heidegger distinctive of modernity and reinforces the emergence of a conception of human beings as subject and ground for the construction of knowledge. Heidegger distinguishes between what it is possible to think in the modern age and what was possible in the age of the Greeks:

> There can be no surprise that, where the world becomes a picture, there humanism comes to the fore. Just as little as it was possible at the time of the Greeks for there to be a picture of the world, so it is impossible to make a humanism function in that context. Humanism in a narrower historical sense is nothing other than a moral aesthetic anthropology. (*HW*: 86)

He explains what he means here by humanism:

> This word does not mean natural scientific research about human beings. It does not mean the doctrine set up in Christian theology about the created, fallen and redeemed human beings. It picks out that philosophical interpretation of human beings which explains, and underestimates, what there is as a totality on the basis of human being and with respect to human being. (*HW*: 86)

It should be noted that this use of the term 'humanism' is unusual. It does not address what is usually meant by the term. Heidegger instead makes a connection between theories assigning value to what it is to be human, given in humanism, and the epistemological and metaphysical roles assigned to theories of the subject, produced in post-Cartesian philosophical theory. The term 'anthropology' picks out the connection between these two.

Anthropology, for Heidegger, is the modern manner of forgetting being as a process operating above and beyond what there is, in this instance above and beyond the powers and interests of human beings. Modernity, for Heidegger, marks a critical phase with the juxtaposition of disproportional images: there is the contrast between the enormous scale of technically based transformation and the microscopic scale of the processes on which that transformation is based. The attempt to think in terms of both scales at the same time elides any sense of the size and vulnerability of the human body, its natural habitat and lifespan. Heidegger concludes the essay with a reading of part of Hölderlin's poem *An die Deutschen*, 'To the Germans', which warns against losing contact with locality, losing the proportions set up by a grounding in '*die eigne Zeit*' by moving out into the boundlessness of '*die Jahre der Völker*'. What is needed is for human beings to recognise that we occupy: 'a place between, in which human beings as beings remain as a part of what there is, and yet remain strangers amongst entities' (*HW*: 88). Heidegger adds enigmatically: 'Hölderlin knew about this.' He then quotes lines from Hölderlin's poem *An die Deutschen*:

Wohl ist enge begrenzt unsere Lebenszeit,
Unserer Jahre Zahl sehen und zählen wir,
Doch die Jahre der Völker,
Sah ein sterbliches Auge sie?
Wenn die Seele dir auch über die eigne Zeit
Sich die sehnende schwingt, trauernd verweilest du
Dann am kalten Gestade
Bei den Deinen und kennst sie nie.

How narrowly bounded is our lifetime
We see and count the number of our years
But the years of nations:
Have they been seen by mortal eye?
If your soul soars yearningly out
Beyond its own time, then, mourning
You linger on the cold shore
Among your own and never know them.

This moving out into a limitless domain, affirming connections to everything that there is, makes it difficult for human beings to make connections to any particular location. It generates a groundlessness and homelessness, which deepens as a result of there being no metaphysical system to provide a grounding. There is a contrast here between being human as a metaphysical, generalised abstraction and as an ethical, located, lived relation. This poem continues with a more hopeful reference to those to come, who are promised, who will be open to the poet's soul or, in the incomplete rewriting offered by Hölderlin under the title *Rousseau*, able to respond to this solitary speech (*einsame Rede*). For Heidegger, a response to the question of being human that does not give the inadequate generalised answer is to be found in Hölderlin's poetry, in solitary speech.

ELUCIDATIONS OF AMBIGUITY

In his readings of texts, Heidegger makes use of several levels of ambiguity: in the terminology used; in the thought developed, contrasting the thought and unthought dimensions of texts; and in the interaction between reader and text. This last is especially important in his readings of his own texts. In his readings of Hölderlin, he discovers a pair of terms which captures his mode of reading: an *Andenken*, commemoration, which is also a *Nachdenken*, a rethinking of the thought of the other which necessarily disrupts that thought. This commemoration is a form of remembrance for which the openness of the future as anticipation is affirmed. What is remembered is inseparable from its transformation in the process of its retrieval in that commemoration. The fixity of the sequence of past, present and future is disrupted and the metaphysics of subjectivity definitively displaced. The elucidation of these ambiguities attempted here juxtaposes three texts from 1943: the *Holzwege* essay 'Nietzsche's aphorism "God is dead"', the address 'Andenken', given on the occasion of Hölderlin's anniversary, and the afterword to 'What is metaphysics?'. In a remark made in advance of repeating the 1943 'Andenken' lecture, Heidegger states that elucidation (*Erläuterungen*) must, if effective, make itself redundant:

> Whatever an elucidation may be capable and incapable of achieving, this remains true: when what is put into poetry in the poem becomes clearer, the exposition must itself break off with what it attempts. For the sake of what is put into the poetry, the elaboration of the poem must itself tend toward making itself superfluous. The last and most difficult step of any interpretation consists in disappearing, with its elucidations, in the face of the pure thereness of what is put into poetry [*dem reinen Dastehen des Gedichtes*]. (*ED1*: 32)

This remark is taken up in the introduction to the second edition and is, I suggest, a description of what Heidegger attempts to do in *Being and Time*, with the aim of elucidating the structures of *Dasein*. Thus I suggest that the methodological remarks Heidegger makes with respect to reading Hölderlin apply to readings of Heidegger's own texts. Once the poem has become clear, then the explanatory apparatus drops away. Once the structure of *Dasein* has become clear, then the process of attempting to describe it and to bring the reader to understand the site of human experience in this way can be discarded, simply leaving the reader with that understanding. This approach to elucidation connects with Heidegger's attempt to read into his earlier works and into the writings of others thoughts at work in them but not fully expressed. Such attempts to come to terms with the incompleteness of *Being and Time* are to be found both in the afterword to 'What is metaphysics?' and in the 'Letter on humanism'. This is also a description of Heidegger's readings of the texts of the philosophical tradition to reveal in them an unthought, a relation between thinking and language, between determinate existence and being, which is not explicitly thematic in them.

Beda Allemann, in his book on the relation between Heidegger and Hölderlin,[8] discusses the title '*Erläuterungen*', which perhaps might be better put as 'resonatings'. He draws attention to an observation from the opening pages of Heidegger's *Holzwege* essay on Nietzsche, also from 1943, 'Nietzsche's aphorism "God is dead"'. The remark runs:

> Every elucidation (*Erläuterung*) must of course not only draw from the text; it must also, without belabouring the point, add unnoticeably something of its own. This addition is that which non-experts, in accordance with what they hold the text to consist in, respond to as an imposition, with this much justice

which they claim on their own behalf, that they criticise it as arbitrary. (*HW*: 197)

The point in connection with the non-experts seems to be that the right to interpret and the right to judge interpretations are simply counterposed forces. Heidegger continues, distinguishing his view from Dilthey's hermeneutics of interpretation, which understands texts better than the authors themselves: 'A justified elucidation never understands the text better than the author understood it, but certainly differently. Yet this difference [*dieses Andere*] must be of such a kind as to touch upon the sameness [*das Selbe*] towards which the elucidated text is thinking' (*HW*: 197). This thinking, the final word in the quotation, is a *Nachdenken*. The juxtaposition here is between *das Selbe*, a sameness, and *das Andere*, an otherness, a different way of understanding that sameness which is offered by the elucidation. The suggestion is that the text cannot be expected to articulate completely what it is attempting to articulate; thus the meaning to be recovered is one which is not fully expressed in the text but is indicated and gestured to as meaning to be brought into expression at some future time. The meaning in the text has the structure of an incomplete event, *Gewesenes*, not of a totalised past, *Vergangenheit*. This '*Nachdenken*' stands in contraposition to '*Andenken*'. It thinks towards the issues which the text to be elucidated seeks to locate. The '*Andenken*' appears to be contrasted to this, but in fact has a very similar structure. It is a retrieval of a past, but a retrieval in relation to an incomplete past, a *Gewesenes*, not a completed, closed-off past, a *Vergangenheit*.

Heidegger elaborates on this in the essay 'Andenken', composed at the same time as the 1943 lecture and published in the second edition of the *Erläuterungen*. There, he responds to the final line in the poem *Was bleibet aber stiften die Dichter*, ('What remains, however, the poets establish'). This line is also discussed in the 1936 essay 'Hölderlin and the essence of poetry',[9] which can be read as explaining why, in the slightly earlier paper from 1935–36, 'The origin of the artwork', poetry is taken to be the primary art form.[10] The line is the fourth of the five quotations around which the 1936 essay is structured. The primacy of poetry as an art form is revealed in the later essay as based in the possibility that in poetry a new word for being may emerge. For Heidegger, Hölderlin's diag- nosis of this as a time of need reveals that what is lacking is a way of naming what there is. This, in Heidegger's terms, is a withholding of being or, with Hölderlin, the absence of divinity. Thus the history of words for being has come to an end in the present epoch because of the extremity of the current withdrawal of being. Neither 'technology' nor 'humanism' are words for being, but are indications of the unavailability of a word for being and of the difficulty of retrieving a relation to being, resulting from the extreme withdrawal of being. In the 1936 essay, Heidegger discusses this line in terms of the ontological difference between being and entities. In the essay written with the 1943 lecture, the emphasis shifts to considering the relation to the future: 'Does the poet "think" about the past which remains, while it remains left over? Why then is there an establishing?

Does this establishing "think" rather about something which is to come [*das Künftige*]. Then the "*Andenken*" of the title would indeed be a remembrance, but of something to come' (*ED2*: 79–80). He goes on: 'Such a "thinking about" what is to come can only be a thinking about what has been, through which we think the difference between what is past [*Vergangenes*] and that which is still in process [*das fernher noch Wesende*].' (*ED2*: 80).

In both *Nachdenken* and *Andenken*, there is a recognition of the incompleteness of the thought to be followed through and commemorated. That incompleteness is complicated by the operations of forgetting within the originary processes of thinking and within the subsequent commemoration. Thus, forgetting is not a process which intervenes between the thought to be retrieved and the attempt to retrieve it, but is structured into what is to be retrieved. The future is necessarily implicated in the gesture of elucidation and commemoration; for only in the future is it possible to elaborate incomplete thoughts. Thus in this reading of Hölderlin, Heidegger explores both the saying otherwise of what the other has already said, as *Nachdenken*, and the *Andenken* of retrieval of an incomplete utterance. The commemoration of the *Andenken* may be a commemoration for states which may never have existed; the *Nachdenken* is an attempt to follow a thought through which has not as yet been and may never be completed. The emphasis on these structures generates an entirely unusual and disruptive mode of reading, with meaning understood as a two-way process of anticipation and retrieval. In them, the account of temporality and the structures designated in *Being and Time* through the analysis of *Dasein* are merged in ways perhaps projected in *Being and Time* but not there accomplished. Relations between past, present and future take precedence over taking these three temporal dimensions as distinct, and there is here a retrieval and following through of the disruption and displacement of subjectivity at work in *Being and Time*.

In the 1943 afterword to the lecture 'What is metaphysics?', Heidegger invokes Hölderlin, without naming him. The passage is introduced through a reworking of the language of care and solicitude from *Being and Time*, *Sorge* and *Besorgen*, into a new pair, *Sorgsamkeit* and *Sorgfältigkeit*, which resonate with the con- cluding lines of Hölderlin's poem *Heimkunft*:

Sorgen, wie diese, muss gern oder nicht in der Seele
Tragen ein Sänger und oft, aber die anderen nicht.

Cares like these, whether he likes it or not,
The bard must carry in his soul, but not others.

Thus the poet is set apart from other people by having cares which reach out beyond everyday preoccupation. The passage opens with a reference to the task of thinking about being: 'Thinking in obedience to the voice of being seeks out the word, the phrase, out of which the truth of being can come into language. Only when the language of historically determinate human being springs from such a word is it in balance' (*WM*: 309). It continues: 'The thinking of being protects the word and fulfils its invocation in this protection. It is the care [Sorge] for the use of language', a remark that reduces those who object to Heidegger's practices of interpretation and use of German to either laughter or fury. Heidegger then adds:

> Out of a long-maintained speechlessness and out of a careful [*sorgfältigen*] clearing of the domain thereby lit up, there comes the saying of the thinker. The naming of the poet is of the same derivation. Because indeed this sameness is only a sameness as a difference, poetry and thought at their purest are similar in the solicitude for the word with respect to the word, both are at the same time divided in their emergence/essence [*Wesen*] to the greatest degree. The thinker says being. The poet names the holy. (*WM*: 309)

The saying of being and the naming of the holy are thus being set out as the sameness through which the philosophical and poetic activities, the projects of thought and of language, are related and set apart for one another. Heidegger then introduces an unattributed remark from Hölderlin: 'One [*man*] knows much about the relation between philosophy and versifying. We know nothing, however, about the dialogue [*Zwiesprache*] of thinkers and poets, who "live close together on wholly separate mountains"' (*WM*: 309). Heidegger here lines out philosophy and verse with the anonymous, disowned mode of existence, *das Man*, which has an empty knowledge of philosophy and versifying. This links back to the anonymous mode of gossip, of *Gerede*, introduced in *Being and Time*. This contrasts to the 'we', which is ignorant of the dialogue between a poetic naming of the holy and a thoughtful saying of being. There is a resonance here with the 'we' which has fallen into perplexity at the beginning of *Being and Time* about the meaning of the term 'being'. There is also a ghastly resonance with the ignorant and self-deceiving 'we' which in 1943 stood back and permitted the Nazis to murder thousands of people in the death camps. Most appalling of all, it seems that it is the defeat of Nazism which finally persuades Heidegger of the increasing unlikelihood of a new naming of the holy, new saying of being.

Heidegger shifts from this view of 1943 that it is still possible for the thoughtful one to say being. In the rewriting of the afterword of 'What is metaphysics?' in a fifth edition in 1949, the focus of attention moves to reflecting on the impact of technical relations, as making such saying of being and naming of the holy impossible. This change resonates, together on most separated mountains, with Adorno's claim that, after Auschwitz, poetry is no longer possible. It resonates with Hölderlin's claim that this is a time of great need in which the gods have withdrawn from mortal existence, leaving those with a sensibility to detect such absence in silent deprivation, solitary speech. William Richardson, in his important early study of the transitions in Heidegger's thinking, *Heidegger: Through Phenomenology to Thought*, asserts that this afterword to 'What is metaphysics?' constitutes a first draft of the 'Letter on humanism', as a rethinking of the project of *Being and Time*, and goes on to discuss this rewriting:[11]

The original (1943) reading was 'Being indeed comes-to-presence without beings . . .'. Now it reads 'Being never comes-to-presence without beings . . .'. Is this not a complete reversal? and indeed on an essential point? And the unkindest cut of all is that the change is made without so much as a word to call attention to it, much less to explain it.

Richardson then seeks to explain how such a reversal could be made without emptying the enquiry of all meaning. He argues that, underlying this reversal, making it explicable, there is a shift of ontological difference back into the centre of attention, away from the question of how individual human beings might come to be aware of being. While there can be a coming to presence of being without human awareness of it, there cannot be a coming to presence of being without a setting out of a difference between being and entities through which ontological difference comes to the fore. The shift from 1943 to 1949, then, is one from struggling to find a thinker or poet who can say being or name the holy to thinking about the medium within which such a saying or naming might take place. It is a shift from attempting to overcome the limits of the epoch in the direction of a new naming of being on the basis of the return of Hölderlin's gods to a meditative reflection on the nature of an age in which there can be no such naming. Because there are no resources for producing a metaphysical word for being, Heidegger supposes philosophy to have come to an end.

Richardson concludes:

> Briefly, the formula of 1943 emphasizes the primacy of being and implies ontological difference but does not name it as such. The formula of 1949 names it as such. Both have legitimate sense and to appreciate the full complexity of Heidegger's problem, we must think them no doubt together. But the second formula expresses better what the author considers to be, as we see in *ID* [*Identity and Difference*], the insight that is uniquely proper to himself. (p. 565)

However, in the context of discussing one of the most important issues for Heidegger's thinking, the relation between being and what there is, the use of the clumsy technical term 'formula' is disconcerting. This reveals that Richardson is perturbed by Heidegger's performance here and seeks to underplay its significance. Richardson reveals his unease by adding:

> Did he not have the right, then, to alter the first formula accordingly, when the occasion of the new edition gave him the chance? of course! If there were reason for criticism, then, this would have to restrict itself to the unannounced manner in which the change was made. But when all is said and done, even this seems to be a matter of taste: how do you take your philosophy? Straight or with a dash of *legerdemain*? (p. 565)

He thus introduces an interesting new category alongside *Dasein*, readiness to hand and presence at hand: light-handedness. While Richardson no doubt intends this in jest, it marks an important problem. Richardson is inclined to underplay this unease of register in his own writing and his unease with Heidegger's procedure here. I am inclined to take the other tack and see this light-handed mode of rewriting texts as characteristic, not of Heidegger himself, who clearly takes his own thinking extremely seriously, but of a 'Heidegger effect' at work in his texts, which functions separately from his own intentions. There is at work in Heidegger's lectures and writings a disruption of what it is to receive a philosophical tradition by reading its texts.

This disruption comes to the fore particularly clearly in his treatment of his own texts, but it is also evident in his readings of others. Heidegger challenges the punctation established for the verse of Hölderlin and Trakl. He disregards standard footnoting procedures. He fails to alert readers to changes of text in subsequent editions. For Heidegger, the development of his own interpretation and understanding is the primary concern, to the exclusion of concern for assisting his readers in following the process of development. The objection that he fails to remark the differences between the first and second editions of *Erläuterungen zu Hölderlins Dichtung* can perhaps be met by stating that Heidegger may be assuming that readers will compare editions. Probably anyone reading 'What is metaphysics?' in 1943 would have recognised the Hölderlin quotation in the afterword, so there was no need explicitly to reference it. Presumably anyone who knows Kant's critical philosophy at all can tell the aberrance of Heidegger's reading: that it is an elucidation of that critical philosophy, not a faithful commentary. But this shift of meaning to which Richardson draws attention cannot be ignored or explained away. It must rather be made the focus for locating how the principles of a reading in the mode of *Nachdenken* and *Andenken* are quite different from those of any ordinary logic of attention to the consistency of the thinking in a text; quite different from those of establishing a generally accepted view of what the aims of interpretation might be. There is here something radically different and radically disruptive at work over which I suspect Heidegger is not entirely in control: hence the introduction of the term 'Heidegger effect'.

Heidegger's readings of his own texts and of the texts of others form a duplicitous dialogue in which there is no interlocutor to question his determination of meaning. His reading of the philosophical tradition reveals not a truth about that tradition but a truth about the current philosophical condition: one in which the issues of past thinkers become unrecognisable. The end of philosophy is thus an event in the contemporary context which blocks access to the meanings of these previous thinkers; and Heidegger's readings of them reveal this blocking with the same gesture with which it constructs a barrier to them. Thus Heidegger's end of philosophy is not a conclusion to a tradition which has carried that end within its beginning. It is a break with that tradition. The question is not whether this end is indeed the culmination of the philosophical tradition, but rather whether the relation between present readers and that tradition stands in the relation of disjunction which Heidegger suggests. Clearly, I suppose that there is something right about the hypothesis which I am ascribing to Heidegger, that the relation to the past constructed in the contemporary context erases the gap between present preoccupation and previous meaning in favour of that present preoccupation. Heidegger's readings reveal just this erasure of any sense of an intrinsic value and meaning for texts from the past. Their value and meaning is constructed in the present and projected back; and in so far as there are disputes about their meanings and significance, they too take place in the present, if anywhere. This loss of a difference between present preoccupation and previous concern is another version of the loss of historicality, leading to an elision of difference, this time not between metaphysics and the everyday, but between interpretation and text. This much becomes clear from Heidegger's violent readings: that the boundary between interpretation and text is thoroughly disrupted and that this is the point of using the term 'reading' rather than the term 'interpretation'.

The encounter with the text of the other in the mode of interpretation presumes some kind of access to the other's meaning. The encounter in the mode of Heidegger's readings is one in which there is no such access, and therefore no possibility of sustaining any claim to an intrinsic meaning and value of the text to be read. The aim is not a preservation of a given meaning but a release of a new one, supposedly hidden within the text through the duplicitous operations of the sendings of being. Access to this hidden meaning is gained by the disruptive modes of *Auseinandersetzung* and *Erläuterung*. There is a distinction to be made between ambiguities in Heidegger's thinking which he deliberately deploys and ambiguities which occur as a result of difficulties in his thinking. As stated, there are two main forms in which the notion of ambiguity occurs in Heidegger's thinking. Both forms are evident in the 1929/30 lectures, from which the epigraph to this chapter is taken. There is the ambiguity (*Zweideutigkeit*) discussed at length in *Being and Time* as an element in the three-part characterisation of the everyday 'thereness' of *Dasein*, along with idle talk, *Gerede*, and curiosity, *Neugier*. There is also the *Zwiesprache*, the conversation or duplicitous dialogue, which Heidegger identifies as taking place between poetry and thinking, in relation to both Hölderlin and Trakl. Beda Allemann points out[12] that Heidegger makes use of this notion of dialogue in the introduction to the second edition of *Kant and the Problem of Metaphysics*, dated June 1950, when discussing the violence of his interpretative practice. This transfer of the term back from a poetic to a philosophical context indicates that the more important interlocutor at this slightly later date is not Hölderlin but Kant. In the section 'Moira', left out of the 1951–52 lectures *Was heißt Denken?*, the emphasis is on the relation between the present thinking and the tradition of philosophy. The dialogue between poet and thinker thus recedes in favour, first, of a dialogue between Heidegger and himself and then of a renewed dialogue between Heidegger and the philosophical tradition.

Allemann does not risk any such hypothesis but simply remarks the shift in the second paragraph of the preface to this second edition of the Kant book, which opens:

> Incessantly, people complain about the violence of my interpretation. The accusation of violation can be made good with this text. Research in the history of philosophy is justified with this accusation, if it is opposed to all attempts to set up a thoughtful interchange [*denkendes Gespräch*] between thinkers. (*KPM*: xvii)

Heidegger thus distinguishes between the normal practice of faithful interpretation of the texts of the tradition and the violent encounter which leads to 'thoughtful interchange'. In the course of the next sentence he introduces the notions of a *Zwiegespräch* and of *Zwiesprache*: 'In contrast to the methods of historical philology, which has its own task, a thoughtful dialogue [*denkendes Zwiegespräch*] has its own rules. These are injurious. In this dialogue [*Zwiesprache*] the breaches are more common, what is lacking more frequent.' He then identifies breaches and lacks in *Kant and the Problem of Metaphysics*, concluding after another short paragraph: 'Thoughtful people learn more enduringly from what is lacking. [*Denkende lernen aus dem Fehlenden nachhaltiger*.]' And it is no accident that this term for what is lacking, *das Fehlende*, is the term for the absent divinities of Hölderlin's hymns. Here are brought together the themes of violence, interpretation, dialogue and the encounter between Heidegger and Hölderlin, between thinking and poetry, between thinker and poet. There are three strands in the use of the term '*Zwiesprache*'. There is the dialogue internal to philosophy; there is the dialogue between poetry and thinking; and there is the dialogue internal to Heidegger's own thinking.

The theme of a dialogue internal to philosophy is identified as such already in *Being and Time* in the split between a fixed *Tradition* and a reinterpretable *Überlieferung*, but this is referred to as a *Zwiesprache* only in the 1929/30 lectures. The remark in the lectures runs:

> Philosophy – an ultimate expression and dialogue [*letzte Aussprache und Zwiesprache*] of human beings, which wholly and continuously permeates them. But what is human being that it philosophises at the base of its essence and what is philosophising? (*GA* 29/30: 7)

Heidegger goes on to analyse three kinds of ambiguity (*Zweideutigkeit*) in the philosophical task of construction. As a result of this, he comes to the conclusion that philosophy cannot be a form of enquiry producing results, but must be one in which the identities of the questioners themselves are transformed. Heidegger sums this thought up by saying: 'What concerns everyone, each must enter into. [*Was jedermann angeht, muss jedermann eingehen*]' (p. 22). This strand can be taken to have a second level in the analysis of *Zweideutigkeit*, of the ambiguity in language and in concepts developed in *Being and Time*. There is the second strand of a dialogue between poet and thinker, or between poetry and thought, which is emphasised in the Hölderlin readings and in the 1953 essay on Trakl, 'Die Sprache im Gedicht', printed in *Unterwegs zur Sprache* (1959).[13] This can become a dialogue between thinkers or a dialogue between poets, but is always structured around the thought of two very different ways of thinking attempting to address a single issue. This strand emerges slightly later in Heidegger's thinking, perhaps most obviously in the 1936 essay 'Hölderlin and the essence of poetry'. In the later essay on Trakl from 1953, the dialogue between thinking and poetry is taken to reveal the essence of language. There is thus a shift from discussing the essence of art, in the 1935 paper 'The origin of the work of art', through discussing the essence of poetry, in the essay 'Hölderlin and the essence of poetry', to discussing, after the Nazi period, the essence of language. However, I suggest there is a continuity in the direction of enquiry underlying these shifts of focus. In these later writings on language and poetry, the enquiries about an essence of art, of poetry and of language are brought together in a meditation on the impact of the withdrawal of being and the unavailability of a word for being in the age of technology.

Heidegger writes in the essay on Trakl:

> It is, however, also necessary from time to time to have a dialogue [*Zwiesprache*] between thinking and poetic language use, because in both there occurs a special, if quite different, relation to language. The conversation [*Gespräch*] of thinking with poetic language use is concerned with calling forward the essence of language, so that mortals can again learn to live in language. (*US*: 38)

Thus, at this later stage, the resolution of the anxiety generated by metaphysical ungroundedness is to take up residence within the possibilities opening out in language. Later in the essay he sums up his considerations by remarking: 'Poetry speaks out of an ambiguous ambiguity. [*Dichtung spricht aus einer zweideutigen Zweideutigkeit*]' (*US*: 75). There is, however, a third strand in this *Zwiesprache*. This is Heidegger's ambivalence towards his own enquiries and the ambivalence evident within his own enquiries. This ambivalence I suggest both motivates and explains the violence of his readings of Trakl, Hölderlin and Sophocles, of Nietzsche, Kant and Leibniz. There is in Heidegger's thinking a recurrent split between twin themes: the account of being, of its forgetting or withholding, and the account of *Dasein*, of the self-concealed nature of what it is to be human. The difficulty of sustaining an enquiry which has a split focus generates the appearance of self-contradiction and makes this hybrid form of grafting discussion onto readings of the texts of the other appropriate. It is this third strand in the dialogue that is concealed if attention is focused on the relation between the first two: between dialogues internal to philosophy and dialogues internal to language. Once these dialogues, within philosophy and within language, are seen as one and the same then the third strand can become the focus of attention, and can, in turn, reveal what it conceals. In that third strand, there are the twin conflicting movements within Heidegger's thought: a move back into presocratic philosophy in order to declare an end of the deviant thinking of philosophy, and a meditation on what it is to be human, projecting a new way of thinking and a move forward into a new way of being. Between these two, I detect at work a revival of philosophy.

HEIDEGGER AND HÖLDERLIN: TOGETHER ON SEPARATE MOUNTAINS

Heidegger's response to Hölderlin is important because through it Heidegger develops the questioning of temporality and of memory begun but left incomplete in *Being and Time*. Heidegger worked especially intensively on Hölderlin during the Nazi years. He gave three sets of lectures on Hölderlin in 1934–35, in 1941–42 and in 1942, now published in the complete works,[14] and he published three different editions of a collection of papers called *Erläuterungen zu Hölderlins Dichtung*, the first of which appeared in 1944.[15] I shall in the main concentrate on papers published in the first two editions of this collection and on some differences between these editions. However, this chapter cannot offer a complete account of Heidegger's response to Hölderlin, even taking only the 1930s into consideration. While Heidegger gave complete lecture cycles on Hölderlin in the 1930s and 40s, he read Hölderlin already in the 1920s and continued to lecture on him into the late 1950s. However, the question of how early and how late the link between the two remains important for Heidegger's thinking goes beyond the limits of this study. Nor will I discuss the violent syntactical alterations which Heidegger makes in support of his interpretations.[16] The connection between Heidegger and Hölderlin will be discussed here not for the purposes of giving a detailed account of Heidegger's relation to Hölderlin, but in order to continue setting out Heidegger's contribution to ethical thinking.

Hölderlin was born in 1770 and died in 1843. He suffered a psychotic breakdown in 1806 and spent the last thirty-six years of his life in varying states of psychological estrangement. He used pseudonyms to sign the verse written after this breakdown. He worked extensively on translating Greek verse into German, especially that of Sophocles and Pindar, testing the limits of the expressive powers of the German language. He sought to transpose into German poetry the verse forms and metrical structures found in that Greek poetry, thus further expanding the resources of the German language. He shares with Winckelmann and Hegel this interest in returning to the Greeks and retrieving the accomplishments of Greek culture into the modern era; and there is a connection from Heidegger's encounter with Hölderlin to Heidegger's relation to Hegel and, more generally, to Heidegger's relation to a German and a European process of self-affirmation. While Heidegger emphasises the elegiac dimension of Hölderlin's reflections on human existence and on relating to a homeland, the political dimensions of collective self-affirmation as a people and as a race are always near the surface. My inclination is to stress the connection between Hölderlin and Nietzsche rather than to stress a connection between Hölderlin and Hegel, but the full basis for this cannot be argued here. The connection with Nietzsche presumes an image of a poet out of step with his own epoch, whereas the connection with Hegel would locate Hölderlin as a part of the process of German self-affirmation, responding to the challenge of the French Revolution and the Napoleonic invasions.

This links into Heidegger's attempts to disclose a self-affirmative 'Germanness' through a reading of Hölderlin's verse.

Heidegger's readings of Hölderlin parallel his increasing disillusion with the possibilities of a philosophical renewal in the emergence of a new saying of being. Through the encounter with Hölderlin, Heidegger explores differences between a tendency within philosophical enquiry to eliminate temporality and a contrasting centrality to Hölderlin's verse of temporal shifts and of reflection on the complexity of temporal structure. Hölderlin's verse forms are particularly conducive to such reflection. Indeed the difficulties Hölderlin encounters in translating the verse of Sophocles and of Pindar in part result from the problem of transposing Greek conceptions of destiny, of history and of temporality into German. The translations are of great importance for Heidegger for this reason, and his approach to Sophocles is affected by them. Heidegger's readings of both Sophocles and Hölderlin reveal a contrast between a nostalgia for a pre-philosophical origin and a hope for a new beginning in a transformation of thinking, beyond philosophy. Heidegger's response to Hölderlin explores a difference between a given immediacy of empirical experience, which imposes a kind of freezing of temporal process for the duration of the givenness of the data to the perceiver, and a conception of such a standstill which also reveals the structure of temporal processes. This is the difference between the 'now' of experience, as a moment in a temporal sequence, and the *Augenblick* as an interruption of temporal sequence. In the first it is possible to distinguish between past, present and future, but as differences viewed externally rather than as lived from within. In the second, there is a split view of this difference, both objectively, as though detached from it, and from the stance of the lived relation. In the external view, the distinctions between past, present and future events are clear-cut; in the lived relation, the connections are stronger than the breaks between them. To have both relations to temporal structure simultaneously is the effect achieved by Hölderlin's verse.

Heidegger explores this effect by developing an unusual account of the relation between human beings and history. In his essay on Hölderlin, 'Hölderlin and the essence of poetry', given in Rome in 1936 as a public lecture, Heidegger writes of human beings as distinct from all other creatures. He asks: 'Who is humanity? [*Wer ist der Mensch?*]' and responds: 'That which must bear witness to what it is [*Jener der zeugen muss, was er sei*]' (*ED1*: 38, *ED2*: 34). He continues: 'Being a witness as a belonging together with entities as a whole [*das Seiende im Ganzen*] occurs as history. In order that history should be possible human beings are given language.' Heidegger then expands this thought about language: 'However, the essence of language is not exhausted in being a means of communication for human beings. With this determination its essence is not yet touched on. Only a consequence of its essence has been elaborated.' Already in this paper, language is not to be conceived of as subordinated to human intention: 'Language is not just a tool which human beings possess along with others.

Language preserves the possibility of standing in the openness of entities. Only where there is language is there a world.' To which Heidegger then adds: 'Only where there is world is there history' (*ED1*: 39, *ED2*: 35). Conversely, where there is no world, there can no longer be history; and Heidegger's analyses of the world reveal that in the age of technology human beings lose the possibility of conceiving of the world and with that they lose any sense of history. Heidegger goes on to add: 'Language is not some tool to be applied, but that very event [*Ereignis*] that prevails over the highest possibility of human beings' (*ED1*: 38, *ED2*: 34). The impoverishment of language so as to appear to be only a tool is one sign of the extreme withdrawal of being that characterises the age of technology.

In the next section Heidegger claims: 'We, human beings, are a conversation. The being of human beings grounds in language; but this occurs genuinely as conversation [*Gespräch*]' (*ED1*: 40, *ED2*: 36). He then develops this notion of conversation, which he finds in Hölderlin's sketch for his poem *Friedensfeier* ('Celebration of peace'). Heidegger writes of a moment at which conservation and a separation of time into past, present and future become simultaneously possible:

> For there to be a single conversation [*Gespräch*], an essential expression must remain connected to a 'one and the same' [*das Eine und das Selbe*]. Without this connection even, indeed especially, conflictual conversation is impossible. This one and the same can only come in view of something remaining and permanent [*Bleibende und Ständige*]. Permanence and re-maining come to appearance only when persistence and the present are made evident. (*ED1*: 41, *ED2*: 37)

Heidegger then makes a connection to a quite specific experience and structure of temporality: to the emergence of history and of the entity human being which has become historical:

> This, however, occurs only at that moment [*Augenblick*] when time opens itself out into its extensions. Since human beings have set something up as remaining in the present, since then they have first set up something as changing, as coming and going; for only what is persisting can change. Only since 'rending time' rent itself into present, past and future, has there been the possibility of uniting oneself with something which remains. We have been a single conversation since the time there has been time. Only since time has emerged and been brought to a stand, since then we have become historical. Both: being a conversation and being historical – are the same age and belong together and are the same. (*ED1*: 41, *ED2*: 37)

For time to emerge it is necessary to bring it to a standstill in a separation of past, present and future in the moment [*Augenblick*] of thought. At this moment, the possibility of history and of speaking emerge simultaneously. This is a moment of originary time, which does not take place within history, within chronological process, but makes both of these possible. Heidegger goes on to claim: 'Since we have been a conversation, human beings have experienced much and named the gods in many ways. Since language became conversation, the gods have come to expression and the world has appeared.' When the possibility of naming the gods is withdrawn and the world disappears, then history also withdraws and our relation to language is impoverished. Heidegger seems to suggest that it is the attempt to take control of language which reduces the productiveness of our relation to language. Being historical, but no longer having a sense of history, would change the relation to language from this stance of responsiveness.

However, there is a major shift from this insistence in the 1936 essay on a single conversation and on a possibility of naming the gods, which may return, to a reaffirmation of an ambiguity, *Zweideutigkeit*, thematised as central to *Being and Time*, through the development of the theme of *Zwiesprache*, which I translate as 'duplicitous dialogue'. Although the shifting use of the term 'ambiguity' in Heidegger's thinking connects with shifts in the place of language in Heidegger's thinking, these parallels cannot be directly addressed.[17] The term *Zwiesprache* is linked to the term *Gespräch* in the essay 'Moira', a section omitted from his lectures from 1951/52, *Was heißt Denken?*.[18] There, Heidegger uses the two terms to indicate differences between traditional forms of interpretation and his own mode of reading the texts in the history of philosophy, with particular reference to Parmenides. Heidegger contrasts his own approach to what he takes to be three mistaken ways of approaching Parmenides. There is, first, a common-sense view that supposes such thinking and texts to be understandable by anyone. Second, there is the Hegelian view that there is a cumulative process at work in the development of philosophical thinking, such that the earlier contributions become fully comprehensible only at the completion of the process. There is a third view, which Heidegger attributes to Plato, of supposing that this thinking and these texts are approximations leading thinking on to a transcendent truth of a super-sensible purity. Heidegger comments:

> Each of these three viewpoints draws the early thinking of the Greeks into a region dominated by spheres of questioning of subsequent metaphysics. Presumably, however, all later thinking which seeks dialogue [*Gespräch*] with ancient thinking should listen continually from within its own standpoint, and should thereby bring the silence of ancient thinking into expression. (*EGT*: 84)

He contrasts these forms of enquiry to a 'proper', or 'appropriating', form of enquiry and then introduces the notion of *Zwiesprache*:

> An effort at proper enquiry [*eigens nachzufragen*] should not end in an historical enquiry which merely establishes the unexpressed presuppositions underlying early thought; that is, proper enquiry is not an investigation in which these presuppositions are taken into account solely with respect to whatever subsequent interpretation either seems true in the light of currently posited truth or seems false as having been superseded by further developments. Unlike this kind of investigation, proper enquiry must be a dialogue

[*Zwiesprache*] in which the ways of hearing and points of view of ancient thinking are contemplated according to their essential derivation [*Wesensherkunft*] so that the call can announce itself in which there can be set up the early, the following and the future thinking, one distinct from another. (*EGT*: 85)

The distinction between early, following and future thinking is between a thinking in advance of the invention of metaphysics, a derivative form of thinking falling prey to metaphysical foreclosure and a thinking out of that foreclosure. The distinction makes it clear that the dialogue supposed to be taking place is not between contemporaries, but between interlocutors separated in time. In dialogue as *Gespräch* between temporally distant interlocutors, there is the possibility of an encounter between two fully formed, distinct kinds of thinking; in *Zwiesprache*, the thinking in the present is transformed through exposure to the thinking in the past, as the thinking of the past is transformed by being taken up into the present context of interpretation. The thinking of the present and the thinking of the past cease to be thought of as having meanings fixed in advance of the encounter between them.

In the contemporaneous essay 'Dichterisch wohnet der Mensch',[19] given as a lecture in 1951, Heidegger again uses his encounter with Hölderlin to locate an issue of central concern for him. The fragment from Hölderlin brings together two key themes for Heidegger: dwelling and verse. Heidegger has come to suppose that without verse, there can be no reconciliation with the homelessness and uncanniness characteristic of the human condition. Here Heidegger is preferring the mode of *poiesis*, the mode of making, in which individual identity is subordinated to that process, as opposed to the *praxis* characteristic of Aristotle's political deliberations, for which self-actualisation is a central concern. Heidegger remarks:

> Thus we confront a double demand: for one thing, we are to think of what is called human existence by way of the nature of dwelling; for another, we are to think of the nature of poetry as a letting dwell, as a, perhaps the, distinctive kind of building. If we search out the nature of poetry according to this viewpoint then we arrive at the nature of dwelling. (*PLT*: 215)

It is in poetry that it becomes possible for the priority of language over human beings to become clear; and it is this priority of language for human beings which Heidegger at this juncture is keen to bring to attention. Heidegger writes: 'For strictly it is language that speaks. Human beings first speak, when and only when they respond to language by listening to its appeal'. Heidegger then proceeds to insist that this dwelling is a relation to the earth, as a grounding for all other human activities, in the world.

Heidegger interposes a remark clarifying his notion of the 'same', which he and Hölderlin have in common: 'Accordingly, Hölderlin does not seek poetic dwelling out as thinking does. Despite all this, we are thinking the same thing that Hölderlin says poetically.' Heidegger clarifies this by claiming that the crucial difference is between sameness, *das Selbe,* and identity or equality, *das Gleiche*: 'The equal or identical always moves towards the absence of difference, so that everything may be reduced to a common denominator. The same, by contrast, is the belonging together of what differs, through a gathering by way of the difference. We can only say 'the same' if we think difference' (*PLT*: 218). Heidegger then introduces the context in which Hölderlin's remark about poetic dwelling occurs. It runs:

> Is God unknown?
> Is he manifest in the sky? I prefer
> To believe the latter. It is the measure of humanity.
> Full of merit, yet poetically humanity
> Dwells on this earth.
> $\qquad\qquad\qquad$ (*PLT*: 219; translation modified)

He then goes on to explain what this measure is and what this manifestness consists in. He claims: 'The upward glance spans the between of sky and earth. This 'between' is the measure for the dwelling of humanity' (*VA*: 189, *PLT*: 220). It is in poetry that this measuring takes place:

> To write poetry is measure-taking, understood in the strict sense of the word, by which human beings first receive the measure for the breadth of their being. Human beings exist as mortals. We are called mortal because we can die. To be able to die means: to be capable of death as death. Only human beings die; and indeed continually, so long as we stay on this earth, so long as we dwell. (*PLT*: 222; translation modified)

Heidegger then poses the question 'what is this measure?' and he responds: 'The measure consists in the way in which the god who remains unknown is revealed as such by the sky' (*PLT*: 223). This unknown has the same structure as that of the concealed in its concealment, the relation which Heidegger takes to be characteristic of being, as distinct from the being of entities as a whole. In this way Heidegger brings together the theme of the concealment of being, from his earlier thinking, with the themes of poetry, of dwelling and of death. This 'between' as measure for the dwelling of human beings links back to the 'between' of the 1938 essay on anthropology, the 'place between, in which human beings remain as a part of what there is, and yet remain strangers amongst entities' (*HW*: 88). It reaches back to the 'between' of *Dasein* in *Being and Time*, as stretched out between birth and death. It also links into the diagnosis of the conversation as a 'between', as *Zwiesprache*, not *Gespräch*.

In the first edition but not in the second of *Erläuterungen zu Hölderlins Dichtung*, there is appended to the lecture 'Heimkunft: An die Verwandten', a prefatory remark which Heidegger made when he repeated the lecture. It is reproduced in the edition published in 1981 as volume 4 of the *Gesamtausgabe*. Here, Heidegger introduces his notoriously difficult notion of a '*Zwiesprache des Denkens mit dem Dichten*':

It is not permissible for us to repeat a celebration of 'remembrance of the poet', even were we to want to. On the contrary, we must always practise the thinking about such a poet afresh in the only way in which it can begin. That is the attempt to think about what is put into poetry [*das Gedichtete*]. Such commemoration [*Andenken*] arises out of the dialogue [*Zwiesprache*] of a thinking with the writing of poetry, without that dialogue itself and what it talks about in the least coming into language [*Sprache*]. (*ED1*: 31, *Brock*: 253)

By contrast with the emphasis on the unity of conversation of the 1936 essay, there is here the theme of dialogue. In the 1936 essay, Heidegger still supposes that through conversation a word for the gods can emerge and bring the world into view:

Since we have been a conversation [*Gespräch*], human beings have experienced much and named the gods in many different ways. Since language became genuinely a conversation the gods have come into words and the world has appeared. However, again it is important to say that the presence of the gods [*Gegenwart der Götter*] and the appearing of the world are not a consequence of the event of language, but are simultaneous. (*ED1*: 41, *ED2*: 37)

And while, in this essay, Heidegger goes on to name this the time of the departed gods, there is still the thought that there might again be an event of language in which the gods might be named, might come into the present tense [*Gegenwart*], in which the world might appear and there be an active relation between human beings and history. It seems as though the world can appear only if the gods can be named in the present tense. I suggest that in the age of technology there is only the present tense, such that no world can appear and such that there can be no naming of a transcendent condition lying beyond the world frame, no revealing of it to be a movable horizon and not a fixed frame. This is what I take to be the significance of the absence of the gods in the present epoch. This absence makes it impossible to conceive of a transition to some other condition and some other epoch, and it makes it impossible to conceive of the present framing [*Gestell*] as only a framing, as a transient structuring rather than a permanent fixed frame of reference.

In 'Hölderlin and the essence of poetry', Heidegger makes an explicit connection between Hölderlin and Oedipus, who stands in a place between human beings and the gods, the supernatural forces. He writes: 'The observation Hölderlin makes concerning Oedipus in the late poem 'In the beloved blueness there blooms' is true of Hölderlin himself: 'Der König Oedipus hat ein / Auge zu viel vielleicht' (v1, 26) (*ED1*: 49, *ED2*: 44). Heidegger then introduces his diagnosis of the times as needy, between gods who have departed and gods who are still on their way. Heidegger remarks on this absence of the gods:

This is the time of the departed gods and of gods who are to come. This is the time of need, because it stands in a double lack and negation: the no longer of the departed gods and the not yet of the ones to come. The essence of poetry which is established by Hölderlin is historical in the highest degree because it sets out in advance the historicality of time. As an historical essence it is the one essential essence. (*ED1*: 49, *ED2*: 44)

This double negation of a time of departed gods and of a time of a return of the gods is in turn erased, in the moment of oblivion, making it inconceivable that there should have been such gods or that there might be a return. This second negation of the first double negation undercuts the basis on which modern notions of history are constituted, for without the residual articulations of divinity, a past or a future idealised epoch and the use of conceptions of history to assign direction and meaning to temporal processes are eroded. Heidegger goes on to say that the times are needy and the poets overrich, thus perhaps putting excessive strain on their psychological strength. He quotes Hölderlin:

But friend, we come too late: it is true the gods still live
But above our heads, over there in another world. They still
have effects over there without end and seem to care little
whether we live; so much do the heavenly ones leave us.

The passage culminates in the famous quotation: 'to what end is a poet in a time of need? [*wozu Dichter in dürftiger Zeit?*]'(*ED1*: 49–50; *ED2*: 44–5), to which Löwith added his question: to what end the thinker in a time of need?

In the later essay, 'Heimkunft: an die Verwandten' (1943), Heidegger again notes this concern with the absence of the gods, commenting on the remark, 'there is a dearth of holy names [*es fehlen heilige Namen*]': 'Certainly the holy can be named and out of this enhanced state the word can be said. But these holy words are not "names" which name' (*ED1*: 25, *ED2*: 26). He explains: 'The absence of god is the basis for this absence of holy names [*Das "Fehl" des Gottes ist der Grund für das Fehlen "heiliger Namen"*].' It is the task of the poet to remain in the region of this absence in order to keep the space open for a return. It is the task of the thinker to show the impact of this opening on the Sisyphean attempts to construct metaphysical systems. In the earlier essay, 'Hölderlin and the essence of poetry', Heidegger invokes the figure of the poet as held in place between the people (*Volk*) and the gods:

Thus the essence of poetry is drawn into the laws which set apart and draw together the indications of the gods and the voice of the people. The poet stands between them, the gods and these, the people. The poet is thrown out, out into that 'between', between the gods and human beings. But it is first of all this between which decides who human beings might be and where they move into their *Dasein*. 'Human beings dwell poetically on this earth.' (*ED1*: 48, *ED2*: 43)

Thus, in order to feel at home, in order to live or dwell, it is necessary to have a sense of the poetic and to live between the mortals and the gods. The poet, like Oedipus, stands between the people and the gods. It is a dangerous place to be;

and in this context the reference to the *Volk* requires comment, for Heidegger in the 1930s sought to stand in the same dangerous opening.

Karl Löwith reports meeting Heidegger, on his way to deliver this paper in Rome in 1936, and seeing the badge of the Nazi party membership in Heidegger's lapel.[20] This links to the affirmations in the 1943 paper of a destiny unique to the Germans as inheritors of the Greek tradition, taking up and transforming the relation between poetry and philosophy: 'Then there is a kinship with the poet. Then there is a homecoming. But this homecoming is the future of the historical being of the German people. They are the people of writing and thinking [*des Dichtens und Denkens*]' (*ED1*: 28, *ED2*: 24). This is the fascist moment in Heidegger's thinking. Astonishingly, he repeats the claim without clarification in the postwar 'Letter on humanism', as though there were no need to disown the exclusive Nazi use of the term 'German':

> 'German' is not spoken to the world so that the world might be reformed through the German essence; rather it is spoken to the Germans, so that from a fateful belongingness to the nations they might become world-historical along with them. The homeland of this historical dwelling is the nearness to being. (*HW*: 335)

Here the connection between his hopes for a philosophical renewal and the success of the Nazi revolution cannot be avoided. This connection provides the political basis for my rejection of Heidegger's loss of commitment to a philosophical renewal. His view is not that after Auschwitz there can be no philosophy. His view is that a renewal of philosophy can no longer be hoped for as following on from Nazism. This connection between Nazism and the destiny of philosophy, however, is contingent on Heidegger's own misguided political commitments and is not essential to philosophy. It can be put aside, but not without remark. It brings to the fore the problem of his remarks about homecoming and of finding a sense of belonging with respect to a specifically German future.

In his prefatory remark to this 1943 address, Heidegger introduces the notion that 'all the poems of a poet who has entered into his or her poetic activity [*Dichtertum*] are poems of homecoming [*Heimkunft*]'. In the text of the 1943 lecture, he develops this notion of homecoming. He claims: 'Only the thinking of the one who takes care is a remembrance of the poet, in so far as it thinks the secret of the retrieving nearness which appears in poetry. In this remembrance there begins for the first time what is a long-running kinship with the poet who returns home.' The poet can return home into the full exercise of poetic power. The philosopher is seeking to do the same, but with even less hope of success. The return home is described: 'Homecoming is a return to the vicinity of the origin [*Heimkunft ist die Rückkehr in die Nähe zum Ursprung*]' (*ED1*: 21, *ED2*: 23). The vicinity of the origin is perhaps best grasped as the gap between the finite and the non-finite out of which an absence of divinity can first be sensed. This is the dangerous gap in which Hölderlin and Oedipus, and indeed perhaps

Heidegger and Nietzsche, are to be found. There is, however, an important shift here in Heidegger's thinking, between discussing homelessness as a problem central to philosophy and discussing it in the elegiac context of Hölderlin's verse. In between these two there occurs the startling reading in the 1935/36 lectures of Oedipus' fate as revealing the truth about the homelessness of human beings, placed between being and entities, between the full force of disruptive destiny and the familiarity of the given. The homelessness of Oedipus lies in a 'between' in advance of any division between a philosophical and a poetic homecoming. I shall discuss the violence of Oedipus in the next chapter, concluding this chapter with a further elucidation of homelessness and ambiguity.

In *Being and Time*, *Unheimlichkeit*, the ungroundedness, uncanniness and metaphysical homelessness of everyday living and of everyday modes of experiencing *Dasein*, is revealed through the analysis of anxiety. These everyday modes are characterised by ambiguity, *Zweideutigkeit*; curiosity, *Neugier*; and idle talk, or what is put into discourse, *Gerede*. This revelation imposes a need to construct an individual relation to death, to identity, to the future and to the past, out of which a possibility of genuine, authentic language, *Rede*, might emerge. The experience of this uncanny homelessness in *Being and Time* opens up an analysis of time through which a difference between an everyday, a metaphysical and an authentic relation to time can be developed. In the 1929/30 lectures, by contrast, there is a remarkable use of a quotation from Novalis which forms a link from this existential placing of homelessness to a connection between homelessness and a critique of philosophy as a misguided quest to make oneself feel at home everywhere. In the opening pages of those lectures, Heidegger recalls a remark from Novalis that philosophy is homesickness and continues:

> Novalis himself explains: 'a drive to be at home everywhere'. Philosophy as such a drive is possible only if we, who philosophise, are everywhere not at home. What is the aim of this longing which this drive seeks out? To be at home everywhere: what does this mean? Not just here and there, and also not simply some place for everyone together one and all, but to be at home everywhere means: at all times and at the same time to be in the midst of the whole. This 'in the whole of things' and its wholeness we call 'the world'. (*GA* 29/30: 7–8)

At this point it becomes clear that it may be wrong to think of this 'world' as a single coherent structure. This would be the false stability offered by metaphysics in response to a sense of homelessness, offering a false hope of reducing the anxiety prompted by homelessness, instead of coming to terms with the thought that homelessness and anxiety cannot be laid to rest. Thus, there is here a contrast between a genuine homelessness through which an originary experience of time can open out and an attempt through philosophical construction to create a false sense of being at home everywhere.

In the 1943 essay on Hölderlin, Heidegger returns to the theme of homelessness through the discussion of Hölderlin's poem *Heimkunft: An die Verwandten*.

Again, here homelessness seems to be going to be transformed into a home-coming. Heidegger writes: 'The most genuine home is already the destiny of a sending, or as we now say this word, history' (*ED1*: 12; *ED2*: 14). Thus, without a sense of location in history there can be no coming to terms with a sense of uncanny homelessness. The problem, Heidegger insists, is that this sending has not yet arrived. There is no receptivity for '*das Eigenste der Heimat*', '*das Deutsche*', which for Heidegger at this time forms the kernel of this genuine home. This non-arrival is the result of human beings, or rather the Germans, failing to be aware of the nearness of this genuine locatedness, a home, as a relation to the divine. This nearness of the divine to the mortal is akin to the nearness which Heidegger locates between the everyday and the authentic in *Being and Time*. At this later stage, Heidegger claims that it is the divine that lies in closest proximity, but is hard to grasp, quoting Hölderlin: 'God is near but hard to grasp [*Nah ist / und schwer zu fassen der Gott*]', lines which immediately precede the more famous lines: 'Where danger grows so does the power of rescue [*Wo der Gefahr wächst / Das Rettende auch*]'. Heidegger brings these themes together by claiming: 'The elegy "Homecoming" is not a poem about home-coming. The elegy is poetry, the homecoming itself, which still occurs as long as the word sounds as the bell in the language of the Germans' (*ED1*: 23, *ED2*: 25). He goes on to say of Hölderlin's translations of Sophocles: 'Certainly Hölderlin's poetic dialogue [*dichtende Zwiesprache*] with Sophocles in the "Translation" and in the "Notes" forms a part of this homecoming, but it is not the whole of it.' There is not just a retrieval of the past, from Sophocles, although this is a major task. There is also a claim on the future: '*Diese Heimkunft aber ist die Zukunft des geschichtlichen Wesens der Deutschen*. (This homecoming is the future of the historical essence [and here I transpose] of human beings)' (*ED1*: 28, *ED2*: 30). The homecoming is to be gathered out of the past and the future. But Heidegger's own words here skew this retrieval of a sense of nearness to the divine and of the genuine in the everyday into a racial triumph for the Germans over other nations and races. For this reason, I substitute 'human beings' here for the scandalous term 'Germans'.

There is here a contrast between three forms of homelessness. There is the homelessness which seems to be overcome in an actual homecoming, presuming a possible time, not now, but sometime, at which that homecoming might occur. There is a homelessness responded to in metaphysical constructions of a familiar, shared, orderly world-view, which dogmatically declares that time of home-coming to be present. There is, third, a homelessness to which struggling into the future, with no fixed hope of homecoming, is the only possible response. It is a homelessness which all the same declares itself at home by constructing for itself a relation to the transcendent. I suggest that Oedipus' homelessness is of this third form. It is neither that of Hölderlin's elegies nor that which turns into the construction of a metaphysical completion. It is this form of homelessness which Heidegger attributes to Hölderlin, despite the fact that Hölderlin appears to be writing about the first form. Being at home for human beings is to be situated in an unsayable divide between what there is and how it comes to be like that; in the language of *Being and Time*, between entities and being; between mortality and divinity, in the language emerging out of the encounter with Hölderlin. This homecoming takes place in the unsayable dialogue between thinking and writing. This relation between thinking and writing is a subject raised but suppressed by Plato at the beginning of the history of philosophy, in an attempt to distinguish between the truths of reason and argument, on one side, and, on the other, between the illusions of fiction and verse. Heidegger seeks to return philosophy to the moment in Plato's thinking at which this separation occurs. Heidegger's dispute with philosophy can then be seen as a questioning of the rationale and justification for separating rigorous argument from poetic language use. It becomes a dispute about how to view the relation between thought and language.

However, I suggest that neither gesture, neither the rejection of poetry with Plato nor the rejection of philosophy with Heidegger, is an adequate response. What Heidegger's gesture of rejection achieves, however, is a reopening of a question apparently conclusively settled by Plato about the relation between poetry and thought. The extremity of Heidegger's gesture matches that of Plato. This is a philosophically significant violence. The violence of Heidegger's attempt to restrict the gesture to some specifically German breakthrough is, I suggest, an irrelevance, which restricts the scope of his thinking. As a result of this emphasis on a specifically German destiny and on a special relation between the Greek origins of philosophy and a German turn towards the future, Heidegger obscures the need to rethink the shifting relations between reason and verse, philosophy and poetry, thinking and creativity, first in classical Greece, then in German Romanticism and finally, and very differently, in the twentieth century. Heidegger draws attention to the contrast between the archaisms of German Romanticism and the brittleness of the time of the world picture, but he does not explore it.

Chapter 5

Freedom and violence

> This interpretation of the expression must seem like an arbitrary trans-
> position, as reading in something which an exact interpretation could never
> justify. That is true. For customary contemporary thinking, what I have just
> said is truly more evidence for the already notorious violence and one-
> sidedness of Heidegger's interpretative procedure. (*EM*: 134)

Violence is central to the 1930s, both historically in the emergence of Nazism and
for Heidegger's thinking, for this is the decade in which Heidegger first endorsed
and then stepped back from an engagement with Nazism. In the notorious
rectorial address of May 1933[1] he sets up a parallel between himself and Plato,
between Hitler's Germany and Plato's *Republic*, with a retrieval of Plato's distinction between reason, agency and activity in the distinctions drawn between
thinking, military service and labour. This too is violence, especially for those
who think that philosophy must be engaged against evil. Both Heidegger's use of
his own philosophical terminology in the 1933 address and Plato's arguments in
The Republic ground an interpretation of social process in a set of conceptual
distinctions, given in advance of society. This grounding of political analysis
presumes a distinction between the political domain to be analysed and a pre-
political domain in which metaphysical distinctions are set out. It is, however,
also possible to read Heidegger's thinking as providing the resources for a
critique of this distinction between politics and metaphysics. The moment of
violence in Heidegger's thought would then be neither his interpretative practice
nor his endorsement of Nazism, but the moment at which the conceptions holding
in place the distinction between politics and metaphysics are disrupted. The
results of this disruption are to be seen in globalisation, the actualisation of
metaphysics and the derestriction of ethics, and in the spread of technology
throughout the world. The conceptions disrupted are a series of oppositions
between freedom and reason, between history and nature, between art and science,
between ethics and metaphysics. In place of the relation between freedom and
reason, there is the relation between freedom and violence to be explored. In place
of the distinction between history and nature, there is the relation between
Andenken, commemoration, and *Nachdenken*, rethinking.

The epigraph to this chapter is from the 1935 lectures *Introduction to*

Metaphysics. It indicates Heidegger's recognition of the controversial status of his interpretations. These lectures give an account of the relation between being and determinate being as figured by the myth of Oedipus. The relation is both violent and destructive. In this chapter, I present a reading of Heidegger's thinking in the 1930s focused on the figure of Oedipus, to show at work the disruptions these oppositions constitutive of the distinction between politics and metaphysics. The emphasis is on the oppositions between freedom and reason, between nature and history. In the 1930s, Heidegger engages in a massively complex trajectory of enquiry, with interdependent readings of Kant, Hegel, Hölderlin, Schelling and Nietzsche. Out of this there emerge his histories of words for being and his diagnosis of the current state of philosophy, leading into the postwar analysis of technology as marking the end of philosophy. This diagnosis results from a disruption of the relation between history and nature, which emerges out of Heidegger's thought in the 1920s and which leads him to reread Kant as showing that freedom is a condition of possibility for there being matters of fact at all. Freedom is revealed to be an ontological condition of possibility, not an ethical characteristic of human beings. This disrupts the Kantian division between conditions of possibility for knowledge and conditions of possibility for moral experience, between knowledge of nature and the status of freedom. Freedom for Heidegger is a feature not just of human beings but of the conditions in which human beings find themselves, as given by being. Freedom is a feature of a relation between human beings and forces above and beyond human control. Thus freedom for Heidegger, like language, takes the analysis beyond the human context, implying a relation to the non-human.

Although the distinction between the arts and the sciences is drastically displaced into the opposition between *Dichten* and *Technik*, Heidegger does not disrupt it completely. This is unfortunate, for it renders unclear the status of mathematics. In the 1935–36 lectures *Die Frage nach dem Ding*,[2] Heidegger challenges the confinement of mathematics to the domain of the natural sciences, at the same time questioning identifications of philosophy as a 'moral science' (*Geisteswissenschaft*), but the challenge is not explicitly developed. Thus, although the invention of new forms of mathematics has had quite as much impact on relations between human beings and technology as has the poetry of either Rilke or Trakl, the questioning of that impact is blocked in Heidegger's thought. The acceptance of the contrast between the arts and the sciences in its transposed form is all the odder, since that contrast works, with the distinction between history and nature, to set up as misleadingly distinct two only too human practices with a shared point of origination. Failing to question this pair conceals how they are grounded in a common, historically specific site of origination in a specific, not a general, set of human preoccupations. Heidegger thus cuts himself off from the full implications of his enquiries which must, if consequentially thought through, lead to the disruption of the supposed division between the poetic work, such as that produced by Hölderlin, and the theoretical work of a nuclear physicist. It is not obvious that one is more capable than the other of calling into existence new epochal formations by giving names to newly emergent structural features, bridging and subverting the divide between thought and reality, between ethics and metaphysics. Heidegger privileges Sophocles over Aristotle and Hölderlin over Hegel, with Aristotle and Hegel serving as standard-bearers for the philosophical. Just as philosophy is shown by Heidegger to have to cede its place to poetry, so perhaps the full inauguration of the new epoch anticipated by Heidegger may require a displacement of the humanist privilege assigned to literature, to poetry, to art, in favour of another form of thinking combining the expertise of science and of artistic creation. Understanding and coming to terms with the transformative capacities of the new mathematics would perhaps be that resource which Heidegger, through his reading of Hölderlin, diagnoses as both threatening and containing its own rescue.

Heidegger's retention of the distinction between the arts and the sciences restricts the impact of his questioning of the relations between freedom, history and nature. However, that questioning reveals one of the conditions for the spread of technology throughout the world: the suspension of traditional patterns of political organisation and hierarchy. If politics is understood as a domain of human activity, negotiating between the forces opposed in the relation 'history' and 'nature', between human freedom and naturally imposed constraint, then these moves made by Heidegger disrupt all political thinking. Out of this disruption, it becomes possible to think about technology in the modern world as the form in which this disruption is taking place. Thus technology can be recognised as a political and an ethical phenomenon. Up until now, politics as a theoretical and as a practical formation has been bound up with a set of metaphysical distinctions and presuppositions concerning the nature of human beings. The impact of technology is to disrupt this connection between politics and metaphysics and to disrupt the tradition linking this connection back into a classical origin. The connection between politics and metaphysics, while derived from the classical world, acquires stable form and meaning only in the early modern period, through the separation of the sacred and the secular. However, there is then a temporal and historical displacement of this connection back from the early modern period into a mythological classical period.

Thus the tradition constructing a link back to the writings of Aristotle and Plato, back to Solon and Homer, emerges in the course of the early modern period. This tradition, like the terms metaphysics and ontology, is an invention of that early modern period. Heidegger disrupts this version of tradition by denying that Descartes' thinking constitutes a break with medieval philosophy and by throwing into question the possibility of continuing the Cartesian project of producing an account of everything there is, as a repetition of the project inaugurated at the beginning of philosophy by the Greeks. While Heidegger supposes this to be the project of the Greeks, he also supposes it to be no longer possible. However, it is also possible to question whether it makes sense to attribute such a project to the Greeks, and to question whether this is a defining description of the project of philosophy. Disrupting this definition of philosophy makes possible a different account of the links from past to present to future, and from future to present and back into an interpretation of the past. This can open the way either to the unthought-of disaster or to the new beginning about which Heidegger wrote. In this chapter, I shall first discuss Heidegger's questioning of the opposition between nature and history, in relation to Karl Löwith's critique of Heidegger from 1953[3] and in relation to Heidegger's lectures from 1935–36, *What is a Thing*. Then I shall discuss the complexities posed by Heidegger's views on history and tradition, before making a connection between Heidegger's violent readings of the texts constitutive of philosophy and the question of the end of philosophy. I shall then introduce his discussion, in the lectures *Introduction to Metaphysics*, of a connection between human beings and violence as personified in the figure of Oedipus.

ON NATURE AND HISTORY

In his book from 1953, *Martin Heidegger: Denker in dürftiger Zeit*, Karl Löwith claims that Heidegger elides the difference between nature and history in the account of *Dasein* in *Being and Time*:

A determinate existence which is not simply in time and in addition has a history, but exists in its essence temporally and historically, is no longer relative to time and history. This historicality, which is existentially absolute and tied to its directedness to a determinate end, its death, is supposed to make the history of the world possible and understandable. (p. 46)

The problem is that these conceptions of history and of time are themselves ahistorical and atemporal. They are, in Löwith's view, naturalised:

First of all, Heidegger displaces historical relativism by grounding and making absolute the possibility of being historical in the involvement of human beings in historical processes and by placing this involvement in historical processes in *Dasein's* being towards a determinate end, death. This radicalisation of historical relativism is possible, however, only because the determinate end of *Dasein* is not a historical process; it is the always identical fact of natural death. (p. 68)

This is important, but Löwith has picked out only one aspect of a threefold process at work in Heidegger's thinking. There is first of all this naturalising of history in *Being and Time*. There are also an historicising of nature and an ontologising of freedom, which are detectable in *Being and Time*, but become clearer in subsequent work. I suggest that these three, the naturalising of history, the historicising of nature and the ontologising of freedom, taken together, provide a conceptual grid through which to identify and grasp the implications of the permeation of our world by technical relations; for they assist in transforming conceptions of technology in line with Heidegger's questioning of the essence of technology. While Löwith's reading of Heidegger helps to bring this out, he does not identify the full implications of his own observations. The fourth term is the transformation of technology from a series of issues within scientific enquiry into a human problem.

Löwith remarks on Heidegger's failure in *Being and Time* to develop the relation between his conception of the world and current conceptions of nature:

> Starting from nature, there is no way of conceiving the mode of being of the world and its worldness; indeed, nature must be interpreted the other way round, starting from the existential structure of being in the world. Nature as such is indeed absent from Heidegger's sketch of a 'natural conception of the world'. (p. 62)

This absence is the result of the phenomenological critique of the supposed 'common-sense' status of this 'natural conception of the world'. Both Husserl and Heidegger seek to bracket off such appeals to 'nature', in order to reveal unquestioned presuppositions at work. It is not so much a 'natural' as a 'natural-ised' conception, and in such naturalisation both Husserl and Heidegger detect at work a subversion of the philosophical requirement of rigorous construction. Löwith is, however, quite right to suppose that nature is not just subordinated in *Being and Time*, but indeed not addressed in its own right at all: 'In *Being and Time* nature in its naturalness is ignored and, in contrast to the readiness to hand of equipment and to the historical existence of human determinate existence, relegated to the most subordinated concept of the merely "present at hand"' (pp. 61–2). This description, while correct on one level, misses out the important point that in this presence at hand Heidegger identifies a persistent failure to mark the ontological difference between the entity for which there is a question of differ- ence and those entities for which difference and making distinctions are not matters of concern. The common-sense conception of nature conceals this difference.

While presence at hand is indeed subordinated in Heidegger's thinking, it is also the focus for critique, since by thinking solely in terms of presence at hand, important differences between kinds of entity are concealed. Presence at hand and an undifferentiated conception of nature are two of the conceptions through which significance, time and the role of philosophy are deleted as issues for philosophical enquiry. Heidegger traces these deletions back to a single meta- physical gesture of forgetting about being and forgetting about the difference between being and beings. The forgetting of being leads to an elision of on- tological difference, and this culminates in a form of philosophical enquiry focusing on methodology and model building rather than analysing the impact of technology and locating the significance of the discoveries of science. This, combined with an emphasis on human uses of technical relations, gives the illusory sense of human control and provides a basis for connecting technical relations to conceptions of history as a process of human self-emancipation, in the manner of Marx. Heidegger's questioning of history and of nature disrupts any such series of connections. The emphasis on a natural process of development, carried out in Aristotelian teleologies, is also put in question by Heidegger's questioning of the relation between nature and history. Heidegger's naturalising of history and historicising of nature disrupts thinking of human histories in terms of Aristotelian teleologies and disrupts Hegelian dialectic with its rigorous distinctions between logic, nature and history.

Löwith supposes that there is a drastic shift in Heidegger's approach to the themes of nature and history: 'Heidegger's account of nature has, like his conception of history, changed in many ways, without achieving a full determinacy. In *Being and Time* nature and history are thoroughly distinct, while later as *phusis* and as the occurrence of being [*Seinsgeschehen*], they become almost identical' (p. 62). However, I suppose that the historicality of *Being and Time* already takes up into itself a conception of nature. Thus, what for Löwith is accomplished only through the rethinking of *phusis*, I suppose has already started to take place in *Being and Time*. Löwith notes in this later move a historicising of nature in parallel with the naturalising of history noted earlier; but he does not seem to recognise the connection between the two. He does not see that part of Heidegger's claim is that there is no uninterpreted nature. Nor does he see the third element, the ontologising of freedom. Löwith does not recognise how these three disruptions are preparatory to transforming the account of being in relation to time, announced but not performed in *Being and Time*, into an account of technology. This ontologising of freedom and insistence in the 1930s on the variability of the sendings of being must be read in parallel with the themes of technology and of the end of philosophy from the 1950s. All four, technology, the end of philosophy, the naturalising of history and the historicising of nature, reveal a process at work in philosophy which misleadingly presents philosophical construction and technological innovations as natural growth. Naturalising the histories of philosophy and of technology makes it unnecessary to consider the genesis and conditions of possibility for technology and for philosophical construction when assessing their claim on reason and their impact on human beings. There is a concealment of the fact that a quite particular relation to time and to human existence is required for the evolution of technology out of modern science. This can be revealed only by questioning the moment of transformation of science into technology. By disrupting the naturalisation of science and technology, it becomes possible to apply ethical categories to the analysis of the impact of technology, instead of simply treating it as a matter of fact. Technology can be shifted from the domain of nature and of matters of fact to that of freedom and human answerability by questioning the boundary between the two domains.

The ontologising of freedom is developed in Heidegger's 1930 lectures on Kant and in the 1936 lectures on Schelling, on the essence of human freedom.[4] The texts of these lectures were probably not available to Löwith when he wrote his commentary on Heidegger, although he presumably heard the lectures on Kant. In the lectures on Kant, *Vom Wesen der menschlichen Freiheit: Einleitung in die Philosophie*,[5] Heidegger argues that freedom is not primarily an ethical issue for Kant, but an ontological one, thus confirming the thought that the point of the term 'ontology' for Heidegger is to cut across the division of themes set up

by a distinction between ethics and metaphysics. Heidegger challenges the distinction between analysing freedom as possibility, subordinated to the forms of
categorial thought, and analysing freedom as effective actuality, articulated through
responsiveness to the moral law. Heidegger attributes priority to the latter, as an
ontological characteristic of actually existing persons. Thus, two strands in
Heidegger's contribution to ethics come together: his disruptive approach to the
boundary and priority set up between ethics and metaphysics and his disruptive
treatment of the thought of other philosophers. This theme of subverting the distinction between metaphysics and ethics is developed in the subsequent readings
of Schelling and Nietzsche. Löwith did, however, have access to the contemp-
oraneously published essay 'Vom Wesen des Grundes' published in a *Festschrift*
for Husserl in 1929. Like the parallel text, 'Vom Wesen der Wahrheit' (1929–43),
The Essence of Reasons is subjected by Heidegger to a series of reinterpretative
rewritings,[6] and both essays pose huge problems for interpretation, since they are
caught up in the shifts in the 1930s in Heidegger's view of the relation between
fundamental ontology, philosophy and history.

In the essay, Heidegger distinguishes between Kant's conception of the world
and his own as developed in *Being and Time* by appeal to the *kosmos* of
Heraclitus, to the the *kosmos* of the Gospel of St John and to the *mundus* of
Augustine. These moves are repeated in the much later essay 'Die Sprache', in
Unterwegs zur Sprache,[7] where Heidegger writes in connection with his thinking
of the fourfold:

> In the golden blossoming tree are gathered the earth and the sky; the divinities
> and the mortals. Its particular fourfold is the world. The word 'world' here is
> no longer meant in a metaphysical sense. It names neither the secularised
> represented universe of nature and history, nor does it mean the theologically
> conceived creation (*mundus*), nor does it mean the whole of what there is
> present. (*US*: 23–4)

The secular universe of nature and history is the modern conception of the world;
the world as God's creation is the medieval European notion of the world; and the
world as the wholeness of what is present here stands for the Greek conception of
the world. In the 1929 essay, Heidegger gives equal weighting to the Greek
tradition, to the New Testament *kosmos* and to Augustine's Platonised, created
world. Heidegger writes of Augustine, with more than a hint of a preoccupation
with his own phenomenological projects: 'Thus, "world" means: being in its
totality as the definitive "how" in accordance with which human *Dasein* positions
and holds itself with respect to being' (*WG*: 113). This repeats the aim in *Being
and Time* of developing a conception of worldness which can accommodate these
and other conceptions of world. However, the attempt can not succeed, and
Heidegger is stuck with a conception of worldness that extrapolates from the
three or four distinct conceptions of world which his tradition makes available to
him; it does not name a transcendentally neutral structure. The *kosmos* of
Heraclitus, the *kosmos* of St John, the Augustinian *mundus* are distinct from each

other and, if brought together in one transcendental structure with a modern conception of world, simply lose that distinctiveness. Significantly, Heidegger does not introduce the distinction drawn by Schopenhauer between the world as will and the world as representation. This splitting of the world marks a stage in the dissolution of a transcendental conception of the world into the positive sciences, erasing the question of truth in favour of the incoherences of orderings specific to particular domains.

In the essay, Heidegger distinguishes between a derivative freedom of purposiveness in action and a more primary ontological condition of being able to form purposes at all. He construes the second as the ontological condition for the Leibnizian project of demanding and deriving reasons or grounds. Thus, already in this essay, Heidegger addresses the Leibnizian principle 'nothing is without reason', and the enquiry, which culminates in 1956 in the lectures discussed in Chapter 2, *The Principle of Reason*, extends over the entire period from this essay in 1929. In this essay, Heidegger still uses the terminology of transcendence to capture an ontological capacity to detach oneself from the given and set up a relation to oneself. However, the later preferred term '*Überstieg*' is used alongside the more traditional term '*Transzendenz*', which is only subsequently identified, in the Nietzsche lectures and in the letter to Jünger, as caught up in the concealed oscillations of metaphysical thinking. Heidegger uses the term '*Überstieg*' to mark a transition from freedom as experienced in choosing between specific, given, ontical, ready-to-hand options to freedom as constitutive of a form of existence, *Dasein*, for which there is a horizon, or world. This distinction links back into his analyses of ontological difference rather than forward into the accounts of words for being. However, the strategy of seeking to reveal a more primordial, ontological structure concealed by an ontical, occasional structure is paralleled in his subsequent attempt to read a broader conception of *phusis*, as in place prior to the emergence of a distinction between *phusis* and *techne*. The distinction between the ontical capacity to choose ends of action and freedom as the ontological condition making such choice possible is introduced as follows:

> Every 'will' must, however, 'develop' a purposiveness [*Umwillen*] as and through a transition [*Überstieg*]. That which projects in advance, in accordance with its essence in the form of a purposiveness, and not just as a chance achievement, is what we call freedom. The transition to the world is freedom itself. (*WM*: 161)

Heidegger thus distinguishes between a chance opportunity and a structural feature of a certain form of existence. The distinction is between the sense of freedom experienced in choosing between paths in a wood and the structural features of a form of existence which makes such an experience possible. He connects this distinction to the distinction from *Being and Time* between a ready-to-hand opportunity and a chosen project that has the more complex structure identified through the analysis of *Dasein*:

> Thus, transcendence does not happen across purposiveness as if on a ready-to-hand value and aim, but on the contrary freedom maintains itself, and indeed as freedom, in opposition to purposiveness. In its transcending self-opposition to purposiveness, there occurs the *Dasein* of human beings, such that it is subordinated to itself in the essence or emergence of its existence [*Wesen der Existenz*], that it can be a free self [*ein freies Selbst*]. (*WM*: 161)

In this essay Heidegger makes the claim: 'Freedom is the origin of the principle of sufficient reason', and the essay concludes: 'For in transcendence, the essence of the finitude of *Dasein* discloses itself as freedom for reasons.' In this way Heidegger definitively rejects any separation between, on one side, ethical and moral aspects of freedom and, on the other, ontological and metaphysical aspects.

In order to understand Heidegger's questioning of the opposition between history and nature and his refusal of the thematics of nature it helps to locate three very different oppositions to nature set up at the end of the eighteenth century, which still function powerfully today. These three can be identified telegraphically with the thought of Hume, of Rousseau and of Kant, and it would be worth considering how the resulting conceptions of nature have greater force in the respective language communities in which they were formed: English-speaking, French-speaking and German-speaking. Hume's preoccupation, crudely put, is with a difference between the observability of natural processes and the non-confirmability of the divine, of miracles, revelation and salvation. Rousseau's preoccupation is with the impossibility of a conception of nature unaffected by the conceptions and practices at work in the context in which that conception of nature is produced. Thus, Rousseau opposes a conception of nature to a conception of society and reveals that conceptions of nature are produced in specific social, historical contexts. Thus, no conception of nature can be natural. The Anglo-Saxon resistance to this thought is another index of a commitment to empiricism and grounds a resistance in the Anglo-Saxon world to the thought of Rousseau, of Hegel, of Nietzsche, of Heidegger, to Derrida and indeed to the conceptual disruptions proposed in the name of feminism. The third opposition, to be associated here with Kant, is between nature and morals. These are for Kant radically distinct objects for thought, splitting human identity and fracturing philosophical enquiry into an impossibly bifurcated dead end. Heidegger's disruption of the opposition between history and nature, between freedom and determinism, disrupts this Kantian dead end.

In the lectures on Kant from 1935–36, *What is a Thing?*, Heidegger questions the stance from which nature is theorised:

> The question about our basic relation to nature, about our knowledge of nature as such, about our mastery of nature is not a question for the natural sciences. This question stands together in question with that question about whether and how we can still be spoken to by entities as such as a whole. (*FD*: 39)

He continues by remarking that it is not open to one person to make a decision on such an issue and suggests that the lack of thorough thinking in this epoch makes an adequate response to this question all the more unlikely:

> Such a question cannot be decided in a lecture, it can only be decided in the course of a century and indeed only then when this century is not just asleep and does not simply put about the opinion that it is alert. The question can be brought to a decision only through the issue being thoroughly taken apart [*Die Frage wird nur zur Entscheidung gestellt in der Auseinandersetzung*]. (*FD*: 39)

This move follows on from the following unusually straightforward remark: 'What is supposed to be "natural" is not at all "natural", which means here, self-evident for any set of randomly chosen existing human beings. The "natural" is always historical' (*FD*: 30). Thus, the essence of nature is not itself natural. There follows a long reflection on different versions of what is natural, with a topical reference to Mussolini's invasion of Ethiopia:

> We call 'natural' whatever is comprehensible on its own terms without any further reference out of the surrounds of everyday understanding. For an Italian engineer, for example, the internal structure of a big bomber is obvious. For an Abyssinian from the most remote mountain village, such a thing is absolutely not 'natural'. It is not self-evident, that is not in context of what this human being and his people can explain without further ado out of comparison with what is already in everyday life well known.

Heidegger contrasts what is natural for Enlightenment and for medieval Europeans:

> For the epoch of Enlightenment what is natural demonstrates itself and lets itself be noted out of determinate basic principles of a self-producing reason, which appropriates every human being and humanity in general. For the Middle Ages, what was natural was that which had its essence, its *natura*, from God, but which then, as a result of this derivation and without further intervention of God, forms itself and in a certain way can sustain itself. What seems natural to eighteenth-century human beings, the rationality of a universal reason detached from any other connection, would have been to medieval human beings very unnatural. (*FD*: 29–30)

This set of remarks prepares for the ensuing questioning of Kant's conception of a thing as a historical, not a philosophically necessary conception. It also introduces Heidegger's questioning of the relation between history and nature.

DIVISIONS WITHIN HISTORY

Central to that questioning is the development in *Being and Time* of a distinction between the adjectives '*geschichtlich*' and '*historisch*'. The difference between the two adjectives can be cumbersomely marked in English by using the term 'history' only for '*Historie*', a narrated history, and 'historicality' for '*Geschicht-lichkeit*', having the character of a historical process. Human death is an event. It is *geschichtlich*; it has causes; it takes place in history and has historical effects. It is a part of the natural history of human beings. It is not *historisch*, until someone has told a story about that death. For Heidegger, then, human death is both natural and historical in the sense of *geschichtlich*. Thus, human death reveals that nature and *Geschichte* are not opposed terms. The difference between the deaths of human beings and those of animals is that animal deaths are not located between historicality and narration. Human death is an event which can be anticipated and to which a relation, even if only one of denial, is constructed by human beings as individuals and as collectives. That relation may then be taken up in the construction of historical narratives, *Historie*, but it may also be articulated through theological or mythological accounts. Thus the assumption that natural history necessarily entails the telling of historical accounts is a prejudice which elides the existence of societies in which theology and myth-ology, not historical narrative, provide the sense of orientation which the ideas of progress and enlightenment provide for modern Europeans.

In *Being and Time*, Heidegger uses the distinction between *Historie* and *Geschichte* to refer historical specificity and the variability of the contexts in which human beings find themselves back to the unvarying fact that human beings are always in some narrative context. Thus, for Heidegger, *Geschichtlichkeit* is a basic existential of *Dasein*. The ontical circumstances change, as do the kinds of story told, but the ontological structure is invariant. Heidegger thus makes use of a set of distinctions which is not readily available in English to demarcate between the facts of the matter of history, including the facts of natural history, that human beings die, and the negotiable significance assigned to them in accounts constructed of them. It is not then Heidegger who erodes the difference between history and nature and who naturalises the basis for human concern with history: there is a natural basis for that concern and for an instability in the distinction between history and nature. Theories of human nature, given in the form of generalised anthropologies, can then be seen as attempts to contain this instability. However, there is a series of shifts in Heidegger's treatment of the instability of the opposition between history and nature. These shifts are easier to understand once this duplicity in conceptions of history has been identified. Similarly, the deliberateness of the subordination of nature in *Being and Time* is easier to understand if these conceptions of both history and nature are placed in a double context. The first half of the context is provided by the 1925 lectures on the history of the concept of time, and the other half by the questioning of metaphysics in his inaugural lecture at Freiburg, 'What is metaphysics?' (1929), developed in the readings of Kant, Schelling and Nietzsche.

The 1925 lectures connect up to a lecture given by Heidegger in 1916, 'The concept of time in the historical sciences', the term for 'historical' here being not '*geschichtlich*' but '*historisch*'.[8] This early lecture appears to accept as basic a distinction between the natural and the historical sciences; but this status is disrupted in a lecture given to the theological institute in Marburg in 1924 and recently published as *The Concept of Time*,[9] in which much of the structure of the existentials laid out in *Being and Time* is already in place. This lecture was closely followed by the 1925 lectures, published in 1979 under a misleadingly Kantian title, *Prolegomena zur Geschichte des Zeitbegriffs*.[10] These lectures propose to thematise the distinction between history and nature as a temporary, not a permanent feature of human thought. The distinct forms of enquiry, with their specific domains of objects, are to be shown to depend on a shared origination in a particular temporal formation. The two are thus no longer to be taken as basic terms of analysis, but rather as themselves in need of a genealogy, tracing them back to a more original, more primordial level of construction. This analysis is to reveal the opposition as limited, not general in application; but the lectures are incomplete, and the genealogy is not provided. In the introduction to these lectures, there are references to the discussions of time by Dilthey, Brentano and Husserl; but the announced history of the concept of time, planned for an unwritten section, names Bergson, Kant in relation to Newton, and Aristotle. The discussion of the horizon for the questioning of being in general, and the being of history and of nature in particular, would have taken place in yet another unwritten part of the lectures. Thus the project of tracing the distinction between history and nature back to a single origin is announced but not performed.

By contrast, in the 1930s it is for metaphysics, and not for concepts of time, for which Heidegger proposes to provide a history, showing how the history of philosophy conceals a more important history of being. The history of philosophy presents the history of being in the reduced form of a history of timeless metaphysical systems, precluding consideration of the temporal processes which first bring those systems into existence and then erode their plausibility. Heidegger constructs this history of metaphysics as a history of words for being which conceals their origin in the sending or history of being. As a result of this drastic reduction of the history of metaphysics to a sequence of words for being, Heidegger reveals the obscuring of being at work in it, as the process through which the impermanence of metaphysical systems is concealed. Heidegger reveals a doubling within the history of words for being, with a history of metaphysics, in which the question of being is obscured, shadowed by a history of being, as the sending of those metaphysical systems. In the course of this, the history of the concept of time of 1925 is replaced by this double history of metaphysics and of being, as a process of sending. In between these two stages lies the publication of *Being and Time*.

In *Being and Time*, Heidegger distinguishes between tradition as handing on, *Überlieferung*, and tradition as fixed system, *Tradition*, echoing the distinction between the process of history, *Geschichte*, and the reconstruction offered in an account, *Historie*. History as open transmission, process and events is reduced to a fixed tradition, a given account. As a result, history is reduced to a domain amongst others for human enquiry. It becomes an ontical domain of entities, not an ontological process in which the question of being can be recognised at work. For history understood as *Geschichte*, there is an internal relation between human beings and events; for history understood as *Historie*, there is an external relation. This difference between an internal and external relation to history is obscured; and there is here an elision of ontological difference. The reduction of history and of tradition from process, in which developments are open-ended, to accounts of a rigid sequence of accomplished events, is then a version of the forgetting of being, through which the contestable and unstable nature of what there is becomes concealed. While it is well known that the forgetting of the question of being is for Heidegger of preeminent importance, this version is not widely recognised. A reduced version of history results from and confirms a failure to understand the nature of the human condition, a failure to produce adequate philosophical enquiry and an insensitivity to processes taking place above and beyond human control. The *Überlieferung* is that which is transmitted and transmittable; it is rewritten in the 1930s as the history or sendings of being. The *Tradition* is what is taken up and affirmed by the receivers of what is transmitted; it is rewritten in the 1930s as the history of metaphysics. In the *Tradition*, there is no guarantee that everything passed on is taken up by those to whom it is passed on; and the same goes for the relation between history as process and events and history as reconstruction and account. There is a concealment of the possibility of conflict about the nature of that inheritance, a concealment of the instability of interpretations of that inheritance and a concealment of the role of an inheritance in setting up connections between past, present and future. There is a reduction of questions about ontological constitution and self-constitution to questions about ontical matters of fact. Having just the one term for the two aspects of history and for the two aspects of tradition suggests that there is just one seamless process, connecting the past to the present to the future, without reservation. It conceals the fact that being in history and having a relation to an inheritance are features of a specific form of existence, the human one. Thus, the English-speaking world has built into its language as a presumption a result which Hegel worked hard, if unsuccessfully, to prove credible: a mapping from events to a rational orderly history.

Heidegger uses both distinctions in *Being and Time*, between history as process and history as account given, between tradition as process and tradition as received. Both distinctions are important for his thinking about the relations between philosophical enquiry, its history and history in general, and are brought together in his proposed destruction of the history (*Geschichte*) of ontology. The point of this destruction, which Heidegger announces in the opening pages of *Being and Time*, is to disrupt an ontological *Tradition* in order to release a philosophical *Überlieferung* and make it possible to pose the question of being. The proposed history of ontology is then a stage between a history of conceptions of time, projected in the 1925 lectures, which do not problematise the historical and temporal dimensions of the stance from which that history is constructed, and the later *Seinsgeschichte*, for which temporality and historicality are the central issue. This history of ontology is radically ambiguous, for the term '*Geschichte*' in the context of the destruction in *Being and Time* is ambiguous between the two senses of history as process and as account. This is one of the reasons for Heidegger's failure to complete the argument as projected in *Being and Time*. Heidegger introduces the destruction of the history of ontology thus: 'If a perspicuity about its history [*Geschichte*] is to be won for the question of being, then there must be an unpacking of the rigidified tradition and release of the concealment which occurs in the temporal structures perpetuated by that tradition' (*SZ*: 22). Heidegger points out that the destruction is not negative with respect to the past; it is negative with respect to present understandings of that past, from which the past is to be released: 'This destruction does not relate negatingly to the past; the critique is directed towards "today" and the dominant way of treating the history [*Geschichte*] of ontology, be it doxographical, intellectual-historical or in a history of problems' (*SZ*: 23). The aim is to identify inadequacies not in the past but in present understanding.

However, at the beginning of the next paragraph, there is an appeal to the past as the past in the references to the 'decisive stages' in the history of ontology:

> In the parameters set up by this enquiry, the purpose of which is to work out the question of being, the destruction of the history [*Geschichte*] of ontology belongs essentially to the question of being and can occur only in the context of that questioning. In the parameters set up by this enquiry that destruction can be carried out only with respect to its grounding decisive stages. (*SZ*: 23)

But Heidegger has enormous difficulty in deciding just what these decisive stages are. The problem is how there can be a definitive account of such a history, rather than several competing ones, depending on the stance from which the history is constructed. The account offered of the 'end of philosophy' also becomes important here; for one interpretation of that end would license a definitive history of philosophy, as cumulatively leading to that end. This would be a Hegelian account, retaining uncritically an Aristotelian notion of essence as given at the beginning of time and realised at the end of a given process of development. While this conception maps closely onto the dynamics of natural growth, as in plants and even human beings, it does not capture the processes at work in technologically constructed processes. Heidegger's use of Husserlian phenomenological reduction and of the Husserlian conception of essence as that which is constructed through phenomenological and eidetic reduction releases his thinking about history from such Aristotelian and Hegelian essentialism. It permits Heidegger to sidestep Hegel's monumental struggle to demonstrate a contiguity between events and conceptual structure, such that systematic connections between all things can be posited and observed.

Hegel seeks to show how events, *Geschichte*, can be ordered into a single *Historie*. *Geschichte*, then, is the name for the processes linking together past, present and future; *Historie* the account given of those processes. By having two terms for the processes and for the accounts given of them, it becomes possible to conceive that there may be more than one way of understanding the relations between past, present and future. By having the one term it becomes difficult to leave open the question of the nature of this linkage and more likely that it will be conceived of in terms of singleness, seamlessness and continuity. There are two versions of an end of history and indeed of an end of philosophy to be distinguished one from the other. There is this Hegelian view of an end of history, perhaps more suitably attributed to Kojève, as the realisation of an essence given at the beginning of history, in God's creation or, in more Hegelian terms, in the transition first from logic to nature and then from nature to spirit. That essence evolves in the course of history and at the end achieves its final form. The end of philosophy would in similar terms be the accomplishment of a task of philosophy, given at the beginning of its history, in a complete account of what there is and how we can know it. This is an end as a completion: a *Vollendung*. There is another version of an end, which comes about not through the realisation of some essence given at the beginning of time, but by a change in circumstances, such that the very form of enquiry and its terms of reference no longer make sense. This is the sense in which Heidegger writes of an end of philosophy in his 1964 essay. It is an end of philosophy not as completion, but as the breakup of the tradition within which philosophy, in a certain form, was possible. For this version of the end of philosophy, philosophy dissolves into the positive sciences and no longer provides overarching generalising theories about the nature of things, about what there is and about the nature of truth. There is then a clear contrast between a Hegelian triumphalist version of an end of philosophy and of history, with an achievement of their aims; and a Heideggerian account, which emphasises a radical change in circumstances cutting present generations of human beings off from the tradition of European metaphysics. The enquiry in *Being and Time* is unresolved between these two conceptions of a history and end of philosophy. The destruction invoked is external to human beings, taking place within the transmission of philosophy. It is not yet identified as a feature of the human condition, as constituted by the relation between being and determinate being.

THE HISTORY OF PHILOSOPHY

Heidegger's destruction of the history of ontology as outlined in *Being and Time* proceeds backwards, from himself to Kant, to Descartes and then to Aristotle. This backward movement indicates that the point of departure, the starting point, has to be the present, but that it is necessary to return to a point of emergence out of which the currently dominant distinctions and preoccupations emerge, in order to retrieve the context within which that point of departure makes sense. This sets up a distinction between a start (*Beginn*) and a beginning (*Anfang*). The start is where the individual thought process begins; the beginning is the point at which the thought process itself starts up. There is also the originary moment (*Ursprung*) through which that beginning is retrieved into the current context. These three have different relations to temporality. A 'start' takes place in the present; a beginning has always already taken place; and an origin brings a start and a beginning together in a moment which cuts loose from the temporal structures of sequence, duration, past, present and future. Heidegger's lectures, however, and indeed *Being and Time*, are notorious for starting but failing to arrive at the proposed beginning point from which this point of emergence might be identified. They thus fail to release that previous thinking into the present context; they fail to locate the *Ursprung*. This failure to arrive at a beginning is matched by Heidegger's hesitations concerning the history of philosophy, already detectable in the work from the late 1920s and never resolved. They are displaced by the turn from the questioning of time and the attempt to destroy the history of ontology to questioning metaphysics and the attempt to construct a history of words for being. This, in turn, is displaced by questioning technology and the ambiguous announcement of an end of philosophy.

There are two distinct levels of development in Heidegger's thinking in the 1930s. There is the attempt to develop a history of philosophy, on the basis of the account of the sendings of being, *Seinsgeschehen*. This leads to the disruptive readings of the texts of others in order to reveal the production of words for being, marking shifts in the sending of being. There are also attempts to trace the emergence of a new kind of thinking, to which these readings also contribute. These two levels, the construction of a history of philosophy as resulting from the sendings of being and the attempt to inaugurate a new form of thinking, anticipate both the declaration in 1964 that the end of philosophy has occurred and the slightly earlier declaration that the new kind of thinking must be primarily concerned with the implications of the spread of technology. These twin aims twist Heidegger's readings of the texts of other thinkers in two incompatible directions. His readings demonstrate the contribution of these previous thinkers, then show their limitations and then seek to break elements of their work free to be used in the new formation. It is the overriding importance of developing this new form of thinking which for Heidegger justifies his impositions onto the texts of Kant, of Leibniz, or indeed Aristotle. The contentiousness of these impositions subverts the attempt to construct a definitive account of those texts, as constituting the philosophical tradition. The simultaneous development of these two layers of enquiry precludes the construction of a single trajectory and single reading of Heidegger's thought. If the second level, producing a new form of thought adequate to modern conditions of existence, is taken as primary, then the ethical commitment of the thinking of the 1930s becomes clear: the enterprise presupposes that it is important to come to terms with the specificity of the new. If the construction of a history of words for being is taken as primary, as a history definitive not just for the twentieth century, but for all time, then the ethical commitment is concealed, in the name of truth. Thus, in Heidegger's thought in the 1930s, there is a contrast between two commitments. There is an openly ethical commitment to an open-ended project of thinking, defying determination as tending towards a fixed endpoint. This commitment is to be justified, if at all, in terms of what it seeks to make possible and in terms of future developments. By contrast, the history of words for being, read as culminating in an end of philosophy as completion, not as interruption, contains a commitment to telling it how it is. Thus each form of enquiry is grounded in a commitment, but of distinctively different kinds. One is an ethical commitment of partiality, directed towards a specific end, in a specific context: of opening out an understanding of a particular future. The commitment to definitive truth-telling is metaphysical.

Heidegger's readings of Kant and of Schelling open the question of Heidegger's relation to the text of the other even more forcefully than his readings of Hölderlin and of Leibniz in *The Principle of Reason*. In the latter there is an interpretation of one element of Leibniz's thought, leaving relatively intact the structure of Leibniz's own enquiries. Heidegger's readings of the texts of Schelling and of Kant take those texts more seriously, as extended philosophical constructions; but they result, from the point of view of Kant and of Schelling, in violent distortions, not sympathetic interpretations of their thought. The same, notoriously, is true of Heidegger's readings of Nietzsche. While these readings have the effect of sending readers back to the texts of Leibniz, of Kant and of Nietzsche, they cannot be taken as capturing an uncontestable truth about the tradition. Less obvious is the connection to his transformation of Husserl's phenomenological method in *Being and Time*. Even Husserl at first failed to notice the radical challenge in that work to his own version of phenomenology. Thus Heidegger gives violent readings of both Descartes and Husserl in *Being and Time*, and proceeds in the 1930s in the same way with Kant, Schelling and Nietzsche. Kant's analysis of the moral/theological conditions of possibility for there being moral experience becomes in Heidegger an analysis of ontological possibility grounded in his history of being. The theorising of the thing-in-itself and of the thing-for-us in *The Critique of Pure Reason* becomes a part of Heidegger's meditations on the reduction of his own preferred tripartite structure, entities present at hand, entities ready to hand and *Dasein* as the kind of existence for which such differences are an issue, to the single dimension of entities which are present at hand. His reading of Kant in *What is a Thing?* develops in the postwar writings into his thinking about technology and his attempt to retrieve an alternative version of what there is as revealed in the fourfold play of forces. Detailed accounts of these readings cannot be offered here. What is important is how the contentiousness of those readings subverts the attribution to Heidegger of any attempt to construct a definitive history of philosophy with a determinate endpoint. What is taking place is a diagnosis of a turn in the relation between a current generation and its history, and a turn in Heidegger's relation to philosophy.

In *Being and Time*, Heidegger displaces the neo-Kantian opposition between history and nature by the opposition between world and time. The central analyses are of *Dasein*, first in relation to its being-in-the-world and then in relation to its multiple ways of being-in-time. In the course of the questioning of metaphysics in the 1930s, Heidegger abandons the opposition between world and time in favour of an opposition between world and earth. This can be understood as displacing the Kantian distinction between history and nature by an Aristotelian distinction between *techne* and *phusis*. The distinction between world and earth is introduced in the essay 'Vom Ursprung des Kunstwerkes'[11] from 1935/36, in which the question of beginnings is taken up through the notion of the origin, the *Ursprung* of the title. This is conceived as a release into the present of originating energies through the organising work of art. There is an extended parallel between the organising, energy releasing work of art and the creation of a state as such an originating event. As discussed in the previous chapter, Heidegger moves from seeing a release of this kind as a current possibility to seeing it as no longer available, but one which might return. The opposition between earth and world opens up a difference between the earth, as a source from which forms emerge, and the world, a domain structured through human understanding. This connects to the Kantian distinction between noumenal reality and phenomenal appearances. It parallels the distinction between *Geschichte* and *Historie*, thus setting out an opposition between *Historie*, *Welt* and phenomena as resulting from human activity and which can be viewed in their entirety from the human stance; and *Geschichte*, *Erde* and noumena which, like freedom and language, exceed that stance and evoke non-human forces.

In the 1939 essay 'On the essence and concept of *phusis* in Aristotle's *Physics*, b,1', Heidegger constructs a complicity between Aristotle and Kant, who, he supposes, operate an elision of nature much more sinister than any Löwith can detect in *Being and Time*.[12] As Löwith points out there is in this essay a threat to the distinction between history and nature, which is replaced as a centre for attention by the distinction between *phusis* and *techne*. Heidegger sets out an opposition between *phusis* and *techne* as a distinction between processes revealing what there is as self-generating growth and construing what there is as controllable process. In this essay Heidegger detects alongside Aristotle's views on matter the residue of a richer conception of *phusis*, not opposed to *techne* as a domain of human control. This he supposes was available to the presocratics and was eliminated only through the subsequent systematising of philosophy. In getting back to this notion of *phusis* prior to the emergence of philosophy in the thought of Plato and Aristotle, Heidegger supposes himself to have got back to a starting point which is a genuine beginning. He poses the question whether Aristotle is not misinterpreting *phusis* as self-producing activity and moves on to Kant, with the same hermeneutics of suspicion:

> Isn't *phusis* here being misinterpreted as a self-producing power? Or maybe there is not misinterpretation here, but the only possible interpretation of *phusis* as a kind of *techne*? It seems so, because in modern metaphysics, in the outstanding form of, for example, Kant, nature is conceived of as a technique, so that this technique which makes up natural entities can provide the metaphysical basis for the possibility, indeed the necessity of encompassing and mastering nature through machines. (*WM*: 287)

This claim about Kant is supported not in the 1939 essay, but in the 1936 lectures

What is a Thing? and the 1930 lectures *Vom Wesen der menschlichen Freiheit*, but this support will not be assessed here.

For Heideggger, the move from Aristotle to Kant contains a shift from a conception of *phusis* as growth to the modern conception of physics as a science amongst others, charting the relations between certain kinds of postulated entity. In parallel with this shift there is the move from the Greek conception of wisdom as virtue, spontaneously producing the right action at the right time, and the modern conceptions of value-neutral science and of a quite distinct domain of universal prescription. Heidegger thus detects in both Aristotle and Kant a nature opposed not to morals but to *techne*, which is then subordinated to *techne*. Thus, for the Heideggerian reading, the oppositions between moral freedom and deterministic nature, for Kant, and between ethical value and metaphysical fact, for Aristotle, mask the more significant opposition between *phusis*, as what there is and how it comes to be, and *techne*, as governing a domain of relations amenable to human control. The subordination of *phusis* to *techne* eliminates any domain other than that subject to human control. This subordination Heidegger traces back from Kant to Aristotle, and it constitutes for him the continuity of the tradition of European philosophy. Heidegger thus identifies in the transmission of the philosophical tradition from Aristotle to Kant a reduction of nature from a set of forces external to human beings, to which human beings are subject, into a set of forces which can be controlled by human beings. This, for Heidegger, is the flight of the gods responded to by Hölderlin; it is the death of God diagnosed by Nietzsche. There is a cumulative denial of superhuman forces at work in the world, bringing that world into existence. This has an effect on philosophical enquiry. Philosophy surrenders its stance of contemplation, wonder and responsiveness to otherness. Instead it intervenes in the construction of the concepts required for the development of positive science and for it to appear that human beings can control their circumstances. Here it is metaphysics, as the stance of detachment, which has been erased in favour of ethics, as the stance of involvement. This is the shift in philosophy Heidegger detects at work between the presocratics and Aristotle, but which takes the intervening period up until the present for its full development in the emergence of modern science and technology.

This transformation of *phusis* into what can be controlled by human beings is the reduction of the earth to nothing but world, nothing but the relations constructed by human beings. Thus, by contrast with the claim in the 1936 essay on Hölderlin, that a construction of world is required in order for there to be history, I suggest that Heidegger comes to the view that a difference between earth and world is required if there is to be history, if there is to be a distinction between chance and destiny. This reduction of earth to world is akin to the process Löwith identifies as taking place in *Being and Time*. Thus the very process that Löwith supposes occurs in *Being and Time* Heidegger himself criticises at a later date. The reduction of earth to world emphatically elides the question whether what there is can be systematically represented and ordered, whether indeed it is entirely available for inspection and can be considered as a totality. The conception of 'world' sets up what there is as representable to and by human beings. There is no unrepresentable other, precondition for what there is and source of transformation into different orderings. Heidegger identifies this reduction of earth to world as a strategy assisting the production of scientific theories of what there is, for it makes it possible to suppose that all processes and entities are observable and measurable. It has the catastrophic consequence of making it difficult to consider processes and entities which have not as yet been observed or which cannot be measured. The unmeasurable, unobservable becomes the uncanny, a source for completely inarticulable unease and disquiet. The erasure of metaphysics in favour of ethics erases the difference between metaphysics as detachment and ethics as involvement; this in turn makes ethics empty. Without the moment of detachment, there can not be involvement, only immersion.

The three-place relation of the inaugural lecture 'What is metaphysics?', between nothingness, being, entities, can be rewritten as earth, sendings of being, world. This three-place relation is then reduced, first, to a two-place relation, being and entities, sendings of being and world, and then simply to the being of entities. Thus, there is a forgetting of earth and of nothingness, and this is a key element in the process leading to the forgetting of being. The loss of the earth, the elision of nothingness, the forgetting of being are the sources of a barrenness extending out of and back into the boredom in human relations to self and other human beings, analysed in the *Grundbegriffe* lectures of 1929–30. They re-emerge in Heidegger's diagnosis of technology as a source of increasing danger, which is usually interpreted as the impending destruction of the environment in the ecological crisis of the current period. This, however, is a one-sided, objectifying, externalising version of the crisis. More important than these objective effects are the transformations in human beings which both result from and cause the processes giving rise to these ecological effects. The reduction of the relation between human beings and non-human environs to one of control and use is a precondition for ecological crisis. This reduction makes human beings the only source of value and focus for respect. The emergence and spread of technology is thus only one of the conditions for pursuing environmental damage to the point of ecological disaster. The willingness of human beings to take part in that destruction is much more important. The critical feature is the elimination of otherness, to which Heidegger gives these various names: being, nothingness, earth. This elimination distorts human orientation and judgement. It leads to a suppression of wonder at strangeness, which is characteristic of philosophy, in favour of the accumulation of knowledge in the positive sciences, for which nothing is alien. This is an important dimension in Heidegger's thinking about an end of philosophy: there is no otherness left at which to wonder. Heidegger urges on his readers an understanding and acceptance that the strange, the alien, the uncanny, the monstrous is within each of us in our relation to a world split betweeen the knowable and the concealed. Otherwise the strange, the alien, the uncanny, the monstrous all the same find a site: they are placed by one group of human beings in other such groups. He explores this violence embedded in strangeness through the discussion of Oedipus.

In the 1939 paper on *phusis*, Heidegger runs off a list of oppositions indicating the instability of the meaning of the term 'nature': nature and grace; nature and art; nature and history; nature and spirit. For Heidegger, if not for English speakers, the term 'nature' is both ambiguous and artificial. It is both set up in opposition to history and is used as a term for what certain entities essentially consist in, so that it is, for example, possible to write of 'the nature of history'. Heidegger construes the meaning of the term 'nature' as resulting from a complicated double history, with both Greek and Christian origins. He contrasts the Greek term *'phusis'* with the Latin translation *natura*, which gives rise to the Christian distinction between *natura naturans* and *natura naturata*, creating and created nature. Oddly, this distinction maps onto a distinction in Aristotle's text to which Heidegger draws attention, between *phusis* as growth, *Wachsen* and *Gewächse*, and *phusis* as self-production, *Machen* and *sich selbst machende Gemächte*; and there is a pressing problem here about whether Heidegger must inevitably find in these 'originating texts' what he looks for, just as he finds a thinker of ambiguity in Leibniz and a metaphysician in Nietzsche. Heidegger's readings of the presocratic Greek texts are perhaps his most contentious, since what he says about Aristotle is at least supported by his ongoing encounter with Aristotle's thinking throughout *Being and Time*. I suggest that Heidegger's claims about the presocratics and his disruptive translations are proposed not as definitive readings of those texts, but as attempts to bring into the present context the conceptual resources needed for developing an understanding of current circumstances. Heidegger's readings of Greek texts are more satisfactory if understood as part of his own constructive thinking of a new beginning for thought rather than as part of a destructive history of ontology, supposedly revealing some concealed truth about the thought of a predecessor and about differences between epochs in the sendings of being. His notion of destructive history is to be complemented by a notion of prospective history, written from the point of view of what it makes possible.

Heidegger interprets texts from the stance of an attempt to reveal the precariousness and parochiality of currently accepted conceptual distinctions: freedom and nature, reason and history. He is using these readings to address himself to current and future conditions, understood to be in a state of extreme crisis. He is displacing the entire tradition of philosophy as constructed in the nineteenth century, but usually represented as unquestionable truth of the matter. His mode of reading is emphatically in conflict with any attempt to pass off readings of texts in the history of philosophy as establishing indisputable matters of fact about those texts. It is hardly surprising then that it is sometimes difficult to recognise in, for example, Heidegger's Aristotle the Aristotle of more conventional readers. For this reason I do not accept that there is a single exclusive account of the history of philosophy here to be defended. Thus I suggest that

Heidegger's writing and thinking from *Being and Time* onwards does not provide a definitive reading of the history of philosophy. It displaces a series of oppositions between freedom and nature and between reason and history which marks the end of a certain kind of philosophy, but one with restricted, not general scope. This displacement functions as a precondition for the emergence of the theme of technical relations and for its disruption of the priority of metaphysics over ethics within philosophy. It is also a precondition for identifying the significance of the erosion of the distinction between the everyday and the metaphysical, discussed in Chapter 1. A failure to grasp this precondition blocks understanding of the significance of the theme of technical relations.

Any attempt to retrieve philosophy from Heidegger's declaration of its end turns on the question of whether philosophical enquiry is still possible after the basic status of the distinctions between freedom and nature, between history and reason has been given up. Heidegger's postwar analyses of technical relations require the surrender of these distinctions; and his wrestlings with the philosophical tradition in the 1930s, indeed maybe his involvement with Nazism, are signs of the extremity to which his thinking is driven in the attempt to cut loose from the controlling forces put in play by taking as basic a distinction between freedom and nature. The question, however, must be posed: are the distinctions between nature and freedom, between reason and history constitutive for all philosophical enquiry, or are they salient only for the modern or indeed only for the German idealist tradition? If, through the shift to questioning the historicising of nature and the naturalising of history, the perspective of Heidegger's enquiries is reduced from one framing a process at work from Anaximander to Nietzsche to a process stretching only from Descartes to the present, then Heidegger's sense of another way of thinking could be seen as an attempt to retrieve an otherness still preserved in the Neoplatonic traditions of Christianity, but definitively put to flight by the relentless naturalisations of the seventeenth and eighteenth centuries. What Heidegger's enquiries could then be taken to reveal is that philosophy, as constituted around the divisions between reason and history, between nature and freedom is a form of enquiry interdependent with those forms of enquiry resulting in the technological breakthroughs of the nineteenth and twentieth centuries. Thus the conceptions of freedom, reason, nature and history which inform Heidegger's thinking about the tradition of philosophy from the Greeks to the modern age would be modern notions, not notions which can be projected into the medieval and classical epochs. An obstacle to Heidegger's attempts to cross the medieval divide and return via Augustine to the Greeks would then be a failure to reveal the theological residues in current notions of freedom, reason and nature.

Heidegger's caution with respect to conceptions of nature in *Being and Time* and his insistence on distinguishing between *Dasein* and animality in the 1929–30 lectures take on a different guise once located in terms of his rejection of conceptions of nature as God's creation and of human beings as the highest form of that creation. The ontologising of freedom and the denaturing of the world,

first in *Being and Time* and then through technology, are disruptive of a theologically grounded Christianity, if not of those forms of Christianity which are antitheo-
logical and in process of self-transformation, often making use of Heideggerian
thinking to do so. Heidegger does not convince me that the otherness he seeks in
a new form of thinking was not already or rather might still have been in play in
the medieval epoch, in the less theologically oriented strands of the Christian
tradition. His own enthusiasm for the thought of Meister Eckhart supports this
view. Since Heidegger provides no extensive readings of medieval texts after his
habilitation thesis on the pseudo-Scotus, he has only the most cursory account of
the forgetting of being in that period; and his remarks about a reduction at work
in the translation of Greek philosophical terms into School Latin are similarly
brief. It is therefore plausible to treat his account of the end of philosophy as
applying only to post-Cartesian philosophy, in relation to a certain view of the
Greek philosophical origins as available in the modern epoch, mediated through
the arbitrary survival of Greek texts and the medieval transmission. The philosophy giving rise to technology as unrelated to human well-being is declared to
be at an end. Other forms of philosophy can and will continue. Heidegger's
threefold manoeuvre, the historicising of nature, the ontologising of freedom and
the naturalising of history, disrupts the centrality to philosophy of a distinction
between ethics and metaphysics, between an enquiry about what it is to be human
and an enquiry about what it is to be. However, I am inclined to suppose that it is
only for post-Cartesian philosophy that this distinction and its parallel oppositions,
between freedom and reason, between history and nature, between art and
science, are constitutive. Heidegger's questioning of the relation between *phusis*
and *techne*, and between earth and world, presumes a context in which these
Kantian distinctions have been displaced. Thus only post-Cartesian philosophy is
concluded when these oppositions are displaced; but even this displacement is not
completed by Heidegger, for he does not fully bring into question the distinction
between art and science. The turn, consisting in an end and a beginning, which is
anticipated by Heidegger cannot be hoped for until a disruption of the distinction
between art and science is under way. That way may be marked by the figure of
the Sphinx and the practice of psychoanalysis, which is neither art nor science.
Heidegger detects this disruption at work in Sophocles' plays; and I now turn to
his discussion of Oedipus in *Introduction to Metaphysics*.

THE FIGURE OF OEDIPUS

In the lectures *Introduction to Metaphysics*, Heidegger identifies human beings
as the strangest of creatures. Heidegger's discussion reveals that the human
capacity for self-destruction and for violence is more significant for his questioning of what it is to be human than any theory of human rational capacities, as a
foundation for knowledge. In abstract anthropological accounts of what it is to be
human the violence is done in advance, by reducing what it is to be human to a
cypher. This then sets up a one-sidedly metaphysical approach to technology,

treating it as simply a matter of fact. This lets loose human destructiveness with the added powers achieved through technical means. An ethical approach, locating the forces of technology in the context of their creation and articulation, permits a binding of those forces, such that they can be retrieved from the domain of fate into the domain of a human exercise of power. Heidegger reads Oedipus as challenging the ordering of the world, such as to make apparent the basic structures of that world. At a certain juncture Oedipus refuses to accept what his understanding has revealed to him. This refusal leads to his insisting on more and more overt revelations of the truth of his origins, which bring about his destruction. Oedipus' fate reveals the overmastering power of destiny over human ends. It reveals that there is a power greater than human power arching over human activity. This is the understanding to be gained from meditating on Heidegger's reading of Sophocles' *Oedipus*, which supports Heidegger's claim that Sophocles can teach us more about ethics than Aristotle. However, it is important to note that this is not a remark about the respective merits of Sophocles and Aristotle, but about what we need to learn.

One aspect of the strangeness of human beings is the loss in the modern world of an understanding of the Greek and Judaeo-Christian roots of European culture. This is also a theme for Nietzsche, whose work Heidegger suggests needs rescuing from his interpreters: 'His work seems not to have the worst of this misuse behind it. If we here speak of Nietzsche, we want nothing to do with this, but also nothing to do with heroising Nietzsche. The task is both too important and too sobering for such things' (*EM*: 28). Heidegger shares with Nietzsche the thought that something important, which was available to the Greeks, has gone missing in the modern world, in part through a loss of a sense of the differences between modern living and Greek culture. This loss connects to a problem of translating the Greek term '*phusis*' with the German term '*Natur*':

> In the epoch of the first development of occidental philosophy among the Greeks, which sets the standard for subsequent thought and through which the questioning of entities as such as a whole took its true beginning, entities were called *phusis*. This basic Greek word for entities is translated as '*Natur*', using the Latin translation *natura*, 'to be born', or 'birth' [*Geburt*]. With this Latin translation, the original content of the Greek word *phusis* is already repressed, and the genuine power of naming of the Greek word is destroyed. (*EM*: 10)

Heidegger goes on to generalise from this one case:

> This is true not just of the Latin translation of this word, but of all other translations of the philosophical language of the Greeks into Roman. This process of translation from Greek into Roman is not accidental and is not harmless, but is the first stage in the process of blocking off and estranging the original essence of Greek philosophy. (*EM*: 10–11)

In Nietzsche's inversion of Plato's ordering of the supersensible above sensibility, of the domain of eternal ideas above the realm of transient sensation,

Heidegger reads a completion of one trajectory from Greek thinking into the modern epoch. There are, of course, other readings of Nietzsche and other readings of the trajectory from the Greeks to the late nineteenth century. My conviction is that Heidegger's reading of these Greek origins is not a discovery or retrieval of a pre-given essence of philosophy, but the revealing of formation needed by Heidegger for his attempt to think a new beginning for thinking. The implications of this move with respect to his readings of the Greeks for his reading of Nietzsche cannot here be explored.

For Heidegger, it is through the productive power of language and thought that human experience takes shape and entities become individuated. 'Things only become and are what they are through word and language' (*EM*: 11); and he goes on to claim: 'The Greeks did not discover what *phusis* is by experiencing natural processes, but the other way around. On the basis of an originating experience of being, through poetic thought, there was opened up to them what they had to call *phusis*.' *Phusis*, Heidegger maintains, 'means originally both heaven and earth, both stones and plants, both animals and human beings; human history as both human and God's work; finally and first of all, the gods as fate. *Phusis* means the emergence of what prevails [*walten*] and what is carried over through that prevalence.' Thus Heidegger disputes attempts to reduce theories of *phusis* to a philosophy of nature, with a built-in distinction between nature and spirit, or between logic, nature and spirit, or between nature and history. *Phusis* is a more inclusive term than that. He then points out: '*Phusis* becomes narrowed down to an opposition with *techne* – which is neither art nor technique, but a form of knowing, a knowing control over a free designing and construction, and control over construction' (*EM*: 13). Already in the Greek origins of philosophy, Heidegger traces the reduction of what there is to simply objects of human knowledge and then, supposedly, subject to human control. Heidegger disrupts any attribution of eternal status to metaphysical and philosophical enquiry by stating:

> Our asking of the metaphysical, basic question is historical, because it opens up the event of human *Dasein* to futures, in its essential relations, that is towards entities as a whole, and with respect to unquestioned possibilities. With that, this asking binds it back into its already occurrent beginning and thus both focuses and makes more obscure its current condition. (*EM*: 34)

It is through this questioning, and not in the historical sciences, that a relation to history can be set up: 'The historical sciences can never set up the historical relation to history' (*EM*: 33). Heidegger claims nature to be not natural, but historical in derivation. He claims conversely that the historical sciences are insufficiently historical for the setting up of an historical relation to history.

He provides a clarification of his notion of *Auseinander-setzung*: 'Through this setting apart and disentangling, there emerges the world. (This setting apart does not divide or destroy unity. It creates it as a binding together [*logos*]). *Polemos* (setting apart) and *logos* (binding together) are the same' (*EM*: 47). He is working on an interpretation of Heraclitus' *Fragment 53* and states just before this: 'The *polemos* named here is a conflict which pertains before all divine and human things; it is not a war in human form. The struggle conceived of by Heraclitus permits what there is first of all to emerge as opposition, allows position and place and hierarchy to draw themselves into existence' (*EM*: 47). This struggle is prior to the emergence even of *phusis*. He continues: 'This becoming of world is genuine original history [*Dieses Weltwerden ist die eigentliche Geschichte*]' (*EM*: 48). Where there is no more struggle of this kind, Heidegger claims:

> What there is becomes merely an object, either for looking at (a spectacle or picture) or for activity, as something made or calculated. The originary emergence of a world, *phusis*, declines into a model for copying and imitation. '*Natur*' becomes a particular domain in contrast to art and to all production and planning. (*EM*: 48)

This translation for Heidegger conceals an impoverishment in thought and in understandings of what it is to be human. In his reply to his critics in 1945–46,[13] Heidegger accepts that this term '*polemos*', struggle, strife, war or setting apart, was used in his *Rektoratsrede* in the context of his endorsement of Nazism, but he seeks to distance his use of it from any straightforward endorsement of the Nazi war machine. While no doubt the reference here and in the rectorial address is to the Heraclitan *polemos* is hard to see how the use of the term could have been understood in any way other than as an endorsement of Nazi violence.

In these lectures Heidegger also discusses Parmenides' views on the relation between being and becoming. He quotes Parmenides and then states: 'Anyone who understands the standards set by such a thoughtful pronouncement must lose all desire to write books' (*EM*: 74). It is in this context that he makes the startling move of insisting that Heraclitus and Parmenides, indeed all philosophers at some level, have the same thought:

> In the history of philosophy, all thinkers say the same. This is of course a serious challenge to everyday understanding. Why then should there be the many-sided and complex history of philosophy, if all philosophers say the same? One philosophy is enough. Everything has already been said. But this 'everything' has an inexhaustible richness of that which as its inner truth is every day as though it were its first day. (*EM*: 74)

For Heidegger, then, at this point there is, strictly, no history of philosophy. There is a peculiar relation between philosophical enquiry and time, which poses inexhaustible paradoxes for human thought, each time as though for the first time. For Heidegger, there is a history of metaphysical systems, because metaphysical thinking takes at face value this appearance of everything being now for the first time, not as embedded in a process of development, not resulting from the history or sending of being, not characterised by a structure of repetition. Because it erases historical context, metaphysical thinking falls into the error of supposing that complete and conclusive conceptual construction is possible. This leads to the cycle between affirming and rejecting the adequacy of such constructions. This generates a 'history', a sequence of such constructions; but this is not 'history' in the sense of *Seinsgeschick*, opening out an ordering of what there is. The history of metaphysics is a response to that primary history as *Seinsgeschick* and is derivative from it. It is a history that conceals the relation between thought and time, between philosophy and temporality, between ethics and metaphysics.

In support of the more limited claim concerning the non-oppositional nature of the relation between the fragments of Parmenides and those of Heraclitus, he makes the startling claim that the distinction between being and appearance emerges at the same time as the distinction between being and becoming. This is perhaps in deliberate conflict with the ordering of concepts set out in Hegel's *Logic*. In this context, he also introduces a reflection on the *Oedipus Tyrannus* of Sophocles:

> We must not simply see Oedipus as an individual who is destroyed. We must see in Oedipus the image of Greek existence in which the basic passion in its widest and wildest form goes forward; the passion of revealing being; the struggle for being itself. (*EM*: 81)

Heidegger then refers to Hölderlin's remark about Oedipus having one eye too many: 'This additional eye is the basic condition for all great questioning and knowing and also the sole metaphysical basis for it. Knowledge and the systematic enquiries of the Greeks are the capacity to be affected [*Leidenschaft*]' (*EM*: 81). Oedipus' third eye is his capacity for suffering; his learning is not made safe by the distances set up in the modes of measuring and observation. There is here an undercutting of the distinction between subject of knowledge and subject as agent. The figure of Oedipus, for Heidegger, presents human beings at a point of transition between the three ways set out by Parmenides' poem: the way of appearance, the way of negation and the way of being. Oedipus' answer to the Sphinx's question shows that he knows about the alterability of what it is to be human; but that he does not at first understand how that alterability applies most of all to his own condition. He is carried from princely status and plenty to complete dispossession, exposed as a newborn child to avoid and fulfil the destiny ascribed to him, to kingship and marriage, to the divine disaster, in which he discovers he has broken every conceivable taboo: cursed himself, defied the divine order, fathered children with his own mother and killed his father. He is carried from homelessness to homelessness, from the mountainside to Colonus, but achieves divinity by seeking in the end to understand, not to flee from this destiny. Heidegger reads in the play a relation between being, revelation, appearance and nothingness, and concludes:

> Since it is as it is with being, revelation, appearance and not-being, human beings, who set themselves up in the middle of being, which opens itself up, and who always out of this setup develop relations to entities, find three paths open. Human beings must, if they are to take up their existence in the light of

being, take up this stance, must hold on to it in and against appearance; must tear appearance and being out of the non-ground [*Abgrund*] of not-being [*Nichtseins*]. (*EM*: 84)

Thus Heidegger describes Oedipus in terms of a Parmenidean threefold tension between being, nothingness and appearances; and this can be seen as a redescription of the threefold relation between being, anxiety and entities within which *Dasein* is held in place in *Being and Time*.

Heidegger then reverts to discussing Parmenides and Heraclitus, after interleaving these reflections on *Oedipus*. However, there is a single theme under enquiry here: what is it to be human? According to Heraclitus, what it is to be human emerges first in the struggle or setting apart of an *Auseinander-treten*, which is on this occasion Heidegger's preferred translation of the term *polemos*: 'Who human beings are emerges (*edieze*: shows itself) according to Heraclitus' aphorism first in the *polemos*, in the separation between the gods and human beings, in the occurrence of the eruption [*Geschehnis des Einbruchs*] of being itself' (*EM*: 107). Heidegger then summarises his discussion so far:

1 The determination of the essence of human being is never an answer but a question;
2 the asking of this question and a decision about it is historical, not only as a generality, but as the essence of history;
3 the question, who human beings are, must always be posed in its essential context, with the question about being. The question about human beings is not an anthropological question but an historically trans-physical [*geschichtlich meta-physische*] question.

In a subsequently appended remark he says that: 'The question cannot be posed in the domain of metaphysics as handed on, which is really only physics' (*EM*: 107). These remarks permit Heidegger to claim that Parmenides must be interpreted not from an assumption of what it is to be human, but as providing the backdrop against which accounts of what it is to be human might be developed. Heidegger reaffirms the importance to human beings of being historical in a second summing up:

Human beings discover themselves and have selves first as a question and as historical entities. The being a self of human beings means that human beings have to metamorphose the being which reveals itself to them in history and have to set up a stance within this. This being a self does not in the first instance mean an 'I' as a particular. Nor does it mean a 'we' and a 'community'.

He explains: 'Because human beings are historical, the question about their own being must shift from the form "what is human being?" to "who is human being?"'. Here again is a retrieval from *Being and Time* of the insistence on asking the question 'who is *Dasein*?' in order to prevent a bland generalisation taking the place of existential analysis, which has to be owned by particular individuals.

Heidegger seeks out in the Greek tragedian Sophocles an alternative view of the relation between human beings and what there is, through a questioning of a 'who', which he finds in the plays. He claims that the thought even of the presocratics, Heraclitus and Parmenides, is already too thoroughly embued with thoughtfulness for them to be unprejudiced in their approach to the question of what human beings are:

> The thought of Parmenides and of Heraclitus is still poetic, which means here philosophical and scientific. But while in them this poetic thought has a priority for thinking, even this thinking about the being of human beings has a particular direction and bias. In order to illuminate this poetic thinking from the other side, which also belongs to it, and so to prepare an understanding of it, we will now consult the thoughtful poetics of the Greeks, and indeed that poetry in which being, and the existence of the Greeks which belong to it, set themselves up: tragedy. (*EM*: 110)

And with this remark Heidegger begins a reading of parts of Sophocles' *Antigone*, with the only too apposite remark: 'The following interpretation is of necessity insufficient, if only because it cannot be developed out of the whole of the tragedy, nor out of the whole of this poet's work' (*EM*: 113). He proposes a reading in three moves: an overview, a construction of the chosen strophes and their contraries, and finally 'we will attempt to take up a stance in the middle of the whole to measure who, according to this poetic speaking, human beings are' (*EM*: 114). Heidegger chooses to begin his quotation from *Antigone* with: 'Many are the forms of strangeness, yet nothing can surpass the towering strangeness of human beings', and he comments: 'Human beings are *to deinotaton*, the strangest of the strange [*das Unheimlichste des Unheimlichen*].' Heidegger traces out an ambiguity in the Greek term, between denoting the most feared, the overpowering power, and denoting an essential feature of the existence of human beings, as the ones who must use force and be arbitrary in order to be what they are. He picks out the remark that for human beings a multiplicity of possible paths open up, *pantoporos*, not just the three outlined in the reading offered earlier of Parmenides; but that they all lead nowhere, *aporos*. This can be understood as a diagnosis of the destinies of all individual human beings as puzzles without exit. In the second move, Heidegger points out that the first strophe mentions a human relation to the sea and the earth, and argues that this primordial relation is richer and stronger than any supposedly cultivated relation of advanced society to what there is. Only one thing restricts this upsurge of power which human beings experience, and that is death.

Heidegger goes on to claim that the higher the pinnacle to which an historical form of existence rises up, the lower the fall into which the loss of momentum will take that form of existence: 'The more towering the summit of historical being, the greater the yawning gulf for the sudden fall into the loss of history that drives itself on into having no way out and at the same time is bottomless confusion' (*EM*: 123). Heidegger then reads into this chorus from *Antigone* the dangers posed by the development of a world order, *techne*, in conflict with the order of the Gods, *dike*. The one who brings about such a development, like Oedipus, cannot be welcome in the everyday lives of ordinary human beings. He quotes:

> great honour is given to him who combines the order of the world with that of the heavens. But he who attempts to bring what does not exist into existence oversteps his place and has no place. I cannot share my hearth with him, nor can I combine his attempts within my understanding.

Heidegger identifies this attempt to bring what does not exist into existence as the occurrence of the event of unconcealment, revealing what there is: 'This opening up is the event of unconcealment. This is nothing other than the event of the uncanny [*das Geschehnis der Unheimlichkeit*]' (*EM*: 127). The event of unconcealment is the opening of being. This opening of being constitutes the homelessness and uncanniness, which is already a theme for *Being and Time* but is not there tied into the relation between *Dasein*, *Sein* and the revealing of truth.

Heidegger discusses a relation between a beginning and an end of a history of what it is to be human which ties in with the themes of a beginning and end of philosophy. At the time of Sophocles, Heidegger suggests, there was clearer relation between human beings and what there is:

> the determination of the essence of human beings which completes itself here at the beginning of Western philosophy is not to be set out through grasping at some characteristics of a living creature, distinguishing 'human beings' from other living creatures. Being human [*das Menschsein*] determines itself out of the relation to entities as such taken as a totality. The essence of human beings [*das Menschwesen*] shows itself here as the relation which first opens being up for human beings. (*EM*: 130)

He adds: 'Being human [*das Menschsein*] is of necessity a perceiving and bringing together of inevitability, in the freedom of taking over *techne*, of an understanding setting to work of being. This is history' (*EM*: 130). This distinction between being human [*Menschsein*] and the essence of humanity [*Menschwesen*] maps onto the difference between constructing a relation to entities as a whole, which is a metaphysical relation, and being open to being, as the condition for there being anything at all. Heidegger thus here identifies history as resulting from being human, *Menschsein*, from setting being to work in a specific way, thus taking a part of what there is, our own partial understandings and responses, as all there is. This view of history as resulting from partiality and from the necessarily limited ends and understandings of human beings is obscured if there is no understanding of the difference between the partiality of *Menschsein*, which in trying to set up a relation to everything that there is, to the being of entities, sets limits on itself, and *Menschwesen*, having a relation to its conditions of emergence, to being.

Heidegger invokes *Being and Time* again, making it clear that he supposes himself to be developing a thinking left incomplete in *Being and Time*. He claims that the analysis of *Dasein* and the questioning of being are closely connected: 'Here, at the beginning of Western philosophy, the question of being already encompasses the grounding of *Dasein*' (*EM*: 133). Heidegger claims that there is at the beginning a *phusis* which requires a bringing together, *logos*, made possible by human beings. At the end, there is a reduction of this relation between human beings and *logos* to a definition of what human beings are:

> To measure the distance between the definition and the beginning opening up of the essence of being human, we can set up formally the beginning and the end over against each other. The end shows itself in the formula: *anthropos = zoon logon echon*. Human beings are the living creature which has reason as part of its equipment. We grasp the beginning in an artificially constructed formula, which brings together the results of the interpretation so far: *phusis = logos anthropon echon*, *phusis* is the same as human beings having reason, *logos*. (*EM*: 134)

But Heidegger emphasises the dimension in this definition which subsequently goes missing: 'Being, as the overpowering appearance, requires the bringing together which has within it human beings and grounds them' (*EM*: 134). This binding together of order imposes system, which tends to disperse and be in conflict. Human beings who become involved in these processes of binding together, like Oedipus, are also exposed to the disintegrating forces. Thus it is the relation to the overpowering forces of being which makes human beings appear the most powerful and the most strange and makes human beings unlike other entities, which do not have this relation. At the beginning of European history, Heidegger suggests, poets such as Sophocles display an understanding of this special status of human beings with respect to being. At the end of this history, which he marks as now taking place, Heidegger identifies awareness and understanding of the special status of human beings as going missing, the forgetting of being as becoming more definitive, with a consequent reduction of what it is to be human and a correlative increase in the scope of the destructive powers to be let loose. At what Heidegger takes to be the end of the history of philosophy, any attempt at a retrieval of being, as risked by Hölderlin and by Nietzsche, becomes more urgent and more dangerous for those involved.

Heidegger sets out a difference between beginning and end:

> There, at the end, there is indeed a remnant of a connection between *logos* and being human, but this *logos* has already for a long time been simply a capacity of understanding, expressing reason. The capacity itself is grounded in the presence at hand of a living creature of a particular kind, the *zoon beltiston*, the best set up animal (Xenophon).
>
> Here at the beginning, there is, on the contrary, a being human which is grounded in the opening of the being of entities [*die Eröffnung des Seins des Seienden*]. (*EM*: 134)

This leads into Heidegger's remark about the common opinion of his mode of interpretation, cited in the epigraph:

In the overview of the customary and dominant definitions and in the overview of contemporary metaphysics, theories of knowledge, anthropology and ethics, which are determined by Christianity, this interpretation of the expression must seem like an arbitrary transposition, as reading in something which an exact interpretation could never justify. That is true. For customary contemporary thinking, what I have just said is truly more evidence for the already notorious violence and one-sidedness of Heidegger's interpretative procedure. (*EM*: 134)

He elaborates: 'Indeed, giving up the customary and returning to a questioning interpretation is a leap [*Sprung*].' This questioning, however, 'does not take place at whim and as little in attachment to a system declared to be the norm. It occurs in and out of a historical necessity, out of the need of historical *Dasein* [*in und aus geschichtlicher Notwendigkeit, aus der Not des geschichtlichen Daseins*].' Oedipus stands between the human and the divine world, between *techne* and *dike*; and Heidegger takes this stance to be characteristic of *Dasein*, although it is not given to all human beings to experience the full force of this condition. He elaborates on the danger: '*Legein* and *noeein*, bringing together and apprehending, are necessary and violent acts against what is more powerful, although they are also on behalf of this greater power. So the doers of these violent deeds must always recoil from the use of this violence and yet cannot turn away from it.' Human beings cannot stop attempting to impose order on what there is, even though this necessarily does violence in taking a part for the whole. Heidegger continues:

In this horrified recoil, which is still the will to overpower, there must blaze up for a moment the suspicion that the overpowering of this greater power will then be most certain and most complete when the concealment is maintained by being, by the emergent dominance, which emerges as *logos*, the being gathered together of that which splits apart, if in a certain sense every form of appearance is refused. (*EM*: 135)

The emergent power of *logos* holds together that which tends to diverge so forcefully that there is no appearance. However, if there is no appearance, there is no finite being, no life, no human existence.

The effect of this on entities with the structure of *Dasein* is to undermine their very essence: 'The refusal of the opening with respect to being, however, means for *Dasein* nothing less than giving up its essence. This requires either stepping out of any relation to being or never becoming *Dasein*' (*EM*: 135). This violence which singles *Dasein* out is most dangerous for the integrity of *Dasein* itself:

Here the strangest possibility of *Dasein* shows itself: in the highest deed of violence it breaks the overpowering power of being against itself. *Dasein* has the possibility not as an empty way out, but it is this possibility, in so far as it is, for as *Dasein* it has to break itself up against being, in such a deed of violence. (*EM*: 135)

The age of technology is one in which the act of violence against being, the attempt to impose definitive divisions on what there is, seems to be going to be successful. Heidegger suggests that this will lead to a disaster far greater than that which befell Oedipus. It may be the disaster of bringing into existence the death camps. Heidegger continues: 'Not to be *Dasein*: that is the greatest victory over being. *Dasein* is the continuing need to throw down and take up again the deed of violence against being. In that way all powerful being overpowers *Dasein* on the site of its own appearing' (*EM*: 136). Then, as abruptly as the discussion of *Antigone* began, it stops again.

In the concluding pages of the lectures, Heidegger retrieves the ontological difference. He connects it to the separations of the *polemos* and to a disentangling process, identified as the site at which *Dasein* discovers its own basic characteristics, its relation to *Sein*, and at the same time puts itself at risk: 'The original separation [*die ursprüngliche Scheidung*], carried out by history as the internal and original stepping apart [*Auseinandertreten*], is the distinction between being and entities' (*EM*: 156); and he reaffirms a distance between an analysis of *Dasein* and anthropological determinations, which do not affirm a relation to being:

> The question of who human beings might be is internally connected to the question about the essence of being. The determination of the essence of human beings which is from here necessary is therefore not an issue for a free-floating anthropology, which represents human beings in the same way as zoology does animals. The question about being human is determined in its direction and full richness alone by the question of being.

The question of what it is to be human is forgotten along with the forgetting of the question of being, since humanity is the site at which being reveals itself:

> The question of being human within the question of being, in accordance with the hidden indication of the beginning, is to be grasped and grounded as the place which makes necessary the opening up of being. Human beings are the there which itself is open. In it, entities come to be and enter into process. In this sense we say the being of human beings is, in the strong sense of the word, the being which is there, which is *Da-sein*. (*EM*: 156)

With this, Heidegger again turns back to his own book, *Being and Time*, and to the juxtaposition of its title. It becomes clear that the enquiry in *Introduction to Metaphysics* concerning the relations between being and becoming, between being and appearance, between being and thinking and between being and prescription has been arranged in order to permit Heidegger to distinguish between these four juxtapositions and the juxtaposition between time and being, from the title of his earlier book. Heidegger concludes these lectures by insisting that the juxtaposition 'being and time' is directed in quite a different way from these other distinctions.

The juxtaposition of time and being opens up an awareness of a kind of knowing as questioning and a willingness to wait by contrast to the insistence that everything should be present at hand:

> To be able to question means to be able to wait, indeed perhaps a whole lifetime. For a whole epoch for which what is real is what quickly goes by and permits itself to be grasped with both hands questioning remains strange to reality, as that which does not let itself be settled up [*nicht bezahlt macht*]. But settling up [*die Zahl*] is not the most essential. What is essential is the right time, that is the right moment and the right duration. (*EM*: 156)

And then Heidegger adds an elusive quote from Hölderlin:

> *Denn es hasset*
> *Der sinnende Gott*
> *Unzeitiges Wachstum.*

> For the thoughtful
> God hates
> Growth out of time.
>   (*EM*: 157)

The growth special to this epoch is that of technology; and this growth is not a natural growth, with an in-built temporality and a relation to the temporalities embodied in other processes, human and non-human. This failure of a relation between technology and time makes it difficult to think about the impact of technical relations on the institutions and practices within which human beings live in anything other than an external way. This obstructs the attempt to construct an ethics encompassing the effects of technology in the world and on human beings. Only by opening out the relation between time, temporality and technology will it become possible to set out a relation between human beings, technology and the context in which technology takes place. The first step in doing this is to refuse the distinction between scientific conceptions of time as only a matter of measurement and historical conceptions of time as having human proportions. These two disjointed conceptions of time must be thought together in their interconnecting inadequacy, if a notion of freedom, in advance of a distinction between freedom and determinism, between history and nature, is to be thought. This notion of freedom is central to *Being and Time*.

Chapter 6

Being and Time

What then is time? If no one asks me, I know: if I wish to explain it to one that asketh, I know not: yet I say boldly that I know, that if nothing passed away, time past were not, and if nothing were coming, a time to come were not; and if nothing were, time present were not.

Heidegger's *Being and Time* begins not once, but at least twice and possibly three, or even four times. This indeterminacy is matched by its incompleteness. Only the first two sections of a projected six-section volume were published; and the second of these is uneven and appears hastily put together. In subsequent writings, Heidegger repeatedly returns to the question of the incompleteness of *Being and Time*, both implicitly and explicitly, most famously in the claim in the postwar 'Letter on humanism', mentioned in Chapter 1, that he could not find a form of language in which to express the turn from *Dasein*, determinate being, to *Sein*, being unqualified. In his discussions of Hölderlin, Heidegger distinguishes between a starting point, identifiable as the first words of the discussion, and a beginning, *Anfang*, the point from which an ordered exposition becomes possible. This distinction makes possible the claim that *Being and Time* has a single starting point but many beginnings, one for each of the different expositions under way in it. There is the questioning of being; there is the thought of the forgetting of being; there is the analysis of *Dasein*; there is the proposed destruction of the history of ontology; there is the alternative history of philosophy projected for the unpublished last three sections. These were to have given a reading of the history of philosophy, through the thought of Kant, Descartes and Aristotle. Because *Being and Time* was published incomplete, it is unclear how these readings were to have connected back to the substantive enquiry. It is unclear how the history of philosophy connects to the analysis of *Dasein* and how the analysis of *Dasein* connects to the questioning of being.

Heidegger's *Being and Time* prompts the response of forceful interpretation. I suggest that the enquiry in *Being and Time* is systematically ambiguous between a philosophical, indeed metaphysical project of construction, with the aim of providing an answer to the question of being, which is not completed; and an open-ended process of thinking through the implications of being human, starting out from the estranging conception of determinate existence, *Dasein*. This process is open-ended not just because each individual human life while lived is incomplete, because still open towards the future. It is open-ended because the complex structure of temporality makes impossible a simultaneous revelation of all the conditions of possibility for reflection on such a state of existence. Heidegger explores these restrictions through the relation between ontical and ontological levels of enquiry, the ontological level capturing the general conditions, pertaining to all instances of *Dasein*, but without existential commitment to actual existence; the ontical pertaining to the existence of specific individuals in particular contexts. The temporal structures of the ontical and the ontological are different and this makes it impossible to think them simultaneously and separately at the same time. Heidegger's fundamental ontology reveals against his own expectation that general analysis must be grounded in the specificity of actual ontical existence. This claim is put in the interrogative mode in the final pages of *Being and Time*: 'can one provide ontological grounds for ontology, or does it also require an ontical foundation?' (*SZ*: 436). If the ontological grounds themselves require an ontical foundation then the analysis is grounded in the temporality of ontical *Dasein*, not in being, understood as time. Ontological enquiry appears to be neutral between instances of *Dasein*; ontical enquiry makes evident that the enquirer occupies a particular place and is not genuinely indifferent between options. Thus ontological enquiry pursued without addressing the particularity of ontical enquiry is self-deluding. Fundamental ontology is that form of ontological enquiry which reveals the irreducibility of the particular nature of the relation between the enquirer and their own existence. Fundamental ontology is that form of ontology which makes clear its founding in the particularity of the existence of specific instances of *Dasein*.

The epigraph to *Being and Time* is a quotation from Plato's *Sophist*:

> For clearly you have long been familiar with what you yourselves intend, when you use the expression 'subsisting' [*seiend*]; we however once believed ourselves to understand it, but are now in difficulty.

By substituting the term 'time' for the term '*seiend*' in this opening quotation, there results a remark very like the epigraph for this chapter which is taken from Augustine's *Confessions*. The relation between this quotation from the *Sophist* about being and its rewriting by Augustine, in terms of time, reveals *Being and Time* to be a response to an already existing dialogue between Greek philosophy and Christianity. This is one very important strand in the enquiry in *Being and Time*: the conception of philosophical enquiry as dialogue with previous philosophers, already in dialogue with each other. The absence of the projected last three sections addressing representatives of the philosophical tradition leaves this dialogue half articulated. The choice of these two authorities, Plato and Augustine, marks the grounding of philosophy, for Heidegger anyway, in at least two traditions: the Greco-pagan tradition, culminating in the writings of Hölderlin and Nietzsche; and the Neo platonic Christian tradition, embodied in Augustine, but continuing through the writings of Descartes, Kant and Hegel into the twentieth century. However, *Being and Time* marks a break between philosophy and theology, not by ignoring the theological inheritance, as in positivism, but by examining in detail the impact of theology on European self-understanding. There are two key presumptions which are transferred uncritically from theology into some twentieth-century philosophy: that enquiry is completable, the objects of enquiry being of such a kind that enquiry about them can be completed; and that there is objective meaning in the world in advance of enquiry. *Being and Time* disrupts both presumptions. For Heidegger not just values but facts, too, are constructed through the structure of being in the world, which is characteristic of *Dasein*. Thus without the entity for which being is an issue, there are no facts.

In *Being and Time*, Heidegger identifies Descartes as retaining elements from medieval philosophy. This both disrupts the customary reading of Descartes as breaking with tradition and provides a link back through that tradition to a Greek origin for philosophical questioning. In his reading of the history of philosophy, Heidegger proposes to reveal a hidden transmission underlying the overtly identifiable tradition, usually set out as consisting in three distinct phases: the Greek, the Christian and the modern. For Heidegger, by contrast, there is a single process: the forgetting of being, which makes the triumph of technological relations possible. Heidegger proposes to reveal this through his destruction of the history of ontology. This destruction is to return philosophy to a genuine philosophical questioning supposedly invented by the Greeks, but which has to be continually reinvented, by returning to its point of inception. Heidegger seeks to go back through medieval scholasticism, on which he wrote his first doctoral dissertation, through the connection between Christian and Greek thinking, as set out in Augustine, to an original questioning which, at this stage, he supposes to be discoverable in the writings of Plato. It is for this reason that Heidegger begins the enquiry in *Being and Time* with a quotation from Plato's *Sophist*. The enquiry that follows will have succeeded if it returns the reader to that point of departure. Since the enquiry in *Being and Time* does not accomplish this return, this point of departure does not come into view. The question is whether it is possible all the same to identify a point of departure for philosophical questioning, independently of any relation to a Greek inception of philosophy.

The importance for Heidegger of retrieving the Greek inception of philosophy is repeated in his notion that technology has emerged inevitably out of a distinctly European history. There is, however, no conclusive argument in favour of tracing a connection between European history and the spread of technology; there is no necessary connection between these two and some supposed moment of constitution in which, with the inception of philosophy and the forgetting of being understood as a single event, Europe emerges as Europe. The irreversible historical event of the emergence of Europe as Europe seems to be conflated by Heidegger with the ontological event of the repeated self-presentation and erasure of ontological difference. There is a failure here to mark the difference between the irreversible temporality of historical processes and the cyclical temporality of repetition characteristic of ontology. This conflates historical and ontological priority. In opposition to this claim, it is possible to suppose that technology happens to have found conditions conducive for its emergence in Europe, in part as a result of the prevalence of a certain mode of thinking abstractly about the nature of entities, which may be conditional on the cultivation of habits of thought characteristic of the Christian tradition, but must not be assumed to be necessarily connected to that tradition, as Heidegger seems to do. It is possible to suppose that this mode of thinking has been found elsewhere in the world and that technology might have emerged in some other historical-geographical location. This makes it possible to say that to arrive at its point of departure, the enquiry in *Being and Time* does not have to return to a Greek origin. It does not have to hypothesise a single trajectory, called European history, in which the emergence of technology out of philosophy plays a dominant role. Thus it is possible for the enquiry to have returned philosophy to a genuine questioning even though it fails to get back to some point at which Heidegger supposes philosophical questioning first became possible among the Greeks.

This line of argument disrupts Heidegger's claim that philosophy is contained within a particular history, marking the distinctness of Europe. It disrupts the role of Germany within that particular history and undercuts the temptation to endorse Nazism. It becomes possible to distinguish between a point at which a forgetting of being begins and a point at which philosophy takes place. The forgetting of being is the forgetting of the difference between those entities for which being is and those for which being is not an issue. This makes metaphysical construction possible and leads to the emergence of technology. The point at which philosophy begins is the moment of puzzlement, indicated in the quotation from the *Sophist*, where what once was clear becomes confusing. While both take place at the site which Heidegger calls *Dasein*, they are separable. Thus, the point of departure for enquiry in *Being and Time* is neither the quotation from the *Sophist* nor its rewriting by Augustine; neither Heidegger's responses to Aquinas and to Husserl nor his appropriations of phenomenology and classical philosophy. The point of departure is *Dasein*, determinate being, a site at which enquiry can either affirm puzzlement, as ethical specificity, or move into metaphysical generality, in which mode being must necessarily get forgotten. Forgetting being then becomes equivalent to an erasure of ethics, understood as an erasure of the specificity of *Dasein* and a consequent forgetting of being. Heidegger reinterprets the question of being as the question of the meaning of being; for the question can have meaning only for an entity with the structure of *Dasein*. Only for such an entity can the question of being and its forgetting even arise; thus the questioning pertains to the *ethos* of entities with the structure characteristic of *Dasein*. However, from this point of departure there can be no predictable goal of enquiry. Thus, while there is a beginning to *Being and Time*, there is no conclusion. It ends with a repetition of the initial questions: what is the meaning of being? Is time the horizon for being? There is here a distinction between a point of departure for philosophical construction and a point of departure for thinking. Thus the distinction between thinking and philosophy, which Heidegger develops much later, helps in diagnosing what is going on in *Being and Time*. The term 'thinking' can be used to reveal the unthought of the enquiry, the impossibility of completing a phenomenological reduction of tradition. The point of departure for thinking in *Being and Time* is *Dasein*; there is no point of departure for philosophical construction, because the sources for that construction cannot be completely retrieved. The elements making up the tradition out of which philosophy emerges cannot be detached from their embedding in the particular histories and brought together into a moment of new beginning. Thus there is in *Being and Time* a failure to move on from a dialogue within a tradition to pure philosophical construction.

As discussed in previous chapters, at times this dialogue ceases to be one between Heidegger and other philosophers, turning into a dialogue between Heidegger and his own writings. There is a temptation to see this interiorised dialogue conducted by Heidegger with his own writings as an attempt to break with a residual humanistic metaphysic of subjectivity in those writings. However, I suggest this dialogue is as much an engagement with the humanist, subjectivist readings to which *Being and Time* was subjected on publication and which Heidegger from the start identified as mistaken. As Robert Bernasconi points out his *Heidegger in Question: The Art of Existing*,[1] already in *The Metaphysical Foundations of Logic*[2] Heidegger seeks to correct humanist, subjectivising readings of *Being and Time* with twelve principles of interpretation. There he speaks of: 'this metaphysics of *Dasein*' (*MFL*: 139). The first principle runs: 'The term "human being" was not used for that being which is the theme of the analysis. Instead, the neutral term *Dasein* was chosen. By this we designate the being for which its own proper mode of being in a definite sense is not indifferent' (*MFL*: 136). The critique that the enquiries in *Being and Time* are decisionist, voluntarist and fatalist presupposes a humanist, subjectivist reading; and the criticisms are best taken together. They all fail to take into account Heidegger's questioning of the Cartesian break, through which Heidegger displaces the modern assumption that the starting point for enquiry is the thinking of an individual human being, a *res cogitans*. Importantly, the starting point for enquiry for Heidegger in *Being and Time* is not a Cartesian *ego cogitans*, but the stance of the disowned 'anybody', *das Man*, which is the stance of everyday *Dasein*. It is the everyday 'anybody' which supposes it knows what it means by the term '*seiend*'. The 'anybody' cannot itself give rise to the accusations of decisionism, voluntarism and fatalism. It is Heidegger's account of the emergence of identity out of this 'anybody' which gives rise to these criticisms.

This chapter explores three aspects of the text *Being and Time*: its inconclusiveness; its hesitant beginning; and the effect of the break between the two published sections. I shall read the themes of guilt, the call of conscience, wanting to have self-awareness (*Gewissen haben wollen*), fallenness, death and care as elements of an ethical enquiry in *Being and Time*, which is acknowledged as such neither by Heidegger nor by his readers. For Heidegger, the problem is his restricted notion of ethics. For his readers, the problem is a reluctance to accept the importance for Heidegger of the Christian tradition and of the concepts and terms which Heidegger derives from it. Heidegger's thinking is heterogeneous; it is sited midway between Greek philosophy and Christian meditation. Aversion to the Christian tradition prevents readers from seeing that just as there is an acceptance beneath the rejection of Platonic philosophy, so there is a rejection underlying the acceptance of insights drawn from Augustine, Aquinas, Eckhart and Luther. The unthought of Heidegger's thinking is its inextricable involvement in the Christian tradition. Since this is also the unthought of Western philosophy, Heidegger's work is both central to developing an understanding of that tradition, and wholly inaccessible to those who cannot accept the need for an encounter with that Christian heritage in philosophy. This unthought also blocks the way to affirming the enquiry in *Being and Time* as an ethical enquiry, which would open up an exploration of the impact on Western thinking of the Christian tradition. Heidegger's disruption of the subjectivism of Descartes' *res cogitans* makes possible a questioning of a connection between freedom, history and nature, as set out in the previous chapter. It permits him to reveal a relation between modern thinking, with its positing of subjectivity as its point of departure, and scientific advances. However, since that questioning reveals a connection back to the preceding theological model of human beings as the bearer of divine reason, it does not erase but rather reveals the impact of Christianity on philosophy. The modern notions of freedom, history and nature may be indelibly marked by the Christian tradition.

Heidegger responds thus to his own opening quotation:

> Have we today an answer to the question concerning what we ourselves intend with the word '*seiend*' [subsisting]? No way. It is suitable then to pose anew the question concerning the meaning of being [*Sein*]. Are we then today also simply in the difficulty of not understanding the expression '*Sein*' [being]? No way. And so it is suitable in advance of this question, first of all to awaken an understanding for the meaning of this question. A concrete elaboration of the question concerning the meaning of '*Sein*' [being] is the intent of the following treatise. The provisional aim is the interpretation of time as the possible horizon for an understanding of being [*des Seinsverständnisses*] of this kind. (*SZ*: 1)

Not only then is there no answer to the question of the meaning of the terms 'being' and 'subsisting'. There is not even a sense of the significance of the question of being. Thus Heidegger proposes to begin by reawakening a sense of its importance. Questioning being, then, is postponed in favour of setting out why the question of being should matter. Heidegger adds: 'Having such an aim, the enquiries which connect up to such a presumption and which are required by it, and the path to this aim, are in need of an introductory sounding out.' With this the preface ends, and the introduction proper begins. Here, there is already an ambivalence between the aim of elaborating the meaning of being, the provisional aim of interpreting time as the possible horizon for an understanding of being and this introductory sounding out of the significance of the question of being. The introductory sounding out, I suggest, is the analysis of *Dasein*. The provisional aim of interpreting time as the horizon for an understanding of being is the upshot of the analysis of *Dasein*; and the elaboration of the meaning of being is the exposition of the problematic of temporality, which Heidegger supposes will result in some kind of answer to the question of being: 'In the exposition of the problematic of temporality, there is for the first time a concrete answer to the question of the meaning of being' (*SZ*: 19). However, Heidegger does not complete this exposition; and the relation between being and time remains unclear. Thus he does not give his supposed answer to the question of the meaning of being. This ambivalence is mirrored by the shift from questioning being to questioning the meaning of being to raising the question of the meaning of 'being'. There are then three versions of the central aim of the treatise and three possible lines of questioning. The incompleteness of *Being and Time* leaves it open what the relation between these aims and lines of questioning might be.

The response to the opening quotation introduces three important themes: a relation between an everyday 'we' and a philosophical 'we'; a relation between familiarity and strangeness; and a relation between subsisting, '*seiend*', and being, *Sein*, which later becomes known as the ontological difference. These three are interlocking. In the gap which opens up between the everyday and the philosophical 'we', Heidegger develops a discussion of the individuation of human beings. He transposes that 'we' into a disowned 'anybody', arguing that this is the mode in which for the most part human beings interact. He then analyses *Dasein* as the site at which there occurs a process of self-constitution, through a process of self-affirming individuation, culminating in the affirmation of *Selbstsein*, being oneself. The incompleteness of the analysis developed in *Being and Time* demonstrates the enormous problems which such a project of self-constitution must encounter. This incompleteness enacts the open-endedness of any project of self-affirmation based on an individual's existence, which, once that existence is cut loose from theological groundings in doctrines of eternal life, must be cut short by death and cannot be thought of as coming to fulfilment and completion at that ending point. The alternative project of self-affirmation in a community is one which has become historically and politically enmeshed in the questions of the place of Europe in the world and of the place of Nazism in Heidegger's thought. Endorsing Hitler is the kind of answer to the question of identity which suggests that the question is best left open. There is a hiatus here between the puzzlement prompted by the absence of theological and meta-physical answers to the question of identity and the babel of political, pragmatic answers. The metaphysical violence of running up against the limits of possibility of sustaining identity is to be distinguished from the political violence of imposed stability. If this metaphysical delimitation of identity were better understood, there would be less desire for an imposed political solution to the problem of unstable identity.

The relation between the familiar and the strange connects up to a relation between the near and the far, which in turn connects to Heidegger's invocation of the pre-ontologically given, but ontologically obscure. Heidegger writes: 'Ontically, of course, *Dasein* is not only close to us – even that which is closest: we are it, each of us, we ourselves. In spite of this, or rather for just this reason, it is ontologically that which is most distant' (*SZ*: 15), a thought which he repeats much later in the enquiry in the following terms: 'The entity which we ourselves are is ontologically the most distant' (*SZ*: 311). This questioning of the near and far, the familiar and the strange culminates in the discussions of anxiety and uncanniness, through which the limited nature of human existence presents itself to human beings. This relation between familiarity and strangeness also plays itself out in the ontological difference, between *Seiendes*, what there is, and *Sein*, that there is anything at all. 'Ontological difference' is mentioned in *Being and Time*, but not explicitly as a term for the difference between entities and being: 'In the first instance it is sufficient to note the ontological difference [*den ontologischen Unterschied*] between being-in as an existential and the internality of the present at hand as a category' (*SZ*: 56). This version of the difference distinguishes between the kind of entity for which being is an issue and those kinds of entity for which it is not; it is marked by the use of the term 'existentials' for the structures characteristic of entities for which being is an issue and the term 'categories' for other kinds of entity. Heidegger introduces ontological difference in the opening pages of *Basic Problems of Phenomenology* in a different way:[3]

> We must be able to bring out clearly the difference between being and beings in order to make something like being the theme for enquiry. This distinction is not arbitrary; rather it is the one by which the theme of ontology and thus of philosophy itself is first of all attained. It is a distinction which is first and foremost constitutive for ontology. We call it the ontological difference – the differentiation between being and beings. Only by making the distinction – *krinein* in Greek – not between one being and another being but between being and beings do we first enter the field of philosophical research. (*BPP*: 17)

In this insistence on the importance of marking distinctions and differences, Heidegger constructs a connection from his version of phenomenology to Kant's critical philosophy.

In a recently published essay, given as a lecture in 1989, Friedrich Wilhelm von Herrmann writes: 'When the manuscript of *Being and Time* was originally delivered to the printer on April 1, 1926, it included the text for division 3 of part 1, entitled "Time and Being". As Heidegger was reading proof for the book, he realised that this last and most important section of the book was not worked out as well as it needed to be. Thus, in early January 1927, he withdrew that portion of the text.'[4] Von Herrmann then points out that the lecture series of that summer semester, published as *Basic Problems of Phenomenology*, was explicitly intended as a reworking of that withheld 'division 3'. These lectures include a long discussion of the temporality of *Dasein*, with which the published version of *Being and Time* breaks off. However, the lectures, like *Being and Time*, diverge from the outline of contents given at the start and present only a part of the proposed investigation. The lectures conclude with a reference to Kant's now well-known essay, 'On an apocalyptic tone recently adopted in philosophy', in which Kant cites Plato's seventh letter and discusses the mistake of supposing it possible to look directly into the sun and thereby to gain knowledge of things as they are in themselves.[5] The attempt to acquire direct knowledge of things-in-themselves has the same structure as attempting to analyse and define being directly. Again there is a loop back here from Heidegger via Kant to Plato, indicating in outline Heidegger's approach to the history of philosophy. However, any attempt to engage with the non-completion of *Being and Time* in these lectures simply repeats the problem already identifiable in *Being and Time*, adding a second problem of incompleteness to the first. The focus for the next section is not the lectures contemporaneous with *Being and Time*, but the relation between familiarity and strangeness in the analysis of *Dasein*.

DISQUOTATIONAL METAPHYSICS[6]

In the same paragraph of *Being and Time* where the reference to 'ontological difference' is to be found, Heidegger draws a distinction between ontological and metaphysical concerns, with 'metaphysics' in quotation marks:

> Not until we understand being-in-the world as an essential structure of *Dasein* can we have any insight into *Dasein*'s existential spatiality. Such an insight will keep us from failing to see this structure or from previously cancelling it out – a procedure motivated not ontologically but rather 'metaphysically' by the naive supposition that human beings are, in the first instance, something spiritual which is subsequently misplaced into a space. (*SZ*: 56)

This approach conceals the different relations to time and to space which hold for *Dasein* by contrast to those which hold for other kinds of entity. Considering human beings as a certain kind of entity, that is considering human beings 'metaphysically', results in a failure to notice the relation between human beings and being, and a failure to identify the differences between those entities for which being is and those for which being is not an issue. Ontology by contrast is concerned with differences between distinct kinds of entity, in their relation to being. The difference between ontology and 'metaphysics' is that ontology addresses entities in their relation to being, whereas 'metaphysics' fails to identify this relation and erases ontological difference. 'Metaphysics' thus presents an account of the nature of entities as though that were a response to the question of being, without that question actually being posed. Metaphysics, by contrast, can take one of two forms. As ontology, it opens up the question of being; as 'metaphysics', it substitutes an enquiry about the nature of entities for a questioning of being. However, this distinction between ontology and 'metaphysics' is not entirely clear in *Being and Time* because at the time of writing Heidegger supposes that he will give an answer to the question of being in *Being and Time*.

Both ontology and 'metaphysics' are addressed by the question of being; the incompleteness of *Being and Time* opens up the gap between answering and responding to the question.

When, in 1929, Heidegger asks the question: 'What is metaphysics?', he claims: 'metaphysics is the occurrence of grounding in *Dasein*, it is *Dasein* itself [*Die Metaphysik ist das Grundgeschehen im Dasein. Sie ist das Dasein selbst*]' (*WM*: 120). This grounding, he goes on to explain, is a grounding in an abyss [*diesem abgründigen Grunde*]. Thus, at this juncture, Heidegger is trying to retrieve a disquotational use of the term 'metaphysics' from the ontological reduction taking place in the history of philosophy. The use of the term with quotation marks, by contrast, indicates Heidegger's critique of the tendency within metaphysics to ignore the abyss, to suppose it possible to go beyond the domain of entities, on the basis of a firm foundation, and give a systematic account of what there is. In *Being and Time* Heidegger seeks to return to the inception of metaphysics in order to retrieve what goes missing in the reduction of metaphysics to 'metaphysics'. However, the retrieval of metaphysics requires a retrieval of ethics, to which Heidegger only implicitly addresses himself. Ethics then would be the event of *Dasein*, revealed as a relation to being. It is an event, which opens out possibilities, rather than an occurrence, which presents what there is. This event is the moment in which ontological enquiry is revealed as ontically grounded, in which *Dasein* can own itself in owning its own limitations. In so doing, the enquiry reveals the difference between determinate being and being as such. 'Ethics' is that form of reflection on human activity which supposes that the question of the metaphysical status of human beings can be settled first, in advance of turning to the traditional ethical questions of action, responsibility, evaluation and judgement. There are thus at least two questions of ethics, as there are at least two questions of metaphysics: one which does and one which does not mark the ontological difference; one which does and one which does not bring into question the separability of metaphysical from ethical questioning. This inseparability, which entails the irreducibility of tradition and of historical context, makes the turn from preparatory analysis to philosophical construction impossible. This thought becomes available only when the non-Heideggerian question is posed: what is ethics? This question asks not for an answer but for a response, in the form of a provisional elaboration of its meaning. The entity for which the question arises cannot be fully taken up in the ensuing analysis. There is a pre-theoretical residue which remains concealed.

Already in the first three pages of *Being and Time*, there is a demonstration of the problem of producing an adequate specification of just what the issue under discussion might be. There is a marked contrast between two styles of enquiry. The meditation on a chosen quotation given in the opening remark simply jumps off from the attempt to translate the Greek of Plato and neatly locates three of the central concerns of the following enquiry. The introduction which follows has difficulty in getting under way. The first meditative response to the problem of translation is much more in line with the tone of Heidegger's postwar publications.

The solemnness and heaviness of the prose style of the following introduction is more characteristic of the enquiry which then follows. Thus, in the first few pages of *Being and Time*, there are two distinct styles of enquiry, one hesitant and one overelaborate; there are at least two distinct enquiries, a dialogue with Plato and a systematic enquiry into the forgetting of being. Within each of these, there are divergent lines of enquiry with a multiplication of questions of being. The introduction opens with no less than three headings: a title for the introduction overall; a title for the first chapter of that introduction; and a subheading for the first section of that first chapter. In each there is mention of a question: the first runs: 'The exposition of the question concerning the meaning of being'; the second: 'Necessity, structure and priority of the question of being [*Seinsfrage*]; and the third: 'The necessity of an explicit retrieval [*Wiederholung*] of the question concerning being'. There are here not one but three distinct questions: the question concerning the meaning of being; the question of being; and the question concerning being. These three questions are systematically linked up in some way, but the incompleteness of *Being and Time* makes it difficult to determine those linkages. These diverging statements of the nature of the question conflict with the forthright first line of the introduction to *Being and Time*, in which these three are presumed to constitute just one question: 'The above question is today fallen into forgetfulness, even though our time counts itself as progressive, since it again affirms "metaphysics"' (*SZ*: 2). Here Heidegger introduces two key themes: the forgetting of the question of being and the suspect status of 'metaphysics'.

The question 'where does *Being and Time* begin?' is matched by the question 'where does the forgetting of being begin?' to which one answer is: at the beginning of philosophy. So there are three beginnings in question: the beginning of *Being and Time*; the beginning of philosophy; and the beginning of the forgetting of being. The point of departure at which Heidegger hoped to arrive is the one at which these three coincide. However, the uneasiness of tone and style suggests an awareness of the problem identified in the 'Letter on humanism' of finding a language sufficient for articulating this. In *Being and Time* itself, there is a remark which can be taken as a comment on the difficulties Heidegger's enquiry encounters: 'Someone who is genuinely on the track of something doesn't talk about it' (*SZ*: 173). They presumably just get on with tracking it. Only when this tracking runs into difficulties of some kind, does it become necessary to cast around for an explanation of these difficulties and for a description of where the track was supposed to be leading. Heidegger continually insists that enquiry can only achieve a clarification of what the enquirer already knows in pre-ontological understanding. Thus there is in *Being and Time* both an appearance of making progress in philosophy, acquiring new understanding, and this conflicting claim that no such achievement is possible. There is instead a retrieval of something previously known but forgotten. Philosophical enquiry can then provide clarification of why puzzlement arose; but it cannot eradicate puzzlement.

Enquiry starts where a practice ceases to work and where there is a problem finding resources in language and thought to address this breakdown. This is the moment at which the everyday givenness of things opens out into a problem or paradox; where the everyday reveals an uncanniness, a strangeness at the heart of the familiar. The primary context is one in which practices and languages are sufficient for the purposes of those engaged in them and can thus be taken for granted. Philosophical enquiry is a secondary phenomenon, arising as a consequence of running up against a limiting constraint within a particular language or practice. Thus thinking has already begun when philosophy begins. For Heidegger, in *Being and Time*, philosophical problems lie in what is most taken for granted. Central to the text is a process of problematising the familiar in order to reveal philosophical problems emerging out of what is familiar. However, the focus of attention must be not the familiar made strange but the familiar not yet made strange. The problem is that analysis immediately makes the familiar strange. Thus there is an oscillation between the familiar and the strange in the insistence that the focus for analysis in *Being and Time* are the states in which human beings are for the most part to be found, in which we customarily find ourselves. By calling this focus '*Dasein*' and subjecting it to analysis this structure becomes strange and unfamiliar; but it is not some occult structure, located in some other region. *Dasein* is the familiar structure of human experience, which is for the most part taken for granted and which therefore becomes strange once it is put in question.

There is a parallel between analysing *Dasein* and analysing language, and a shared relation to temporality. Understanding language requires a grasp of the simultaneous interdependency of meanings and of its necessary articulation through time. This ambiguous temporality is characteristic of the structure of *Dasein* and of human experience. When using language it is possible to take for granted an understanding of language and time, and of the connection between them, which on inspection turns out to be inexplicable. It works without a 'why'. In his use of language in the analysis of *Dasein*, however, Heidegger puts intensive pressure on existing meanings, which points up the arbitrariness and precariousness of meaning, of our grasp on meaning and of the grasp of meaning on us. He develops his analysis through the device of introducing new words into the language, by nominalising verbs and adverbs and by turning nouns into verbs. Central to *Being and Time* is the use of adverbial phrases to mark shifts in the focus of enquiry: *Dasein, Insein, Mitsein, Zusein; sich-vorweg, schon-sein-in, sein-bei*. Thus, in the very language used, there is at work a process of rendering the familiar strange. It is then unfortunate that Heidegger does not make a connection between familiarity, strangeness and the nature of language. He does not make explicit the relation between fallen, taken-for-granted forms of language and revealed, authentic forms of language, even though he has the contrast between *Gerede*, language as spoken, and *Rede*, a pure order of discourse. Nor does he make a connection from this distinction to the distinction of the later writings between *Denken* and *Dichten*. The use of language in *Being and Time* is more like the language use of *Dichten* than like that of customary philosophical analysis. This subverts claims that only later in his enquiries does language become an issue for Heidegger. Instead of respecting the given meanings of language and inventing technical terms to express previously unidentified features, Heidegger twists meanings into proximity with the thought he is trying to articulate. This parallels his interpretative practice discussed in previous chapters. For those expecting direct propositional communication, the use of language in *Being and Time* is an unpleasant shock.

By interrogating the meaning of the term '*seiend*' it becomes possible for Heidegger to distinguish systematically between a question about being and a question about the nature of particular kinds of entity. Understanding the significance of the expression '*seiend*' is made more difficult by a forgetting of the question of being, which in turn elides the fact that there is a question about the meaning and significance of being at all. This understanding is blocked by the erasure of ontological difference, the relation between being and that for which there is a question about being, *Dasein*. The failure to identify these questions, their forgetting and erasure are for Heidegger characteristic of 'metaphysical' enquiry. According to Heidegger, this failure is built into the philosophical tradition and makes necessary the destruction of the history of ontology, announced in the introduction to *Being and Time*. This destruction is preparatory to an equally important retrieval of the truth of tradition as transmission, *Überlieferung*, which is to make possible a repetition or retrieval, *Wiederholung*, of the inception of philosophy. One major problem left unresolved at the end of *Being and Time* is the status of this history of philosophy constructed through the double movement of destroying a rigidified tradition of interpretation and releasing a more primordial process of enquiry concealed within that tradition. The problem is whether there is one true reading of the history of philosophy or whether there are as many readings as there are circumstances in which readings of that tradition are possible. This problem displaces the question of being and its forgetting from the centre of concern in favour of the theme chosen as the means of access to it, the analysis of *Dasein*. Distinguishing between a question about a single inception of philosophy with an irreversible history and a question about a recurrent point of departure for philosophical enquiry makes it possible to separate the analysis of *Dasein* from the aim of retrieving and completing the history of philosophy in a new beginning. The question of being and its forgetting are the stated themes for the enquiry in *Being and Time*; but it is not just the question of being which is forgotten.

The structure of *Dasein* is also marked by forgetting; and in the dynamic at work between a forgetting, as repetition, of one's own specificity and the retrieval, as destruction, of a primordial structure, there is a trace of Nietzschean thinking. For Heidegger, the forgetting of being at the beginning of the history of philosophy is displaced by the forgetting by entities with the structure of *Dasein* of their specificity. In the third starting point of *Being and Time*, the start of the first division, there is the following discussion of *Dasein*:

Dasein's average everydayness, however, is not to be taken as a mere 'aspect'. Here, too, and even in the mode of inauthenticity, the structure of existentiality lies *a priori*. And here too *Dasein*'s being is an issue for it in a definite way; *Dasein* comports itself towards it in the mode of average everydayness, even if this is only the mode of fleeing in the face of it and forgetting of itself. (*SZ*: 44)

However, this forgetting takes place at a clearly identifiable location: everyday human experience. Heidegger claims explicitly that the questioning of being must start with *Dasein* because of its dual ontical and ontological status: '*Dasein* is ontically distinctive in that it is ontological' (*SZ*: 12); but it is as important that *Dasein* is marked both by this provisional understanding of being, given to it pre-ontologically – that is, in advance of enquiry – and, most importantly, by this structure of forgetting its own and, concomitantly, being's distinctiveness. While Heidegger supposes a primordial understanding of being to be evident in the first moves of philosophical questioning, at the beginning of the tradition, it is also given in advance to human beings in a pre-ontological, pre-theoretical understanding. Indeed: 'Understanding of being is itself a definite characteristic of *Dasein*'s being' (*SZ*: 12). However, we lose access to this understanding by taking on dominant distorting ways of thinking, by interpreting ourselves not in terms of our relation to and understanding of being but by analogy with those entities in the world which do not have this access: 'The kind of being which belongs to *Dasein* is rather such that, in understanding its own being, it has a tendency to do so in terms of that entity towards which it comports itself proximally and in a way which is essentially constant – in terms of the "world"' (*SZ*: 15). All the same, any theorising of entities involves a reference back to *Dasein*, as that entity which is endowed with the capacity for such theorising:

> Thus *Dasein*'s understanding of being pertains with equal primordiality [*gleichursprünglich*] both to an understanding of something like a 'world', and to the understanding of the being of those entities which become accessible within a world. So whenever an ontology takes for its theme entities whose mode of being is other than that of *Dasein*, it has its own foundation and motivation in *Dasein*'s own ontical structure, in which a pre-ontological understanding of being is comprised as a definite characteristic. (*SZ*: 13).

This is sometimes taken to mean that the analysis of *Dasein* provides a determinate foundation for all enquiry. However, fundamental ontology can be thought to be foundational in this way only if the nuance and paradoxes of Heidegger's exposition of it are left out of account. This is a founding only in the sense that each enquirer must ground themselves, through a confrontation with finitude.

Heidegger indicates the importance of the everyday: 'Everydayness is all the same being "between" birth and death' (*SZ*: 233). This everydayness has a triple structure. It is the structure in which conditions of possibility are just taken for granted and function unremarked. Thus everydayness reveals itself as the opposite of the disruptions of common sense brought about by philosophical analysis. However, it is also the structure within which those conditions can be revealed, thus distorting that everydayness into a state of unfamiliarity and uncanniness. Everydayness is the domain in which, as a matter of course, there is experience of the uncanny, of anxiety and of ecstasy. Thus there are distinctions to be drawn between a naive everyday, understood as unproblematic and not in need of clarification, an everyday in which the uncanny experienced as anxiety takes place and an everyday rendered strange by being subjected to analysis. There is also a sophisticated reconstruction of the everyday, containing all three of these and the associated aporias and paradoxes of attempting to think these together. There is a hypothetical everyday, constructed by theorists who want to pretend that how the everyday seems, its seamless simplicity, is indeed all there is to it. This hypothetical everyday enacts the gesture of denying bivalence and reducing difference. It blocks the thought that the everyday both is and is not a simple structure; that the everyday both is and is not aporetic and paradoxical. This switching of places between strange and familiar, near and far, first and last is a recurrent feature of Heidegger's thinking and writing. The discussion in *Being and Time* of the submersion of individuality in an anonymous 'anybody' can then be shown to recapitulate these moves. This submersion is a precondition for an individual emerging with any individuality at all, since only by passing through engagement in practices constituted by others is it possible to acquire language; an inherited set of practices is a precondition for having a sense of what the possibilities for human existence are.

Heidegger shows that the possibility of seeking to constitute oneself as an autonomous 'I' is conditional on the existence of the 'anybody', on coming to terms with what that 'anybody' entails. The project of self-constitution emerging out of immersion in the 'anybody' connects closely to two other strands in *Being and Time*: an analysis of truth and an account of temporality. *Dasein* denotes this structure of everyday human experience, but in the course of analysis the every-day is revealed as grounded in the wholly unfamiliar structures of ecstatic temporality. Indeed, this can be thought of as the promised but unattained conclusion for *Being and Time*: the moment at which it might have become clear that everydayness and ecstatic temporality are one and the same; that they merely appear distinct for those enmeshed in the disjoining forces of natural existence, extended between birth and death. The stretching out of *Dasein* between birth and death tends to be obscured:

> At bottom, even in the ordinary way of taking the 'connectedness of life', one does not think of this as a framework drawn tense 'outside' of *Dasein* and spanning it round, but one rightly seeks this connectedness in *Dasein* itself. When, however, one tacitly regards this entity ontologically as something present-at-hand 'in time', any attempt at an ontological characterisation of the being 'between' birth and death will break down. (*SZ*: 374)

Only as care can *Dasein* take up and affirm this in-between structure: 'As care,

Dasein is the between' (*SZ*: 374). Ordinary understanding elides the difference between presence at hand and the mode of existence of *Dasein*; the complexity of the relation between *Dasein* and time goes missing. The danger, once that complexity has been retrieved, is to suppose that no sense and unity can be found in it. The structure of temporality of *Dasein* is experienced in the fleeting moment of illumination, the *Augenblick* of mystical experience, the religious moment of Kierkegaard's writings and the Aristotelian *kairos*. In this moment *Dasein* acquires the structure of *Entschlossenheit*, the mode of truth in which simultaneously its own structure and the structure of temporality becomes clear to *Dasein*.

Ecstatic temporality and everydayness appear distinct because human beings experience themselves and time as differential, as extension through time, not as single complex structures. The 'metaphysical' temptation is to impose a reduction on this complexity, thus making the singleness of this structure easier to affirm. The 'ethical' temptation is to insist on absolute singularity and isolation. The philosophical imperative is to resist both reductive gestures and to recognise the sameness at work across the distance set up by the separation and separability of time and *Dasein*. The problem with any analysis of the basic structures of human experience is that the enquiry itself takes place within those structures and takes up a specific angle of entry into them. What is to be revealed through analysis is both most immediate and therefore least accessible. In order to reveal those familiar immediate structures, it is necessary to make them appear strange. The very process of revealing these structures in order to describe them transforms them from self-evident immediacy to strange distance. It is thus the intervention of analysis and the desire for explanation which makes the familiar strange. The everyday is transposed into the extraordinary, and the extraordinary efforts of philosophical analysis result only in a return to and clarification of the everyday. *Being and Time* can thus be read not as a failed move from the everyday to some other temporal structure, nor as a failed move from the relatively familiar structures of determinate being to an account of the indeterminacies of being, but as revealing the complexity of the temporal dimensions contained within the everyday and, analogously, as revealing the fullness of being in the existence of determinate being.

THE ANALYSIS OF *DASEIN*

In his analysis of *Dasein*, Heidegger combines three distinct forms of enquiry. There is the phenomenology of Husserl, analysing the connection between thought and its objects through the conception of intentionality. There is the hermeneutics of Schleiermacher and Dilthey, emerging out of the biblical and historical traditions, in which texts and language are analysed as preservers of truth, with the underlying presumption that the order of things and the order of language are two parallel articulations of God's creation. Combining and disrupting these two, Heidegger develops a theory of signification (*Bedeutungslehre*) as 'rooted in the ontology of *Dasein*' (*SZ*: 166), which must resolve the apparent conflict between

the aim of phenomenology to give access to things themselves and the commitment in hermeneutics to the embedding of thought in systems of meaning. These
three come together in the fundamental ontology developed in the first section of
Being and Time. From the hermeneutics of Dilthey and Schleiermacher,
Heidegger takes the notion of meaning as always systematic and historical, while
breaking with the theological presumption about completeness and complet-
ability. From the phenomenology of Husserl, Heidegger takes the notion of
intentionality, of meaning as constituted through a relation between thought as
cognition and thought as that which the thought is about, with a fulfilment of
meaning in the actual existence of the object; but he transforms Husserl's
grounding of intentionality in a transcendental ego and brings into question the
theological commitments of transcendental phenomenology. In *Being and Time*,
Heidegger does not discuss intentionality directly, although there is a reference to
intentionality, in a footnote, as grounded in the ecstatic unity of *Dasein*:

> The thesis that all cognition has 'intuition' as its goal has the temporal
> meaning that all cognition is making present. Whether every science, or every
> philosophical cognition, aims at making present need not be decided here . . .
> This 'temporal' way of describing this phenomenon must have been suggested
> by the analysis of perception and intuition in general in terms of the idea of
> intention. That the intentionality of consciousness is grounded in the ecstatical
> unity of *Dasein* and how this is the case will be shown in the following section.
> (*SZ*: 362)

The ecstatical unity of *Dasein* is its simultaneous relation to past, present and
future and the complex temporal structure (*Zeitlichkeit*) which emerges out of this
simultaneity. While the English translation has 'division' instead of 'section', the
German has '*Abschnitt*', referring thus not to the unpublished discussions of
Kant, Descartes and Aristotle in the second division, but to the unpublished third
section of division one, on time and being.

In the lectures *Basic Problems of Phenomenology*, Heidegger argues that this
intentional structure, in which meaning is grounded, is itself possible only on the
basis of the articulations of temporality. Thus, for Husserl, meaning grounds in
intentionality, intentionality in consciousness, and consciousness in a transcendental ego. For Heidegger, intentionality grounds not in consciousness but in
Dasein, the meaning of which is revealed in the course of *Being and Time* to be
first care, *Sorge*, and then temporality. This ground is immanent in time and
human, not divine and transcendent. Through his appropriation of phenomenology and hermeneutics Heidegger supposes the structure of *Dasein* can be
shown to put on one side sceptical doubts about the existence of the world.
Heidegger writes of Kant's attempted refutation of scepticism:

> The 'scandal of philosophy' is not that this proof has not yet been given, but
> that such proofs are expected and attempted again and again. Such expect-
> ations, aims and demands arise from an ontologically inadequate way of

starting with something of such a character that independently of it and 'outside' of it a 'world' is to be proved as present at hand. If *Dasein* is understood correctly, it defies such proofs because, in its being, it already is what subsequent proofs deem necessary to demonstrate for it. (*SZ*: 205)

Through hermeneutics, Heidegger displaces the understanding of the being of human beings as 'the living creature whose existence is determined by being able to talk' (*SZ*: 25). For Heidegger, human beings do not have language as a capacity added on to a pre-existing structure. Human existence is structured through given meanings and the production of new meanings, in the twin structure of thrownness and projection. Human beings are placed within systems of meaning which are given in advance in the thrownness and historicality of the situation in which human beings find themselves. The structure of meaning within which we find ourselves gives the world and the existence of others to us in advance of any articulation of doubt about their existence.

Heidegger claims that hermeneutics is superior to dialectics: 'As the onto-logical clue is progressively worked out – namely in the 'hermeneutic' of the *logos* – it becomes increasingly possible to grasp the problem of being in a more radical fashion. The 'dialectic', which has been a genuine philosophical embarrassment, becomes superfluous' (*SZ*: 25). Heidegger distances his enquiry from the Hegelian dialectical procedure in the next section, where he discusses the meaning of the term 'phenomenology' and sets aside the Hegelian subordination of a realm of appearances to a superior domain of conceptual completeness. For Heideggerian phenomenology, appearances are appearances of the things themselves. The problem is to have the right angle of approach and to see those appearances clearly, rather than permitting them to remain concealed. However, already in *Being and Time*, there is the image of enquiry as wresting what there is out of the concealment in which it lies hidden:

> The way in which being and its structures are encountered in the mode of the phenomenon is one which must first of all be wrested from the objects of phenomenology. Thus the very point of departure [*Ausgang*] for our analysis requires that it be secured by the proper method, just as much as does our access [*Zugang*] to the phenomenon, or our passage [*Durchgang*] through whatever is prevalently covering it up [*herrschende Verdeckung*]. (*SZ*: 36–7)

This covering up conceals from *Dasein* its own structure and its own basic uncanniness, as the entity which has to give itself meaning and to provide itself with it own grounding, in the absence of any objectively given ground. Heidegger writes of this: 'In the self-evidence and self-certainty of average interpretations, however, there lies concealed the uncanniness of the state of suspension, in which *Dasein*, under the protection of its actual occurrence [*jeweiligen Dasein*] can pursue a mounting loss of groundedness' (*SZ*: 170). This mounting loss of groundedness is the modern condition, in which traditional purposes are eroded and nothing put in their place. Heidegger points out that 'phenomenology' names a method for revealing entities, without any commitment about the nature of the entities to be revealed: 'This expression does not characterize the "what" of the objects of philosophical research as subject-matter, but rather the "how" of that research' (*SZ*: 27). This leaves it open for him to make the following connection between phenomenology and ontology: 'With regard to its subject-matter, phenomenology is the science of the being of entities, ontology' (*SZ*: 37). He then makes a series of connections between these three methodological approaches: 'Phenomenology of *Dasein* is hermeneutics in the original sense of the word, according to which it indicates the activity of interpretation' (*SZ*: 37). To make the connection between phenomenology and ontology clear, he then asserts:

> Ontology and phenomenology are not two different disciplines which among others belong to philosophy. The two titles characterise philosophy itself according to its object and its manner of treating that object. Philosophy is universal phenomenological ontology, starting out from the hermeneutic of *Dasein*, which, as the analytic of existence, makes fast the endpoint of the thread of enquiry to the point at which it emerges and to which it returns.

This, then, backs up the claim that the point of departure for the enquiry in *Being and Time*, to which it is supposed to be going to return, is not some mythical point of origin for philosophical enquiry at the time of the Greeks, but *Dasein*.

In the introduction, Heidegger claims that an understanding of time will give an answer to the question of the meaning of being: 'In the exposition of the problematic of temporality, there is for the first time a concrete answer to the question of the meaning of being' (*SZ*: 17). Heidegger starts by claiming that temporality is the meaning of the being of *Dasein*: 'The meaning of the being of the entity, which we call *Dasein*, is temporality [*Zeitlichkeit*]' (*SZ*: 17). Heidegger then states, but does not explain, that revealing the centrality of temporality to *Dasein* will help demonstrate a connection between being and time: 'The originating explication of time as the horizon for an understanding of being emerges out of temporality, [*Zeitlichkeit*], as the being of *Dasein*, the entity which has an understanding of being' (*SZ*: 17). Thus, the temporality which in the previous quotation is identified as the meaning of the being of *Dasein* is here identified as the being of *Dasein*, suggesting that the meaning of being, *Sinn von Sein*, and being, *Sein*, are, for Heidegger's phenomenological purposes, the same. For Heidegger, only *Dasein* has an understanding of being, and only for *Dasein* is there meaning. Furthermore, only human beings, for Heidegger, can have the characteristics of *Dasein*. Thus there is meaning and an understanding of being only for human beings. Implicitly, there is here an exclusion of other natural kinds participating in *Dasein*. The justifiability of this cannot here be explored. Heidegger distinguishes between the temporality of *Dasein*, *Zeitlichkeit*, and the *Temporalität* of *Sein*, but he does not explain how an understanding of the one leads into an understanding of the other. Nor does he specify the difference between them, although the temporality of being must be unconditioned, whereas the temporality which constitutes the meaning of *Dasein* depends on there being instances of *Dasein*. The surprising move Heidegger makes is to argue that the unconditioned conception is derived from the conditional conception, not the other way around.

Dasein as temporality, *Zeitlichkeit*, is the concealed event of the occurrence of time, on the basis of which an analysis of time and temporality becomes possible. One outcome of this analysis is to be a demonstration of the validity to the ordinary conception of time. Heidegger writes of 'an originary explication of time as the horizon for the understanding of being, out of temporality [*Zeitlichkeit*] as the being of the determinate being which has an understanding of being'. He goes on to claim:

> In the whole of this undertaking there is the challenge of distinguishing this conception of time from the ordinary understanding of time, which has become explicit in an interpretation of time showing how time has been restricted in the traditional concept of time, which has endured from Aristotle down to Bergson. With this it is to be made clear how this concept of time and the ordinary understanding of time emerge out of temporality. This returns a genuine validity to the vulgar conception of time, against the thesis of Bergson that this ordinary conception of supposed time is space. (*SZ*: 18)

Thus Heidegger does not reject what he calls the ordinary conception of time. He specifies the limits within which it is valid. In the concluding pages of the book he claims that this ordinary conception of time emerges in Aristotle's philosophy and that it leads to a 'natural' way of understanding being (*SZ*: 421). This ordinary conception of time represents events and entities as taking place within time. Heidegger seeks to reveal instead how time and temporality are internal to the structures of both *Dasein* and *Sein*. This makes possible the conception of time as that within which events and entities take place, alongside other conceptions of time, the everydayness already discussed and the ecstatic temporality in which identity is affirmed and revealed to instances of *Dasein* in the moment of resolution, *Entschlossenheit*. There are, then, different ways in which these three can be experienced, as exclusive of each other, or as mutually interdependent, if incommensurable. In the second section of *Being and Time*, Heidegger discusses the transformation of ordinary time, as being within time, into notions of measurement, chronology and world history. Being within time is the mode of temporality in which differences between modes of temporality are erased.

The structure of the enquiry which follows on from the introduction splits the analysis of *Dasein* in two: into an analysis of being in the world, entitled 'the preparatory fundamental analysis of *Dasein*', and an analysis of being in time, entitled '*Dasein* and temporality [*Zeitlichkeit*]'. The first part appears to end with an analysis of care, *Sorge*, as the being of *Dasein*. The title of that chapter is: 'Care as the being of *Dasein*'. However, the analysis is diverted into a discussion of truth and reality, with a double conception of truth as both occasion of discoveries about entities, *Entdeckung*, and as the condition making discovery possible, openness, *Erschlossenheit*. The relation between the discussion of truth and the proposal to understand *Dasein* as care is made only in the subsequent section. Thus the first section ends with a puzzling juxtaposition of a discussion of care and an analysis of truth, with an account of how an understanding of truth reveals the difference between entities for which truth is and those for which truth is not an issue. Undifferentiated conceptions of reality play a role in concealing the difference between *Dasein* and other kinds of entity: that it is temporally structured; that it is capable of concern for itself and for other entities in the world; and that being is an issue for it. The second section concludes with discussions of three aspects of *Dasein*'s temporality: everydayness, historicality and being within time. Everydayness is characterised by the tendency to elide the difference between *Dasein* and present-at-hand entities; historicality introduces a distinction between a present-at-hand version of history and a version of history which is not simply a way of relating to past events but one which reveals that there are purposes at work in the occurrence of events above and beyond human control and beyond conceptions of entities as simply present or ready to hand. The third term, temporality as being within time, if taken on its own, is equivalent to the ordinary conception of time. There is a fourth mode, ecstatic temporality, in which *Dasein*, through anxiety and awareness of mortality, becomes aware of its limits. By contrast to this ordinary conception of time, as a structure within which events occur and kinds of entity are distinguished one from the other, Heidegger shows that there is a complex structure of shifting relations between past, present and future, revealed in the ecstatic moment. Out of this moment, there emerge the questions of meaning, identity and truth for the entity, *Dasein*, for which its own identity is an issue. These questions prompt philosophical puzzlement and then the responses of either setting out a relation to these questions, in ethical enquiry, or attempting to answer the questions, through metaphysical construction.

Heidegger explains the relation between the two sections thus: 'What was already set out in the preparatory existential analysis of *Dasein* in advance of the exposition of time is now brought back into the originary structure of the wholeness of the being of *Dasein*, that is temporality [*Zeitlichkeit*]' (*SZ*: 436). The exposition of *Dasein* is, however, only a passage; the aim is still to articulate the question of being. The later claim that his work is better understood as ways and passages than as results can be used to advantage here to suggest that, all the same, the emphasis must not be shifted to a hoped-for completion in an account of being, but must stay with the analysis of *Dasein*, as the only account of being possible. By contrast to the twofold structure of the enquiry, the structure of *Dasein* is a threefold split, into being-in, being-with and being-towards. This threefold splitting maps onto the threefold structure of time – present, past and future – and onto a threefold structure of different kinds of entity: entities with no relation to being, entities with a relation to being, and oneself. The analysis of *Dasein* culminates in an account of being-oneself, *Selbstsein*, which is achieved through the possibilities opened up by a third conception of truth, resolution, *Entschlossenheit*, alongside discovery and openness. Being-in is developed into the analysis of being in the world; being-towards is developed into the analysis of being in time; and being-with is connected up to the shared structures of meaning and significance, *Bedeutsamkeit*, which are the conditions of possibility for assigning meaning to particular states of affairs. Thus, in between the worldness and temporality of sections 1 and 2 of *Being and Time* as published, there is this third structure, that of significance. Just as there being a world recognisable as such is conditional on there being an entity which has the structure of being in a world, and just as the structure of time for Heidegger is conditional on there being an entity which is aware of itself as in time, so, for Heidegger, meaning and truth are conditional on there being relations of significance within which entities with the structure of *Dasein* find themselves. These relations of significance are grounded in the structure of *Dasein* as care, which occurs either at an individual or at a collective level, making possible Heidegger's reference in the 1933 *Rektoratsrede* to the *Dasein* of a people. While *Dasein* is individuated through its confrontation with its own death, the identity of a people must be grounded in a simultaneous affirmation of both birth and death as located within the continuity of a community. The dangers of such a position are clear in the context of Heidegger's endorsement of Nazism and in our contemporary context of so-called 'ethnic cleansing'. However, contrary to those who claim that there is no ethical concern in *Being and Time*, Heidegger makes it clear that there are better and worse ways of exercising care, on an individual level, which can be extended to insisting that the affirmation of collective *Dasein* must take place at the level of human beings as whole, as suggested in Chapter 4, and not at the level of arbitrarily delimited subgroups based on nationality or race. I shall discuss these better and worse ways of exercising care and then go on to look at how the analysis of *Dasein* is and is not an ethics.

FUNDAMENTAL ONTOLOGY AS ORIGINARY ETHICS

In the ordinary course of events, these three structures, worldness, significance and temporality, go unremarked. If they are to be observed, the ordinary pattern of expectations must have been disrupted. The structure of the world is revealed when a piece of practical activity goes wrong; the structure of meaning is revealed when concern and care open up a gap between an individual and whatever the object of their care and concern may be; the structure of time is revealed when an individual instance of *Dasein* comes to terms with its own finitude by understanding the meaning of its own death. The failure of practical activity is analysed in the first section, in the analysis of worldness. The event of death is analysed in the second section as revealing temporal structure. Significance is in play in both sections. It is discussed in relation to being in the world and to truth; it is reintroduced in the second section in relation to the retrieval of the four existentials associated with openness, when they are rediscussed in relation to temporality. These four existentials are understanding (*Verstehen*), dispositionality (*Befindlichkeit*), fallenness (*Verfallen*) and discourse (*Rede*).

The relation between significance and temporality is not directly discussed, although significance provides the first indication of the directedness of *Dasein* into the future out of its past. The analysis of anxiety reveals when significance collapses not just in relation to the failure of practical activity in the non-functioning of some specific piece of equipment, but in general. Heidegger writes of 'the loss of significance of the world which is opened up in anxiety' (*SZ*: 343). This loss of significance in anxiety is identified by Heidegger as uncanniness, homelessness, *Unheimlichkeit*, which connects up to the uncanniness discussed in relation to Oedipus. However, the givenness of meaning and of significance, in pre-ontological everyday relations is also uncanny. It is grounded in the mode of *Dasein* as *Mitsein* and licenses Heidegger's references to the construction of a generation. The connections between significance, *Mitsein* and this notion of a generation connect up to the existential, *Geschichtlichkeit*, but are not fully thought through in *Being and Time*.

Uncanniness disrupts the absorbtion of *Dasein* into the everyday 'anybody': 'This uncanniness pursues *Dasein* continually and is a constant threat to its lostness in the "anybody"' (*SZ*: 189). It reveals to *Dasein* its own genuine capacity for being: 'This stunnedness [*Benommenheit*] does not simply take *Dasein* out of "worldly" possibilities, but gives it at the same time the possibility of a genuine capacity for being' (*SZ*: 344). Uncanniness and stunnedness are the states in which the fact of being in the world, the givenness of meaning and of the existence of others can be revealed to the bearers of those states. Heidegger designates everyday being-oneself in the first section as the 'anybody' self. In the second section, the possibility of being self-owning is diagnosed as emergent out of this 'anybody' self. Thus the first section, the preparatory fundamental analysis of *Dasein*, shows the self as lost in the 'anybody', and the second transposes the analysis into one of temporality showing this self as emergent through the analysis of temporality. The third, withheld section might perhaps have demonstrated that in its self-owning, *Dasein* can set out the ontological difference between itself as determinate being and being as temporality, thus affirming a connection between a sense of self and a sense for being. The two are closely connected. Heidegger indicates a connection between the 'anybody' self and a retrieval of a genuine self thus:

> Even in its preparatory characterisation of everydayness, our analytic has already come up against the question of *Dasein*'s 'who?'. It has been shown that proximally and for the most part *Dasein* is not itself, but is lost in the anybody-self, which is an existential modification of the authentic self [*des eigentlichen Selbst*].' (*SZ*: 317)

In the course of introducing the abstract notion of the self, *Selbstheit*, there is one of Heidegger's long footnotes, concerned with Kant's conception of the self. Thus, this move from the 'anybody' self to the genuine self is part of a rethinking of Kant's notion of the self and of the split between the theoretical and the practical dimensions of the self in Kant's theory.

The following remark suggests that this genuine being-a-self does not present itself for analysis, but simply exists:

> *Dasein* is genuinely itself in the originary individuation of a silent openness which attributes to itself anxiety. This genuine *Selbstsein* says, as the one which keeps silent, exactly not 'I . . . I', but 'is' in this silence, the thrown entity, as which it can genuinely be. The self, which is exposed by the keeping silent of resolute existence, is the basic phenomenal basis for the question about the being of the 'I'. (*SZ*: 322–3)

Heidegger goes on to say that this might provide a basis for deciding on the validity of conceptions of substantiality, simplicity and personality as characteristics of abstract selfhood. However, it appears that this genuine occurrence can only be experienced in silence; once it has become an object for analysis and breaks the silence, it slips back from *Selbstsein*, being an existing self, to *Selbstheit*, a possibility of self as an abstract structure. There appears to be either identity or articulated meaning, but not both. The notion of the *Dasein* of a people is then the temptation of accepting an articulated meaning in a collectively posited identity, in place of the silence of individuation. The move is from the internalised sufferings of Oedipus, Hölderlin and Nietzsche to a sustainable, articulable identity, which in all probability necessarily results in the release of violence and aggression towards other groups of human beings. For an analysis of just what such a collective identity might offer and for reassurance that it would not result, as with Nazism, in the destruction of groups marked 'other', there is a need for a much fuller account of the relation between significance and temporality, through a fuller discussion of being with (*Mitsein*) in specific historical contexts. The problem is dual: in what social, historical conditions is it possible for an individual sense of self-worth to transpose itself and ground itself in a constructive social and historical project? Or are such projects bound to release the metaphysical violence of Oedipus into the actual destruction of life in human history? Heidegger's appalling answer in 1933 is not encouraging.

The analysis of *Dasein* demonstrates an interdependence between an analysis of truth, an analysis of temporality and an analysis of the self-constitution of human beings as individuals. This process of self-constitution is developed through the rewritings of *Dasein* as *Insein*, as *Mitsein*, as *Zusein* and finally as *Selbstsein*. *Dasein* as *Insein* and as *Mitsein* are introduced in the first section, in the preparatory discussion of everyday *Dasein* as being in the world. *Dasein* as *Zusein* and *Selbstsein* are introduced in the second section and are closely connected to the analysis of the difference between the temporality of *Dasein* and that of other kinds of entity. In part, this analysis of self-constitution is overlooked because the transition between the two sections of division 1, as published, breaks the continuity of the enquiry. While Heidegger claims his enquiries are morally neutral, the analysis of the self-constitution of human beings as individuals is an ethical concern. Failure to note this supports the hypotheses that *Being and Time* is not concerned with ethical issues, or that it is morally irresponsible in preparing the way for an endorsement of Hitler, or both. The crucial term here is *Entsch-lossenheit*. The three forms of enquiry, phenomenology, hermeneutics, ontology, and the three themes in the analysis of *Dasein*, temporality, individuation and truth, are brought together in the development of the controversial conception of resolution, *Entschlossenheit*. There are three ways in which this notion has been connected up to Heidegger's subsequent endorsement of Nazism, which turn on misunderstandings of his notions of identity, of meaning and of truth. The first is that far from achieving a moral neutrality, the analysis of identity in *Being and Time* requires an endorsement of authoritarian rule. This appears to be Habermas's view.

It gains support from Heidegger's notion of the fate of a people, in which individual instances of *Dasein* are bound together in a collective project, grounded in a group identity. Heidegger indicates a possible line of enquiry in the concluding pages of *Being and Time*: 'if fateful *Dasein* as being-in-the-world exists essentially as being-with-others, this historicising is a co-historicising and is determinative for it as destiny [*Geschick*]. This is how we designate the historicising of the community, of a people' (*SZ*: 384). He then adds: 'Only in communicating and struggling does the power of destiny become free. *Dasein*'s fateful destiny in and with its "generation" goes to make up the fateful authentic historicising of *Dasein*'. This, then, sets out a difference between the fate of *Dasein*, taken as individuals, and the destiny of a generation, understood as *Dasein* existing essentially as being with others. The difference between individual fate and collective destiny, and this notion of a generational understanding of history is not developed at this point. Scandalously, it is precisely here that six years later Heidegger inserts his *Rektoratsrede* of 1933, endorsing Hitler. He writes in *Being and Time* that a generation may choose its hero (*SZ*: 385) as a basis on which to respond to the openness of the future. It may even choose the 'anybody' as its hero (*SZ*: 371). While large sections of the German people, including Heidegger, do seem to have chosen Hitler as such a hero, this could be diagnosed as having taken place exactly in the mode of the 'anybody', and not in the mode of authentic *Dasein*. The collapse of Nazism in 1945 provides empirical evidence for the inauthenticity of that choice, in its failure to open up a future for those making it. Thus, while the account of identity, linking individual destiny with that of a generation resonates with Heidegger's choice for Hitler and Nazism, it is also possible to read the fate of Nazism as revealing the modern condition as one in which there can be no such sense of collective belonging. The postmodern condition would then be a recognition that there never has been such collective belonging.

The relation between traditional, modern and postmodern understandings of identity is complicated. If traditional identity as belonging is understood as given in advance, modern understandings of identity can be seen as defying the traditional constitution of identity as belonging and as seeking to construct in place of customary recognition a rationally binding mutual respect as a ground for identity. The modern experience would then be one in which this rational ground of respect proves incapable of securing either individual or collective identity. If metaphysics is understood as preoccupied with identity, then this would make modernity not the occasion for an overcoming of metaphysics, but its triumph in a nihilism through which collectively established value and identity become impossible, but the value of identity remains unquestioned. The postmodern turn would be the recognition that this nihilism is generated by the quest for collective identities which are not available in the present context but were not available in the past, either. The error of modernity would then be the presumption that establishing identity is the basis for human happiness and the doubly mistaken presumption that what previous societies constructed through superstition and prejudice can now be constructed through reason and debate. The question of identity then poses a dilemma: is it unavailable but desirable, or undesirable but available? This in turn generates various different forms of nihilism. While Heidegger diagnoses Nietzsche's response to nihilism in an affirmation of will to power as inadequate, his own response of declaring an end to philosophy is no more satisfactory. The remedy for the triumph of nihilism in metaphysics is not the affirmation of nothingness but rather a revival of another aspect of the philosophical tradition, an ethical affirmation of the possibility of transforming not just the self, as in will to power, but the self in relation to being, to world, time, meaning and tradition.

Divergent responses are evident in *Being and Time* in the double structure of thrownness and projection, thrownness into a metaphysical nothingness and projection into another kind of future. In the development of the former, Heidegger's destruction of the history of ontology plays a major role: the critique of Kant's division of analysis into the theoretical and the practical; the critique of Descartes' conception of reality; and the critique of Aristotle's conception of time. In the development of the latter, he retrieves crucial elements from the analyses of Kant, Descartes and Aristotle: the concept of autonomy, the concept of the self, and the practice of non-universalisable wisdom. These are features of the condition of *Dasein* as *Entschlossenheit*. Thus the question of identity and the reading of the history of philosophy as in need of drastic disruption come together in Heidegger's theory of resolution. The second form of connection from *Entschlossenheit* to the endorsement of Nazism is to claim that, in Heidegger's philosophy, meaning and value become arbitrary and decisionistic, depending on the whim of an individual. Thus it is alleged that his philosophy is rendered immoral and ethically irresponsible as a result of a supposed emptiness in this term 'resolution', the content of which is left open for determination at the ontical level of the individual instances of *Dasein*, in the situation in which it finds itself resolved. Thus it is supposed that any ethical or political endorsement is compatible with the analysis of *Dasein*, which can then be supposed capable of 'an authentic Nazism'.

On this view, Heidegger's analysis of *Dasein* is flawed because it fails to protect Heidegger from the temptation to endorse Hitler. This account is supported by limitations in Ernst Tugendhat's otherwise admirable study *The Concept of*

Truth in Husserl and Heidegger.[7] Tugendhat's analysis of Heidegger's conception of truth is flawed by its failure to recognise the linkages between the three parts of Heidegger's account of truth and to see its relation to Heidegger's critique of separating out interdependent areas of philosophical enquiry. Truth, for Heidegger, is first of all an epistemologically grounded notion revealing facts of the matter in the world; but he grounds that notion first in a set of quasi-transcendental conditions of possibility, which he sums up with the term *Erschlossenheit*, openness. This, in turn, he grounds in the interests of the entity for which its own identity is an issue and for which being is an issue. The moment in which that entity constitutes itself as an individual is the third moment of the analysis of truth, *Entschlossenheit*. Tugendhat is unimpressed by Heidegger's attempt to ground the analysis of truth in the fact that the entity for which truth is an issue is concerned with its own identity. He fails to recognise that, for Heidegger, truth is not simply a question of knowledge and meaning, but a question of identity and purpose. His critique also overlooks the connection between the account of truth and the analysis of *Dasein* as care and as essentially concerned with affirming itself as a self with a future.

Heidegger's account of truth starts with the most immediate occasion on which truth claims are made: when a state of affairs presents itself and is recognised as such. This Heidegger picks out with the term *Entdeckung*, uncovering. He claims that, in order for this kind of truth to be possible, there must be both a world, in which there are states of affairs present to an observer, and a language in which to articulate truth claims. These are the twin conditions of possibility, worldness and signification, *Weltlichkeit* and *Bedeutsamkeit*. Even while *Dasein* is inclined to fail to distinguish itself from other kinds of entity, its position within these networks of worldness and significance constitutes its difference. Heidegger analyses these conditions through the exploration of the second notion of truth, *Erschlossenheit*, openness, which is a structural feature of *Dasein*. Thus, just as being is an issue only for *Dasein*, so truth is an issue only for *Dasein*. In a key transitional passage Heidegger writes: 'The being of truth stands in an originary connection with *Dasein*. And only since *Dasein* is constituted through openness [*Erschlossenheit*], which calls for understanding, can there be an understanding of being, making an understanding of being possible' (*SZ*: 230). The account of *Erschlossenheit* sets up the characteristics required in an entity which can make judgements about matters of fact. Heidegger writes: 'The fundamental existentials which make up the being of the there, the openness of being-in-the-world, are dispositionality and understanding. In understanding there is contained the possibility of interpretation, which is the appropriation of what is understood' (*SZ*: 160). Heidegger attempts to show that this insight is incompatible with a conception of reality as developed by Descartes, where there is no insistence on an ontological difference between entities for which truth is an issue and those for which it is not. This Tugendhat accepts. However, Heidegger specifies a further level in the constitution of truth, the capacity of the entity for which truth is an issue to accept or reject its own distinctive form of existence. This is *Entschlossenheit*, resolution, in which the openness of the being of the 'there' is determined as one which is lucid about its own condition.

There is a transformation here of a general structure of openness, as a condition of possibility for there being an entity which can make truth claims, into a specific, individuated self-affirming recognition of the limited nature of any individual lifespan, and of the limited range of options open in that lifespan. This is the moment at which generalising ontological enquiry is revealed as grounded in the ontical specificity of the existence of particular instances of *Dasein*. This in turn leaves Heidegger open to the accusation of an arbitrary determination of truth in the interests of specific individuals. While it is true that Heidegger grounds his conception of truth in a conception of identity, identity is constituted at the ontological level, and ontically existing *Dasein* attains it only through the moment of resolution. The moment of resolution presupposes an affirmation of the conditions of possibility for an individual identity; and the incompleteness of *Being and Time* suggests that, in the modern context, this cannot be done. As will be shown in the following analysis, Heidegger himself imposes constraints on the states which can give rise to resolution. *Entschlossenheit* is not characteristic of all strongly affirmed human conditions; there are, for Heidegger, objective constraints on what can and what cannot be taken up resolutely.

The relation between these three conceptions of truth, discovery, opening and resolution, has the same complex structure as that between the three kinds of entity, presence at hand, readiness to hand and *Dasein*, as the site at which the difference between the three presents itself. The two tripartite structures are also interdependent; and no one element takes absolute priority over the others. If there were not readiness to hand, in the everyday practices of using things, there would not be present-at-hand entities to be described about which truth claims might be made. If there were no opening within which presence at hand might take place, there could be neither presence at hand nor discoveries. However, it is presence at hand and discovery which reveal openness as their condition of possibility. The same state of affairs can be described both from the point of view of present-at-hand discovery and from the point of view of ready-to-hand openness. In turn, each of these is grounded in the structure of *Dasein* as potentially resolute in recognition of its own structure, but in that moment, presence at hand and readiness to hand become theoretical possibilities, not actually occurrent states. The complexity of these relations makes it impossible to specify a definitive ordering between the three elements in each relation, presence at hand, readiness to hand and *Dasein*; discovery, openness and resolution. Nor can they be simultaneously conceived. The same complex set of relations between interdependent, mutually conditioned, but non-simultaneous structures occurs in the analysis of temporality. *Dasein* is within time, and everyday, and historical, and ecstatic; but it is impossible to experience this simultaneously. The difficulty, then, is not that Heidegger's account of meaning and its grounding in truth leaves his thinking open to Nazi adventurism; but that this account in the end makes sense only as an ethical project of self-discovery; not as an objectively written descriptive treatise.

A third version of the claim connecting the argument of *Being and Time* to Heidegger's endorsement of Hitler supposes that Heidegger proposes a thorough-going historical relativism, removing all criteria for moral choice. This claim is made by Joseph Margolis in his essay in *The Heidegger Case: On Philosophy and Politics*.[8] Margolis sees Heidegger's account of truth as making truth relative to individual points of view and value relative to historical context. This misses the importance of the distinction between the ontological and the ontical levels of enquiry. Truth claims, for Heidegger, are grounded in an ontological structure, one aspect of which is the fact that human beings find themselves in historically variable contexts. This structure is not in history, until it is occupied by a particular instance of *Dasein* with ontical, existential specificity. Thus, *Entschlossenheit* names a context-independent ontological structure, which nevertheless is grounded in the historical context of its bearer. Having a relation to being and having an identity to affirm are conditions of possibility for making truth claims; but those truth claims are about real, independently existing structures and are thus falsifiable. Thus the belief in the thousand-year *Reich* was both false and falsifiable.

Margolis draws implicitly on Leo Strauss's remarkably generous response to Heidegger's philosophy, in an essay printed in his *The Rebirth of Classical Political Rationalism*.[9] Strauss writes: 'Heidegger is the only man who has an inkling of the dimensions of the problem of a world society' (p. 43), and elaborates:

> Cassirer had transformed Cohen's system into a new system of philosophy in which ethics had completely disappeared. It had been silently dropped: he had not faced the problem. Heidegger did face the problem. He declared that ethics is impossible, and his whole being was permeated by the awareness that this fact opens up an abyss. (p. 28)

Strauss notes that Heidegger's 'understanding of existence was obviously of Christian origin (conscience, guilt, being unto death, anguish)' (p. 38). However, Strauss argues that Heidegger rejects existentialism because it leads to the relativism of the context dependency of affirming value on the basis of an individual's idea of existence, which cannot but be referred back to the individual's horizon of experience. He therefore notes that Heidegger's turn to discussing the sendings of being, different in each epoch, is an appeal to a non-relative, non-subjectivistic ground. This gestures towards a retrieval out of the abyss into which Western ethics descend once the validity of the religious foundation has been brought into question. Strauss suggests that this makes possible an encounter between the peoples of the West and those peoples and histories excluded by the joint foundation of Western thinking in the Greek affirmation of reason and in Christian revelation. Thus Strauss remarks, as Margolis does not, that far from being a relativist, Heidegger is the most persistent critic of both relativism and historicism, as indeed he is a critic of subjectivism and scepticism.

Heidegger does not deny the existence of good and evil; what he claims is that the analysis of *Dasein* takes place at a level before, or beyond, the distinction between good and evil. This claim is made in the analysis of *Dasein* as care:

> Not only can entities whose being is care load themselves with factical guilt; they are guilty in the very basis of their being. This 'being guilty' is what provides above all the ontological condition for *Dasein*'s ability to owe anything in factically existing. This essential being guilty is equi-primordially the existential condition for the possibility of the 'morally' good and for that of the 'morally' evil, that is for morality in general and for all the possible forms which this may take factically. The primordial 'being guilty' cannot be defined by morality, since morality already presupposes it for itself. (*SZ*: 286)

Thus morality, as a set of distinctions between good and evil, is for Heidegger derivative of a more basic structure. It is not good and evil which make judgements possible, but the possibility of judgement which makes the distinction between good and evil make sense. Heidegger's account of being guilty, then, is not primarily to do with failing to fulfil some obligation or being in breach of some law; it is concerned with specifying the nature of the entity which can be thus in breach or fail: how it is possible to be both judged and judging. It is an ontological feature of *Dasein* that it has a relation to itself and is sufficiently underdetermined to be held responsible for its acts and omissions. This results from its structure of incompleteness, both in advance of itself in its engagement with future prospects and behind itself, in being caught up by its previous involvements and already established networks of meaning and significance. It is no longer what it has been and not yet what it will be. This incompleteness is the basis for what Heidegger calls '*Schuld sein*', being guilty, or better 'being indebted', in the sense of not being self-sufficient. This 'being guilty' is not an infraction of some rule or expectation. It is a nothingness, a lack of determination, making it possible for *Dasein* to have an existence, a self to which to have relation. This makes freedom possible: 'The intended nullity belongs to *Dasein*'s being free for its existential possibilities. Freedom, however, is only in the choice of one possibility – that is in taking on not having chosen and not being able to choose the others' (*SZ*: 285). Thus freedom is also, for Heidegger, a privation: the inability to opt for all the available options; indeed the inability even to be apprised of all the possible options.

In developing his thought, Heidegger retrieves elements from the language of Christianity, while rejecting theology. Theology for Heidegger is an illegitimate attempt to give an account of everything that there is, *das Seiende im Ganzen*, which forgets the question of being, about how it comes to be like that. In place of the perfection and completeness characteristic of God's creation as understood in Christianity and in place of the notion of Christ as exemplary perfect human being, Heidegger emphasises the deficiency of everyday modes of *Dasein* and the self-concealedness in which *Dasein* is customarily to be found. He focuses attention on the deficient modes of *Dasein*'s everyday existence: the tendency to fall into given patterns rather than to accept responsibility for choosing them, to fail to recognise significant differences. The analysis of care is crucially indebted to transformations of terms from the Christian tradition; and perhaps for this reason its position as a third term between world and time is often overlooked. There are four key terms which Heidegger retrieves from the Christian tradition: being guilty (*Schuld sein*), wanting to have conscience (*Gewissen haben wollen*), hearing the call (*Ruf hinhören*) and fallenness (*Verfallen*). However, in using these terms, Heidegger transforms their meaning. When Heidegger analyses the phenomena of having a good or a bad conscience, he is showing what structure must be in place before any such phenomena can occur. This structure is not a relation between the mortal and the divine. Heidegger argues immanently that there must be a capacity for being answerable for one's actions and omissions. This structure he gets at by analysing a receptiveness to a call to be oneself, *Gewissen haben wollen*, wanting to have a conscience, or wanting to have a certainty. This certainty is a certainty not about external matters of fact but about having a life; having an existence to which to construct a relation; being the entity which has its own being as an issue for it. It can turn into either a willingness to take responsibility or an evasion of responsibility: 'In understanding the call, *Dasein* is in thrall to its ownmost possibility of existence. It has chosen itself' (*SZ*: 287). Even in not choosing, *Dasein* chooses itself. Freedom is inescapable.

He adds on the next page: 'In understanding the call, *Dasein* lets its ownmost self take action in itself in terms of that potentiality for being which it has chosen. Only in this way can it be answerable [*verantwortlich*]' (*SZ*: 288). Responsibility presupposes responsiveness. It is this responsiveness to the call to be oneself which Heidegger calls resoluteness: 'This distinctive and authentic disclosedness, which is attested by *Dasein* itself by its conscience, this reticent self-projection on one's most intimate being guilty in which one is ready for anxiety, we call *Entschlossenheit*' (*SZ*: 297). It is the call which retrieves *Dasein* out of a fallenness into the 'anybody':

> Losing itself in the publicness of the 'anybody', it fails to hear its own self in listening to the anybody-self. If *Dasein* is to be able to be brought back from the lostness of failing to hear itself, and if this is to be done through itself, then it must first be able to find itself – to find itself as something which has failed to hear itself and which fails to hear in that it listens away to the 'anybody'. (*SZ*: 271)

That which calls is not some supernatural creature but as Heidegger suggests: 'What if this *Dasein*, which finds itself in the very depths of uncanniness, should be the caller of the call of conscience?' (*SZ*: 276). It is the call of conscience which establishes the function of uncanniness as retrieving *Dasein* from being lost in inherited custom: 'The call of conscience, existentially understood, makes known for the first time what we have hitherto merely contended, that uncanniness pursues *Dasein* and is a threat to the lostness in which it has forgotten itself' (*SZ*: 277). Thus uncanniness is the experience through which forgetting is overcome. However, uncanniness shifts the register from that of Christian dogmatics to that of Greek tragedy, for uncanniness is *moira*. The problem then becomes: can this notion from Greek tragedy be thus connected into a discussion structured through this Christian terminology? The tension between the two itself generates an unease, almost an uncanniness.

Heidegger makes a connection between being guilty, care and uncanniness: 'Being guilty constitutes the being to which we give the name "care". In uncanniness, *Dasein* stands together with itself primordially. Uncanniness brings this entity up against an undistorted nothingness, which belongs to the possibility of its most individualised possibility for being' (*SZ*: 286–7). Heidegger distinguishes between the mode of action of such an individual brought up against its own individuality and the mode of action of someone in the mode of disownment:

> The understanding of the anonymous individual knows only fulfilling and failing to fulfil the requirements of rules of thumb and public norms. Such understanding notices breaches of these and seeks recompense. It creeps away from its own existence as indebted, in order to discuss all the more loudly obvious faults. In the call of conscience, however, this anonymous being is brought back to its own existence as owing to itself a self. Understanding this call is choosing – not conscience which cannot be chosen. What is chosen is having a conscience and becoming open to one's own state of indebtedness. (*SZ*: 288)

This is where care is no longer deflected outwards towards states of affairs in the world or towards the condition of others. It is a relation to the self, from which the other forms of care are derived. Heidegger distinguishes between care, solicitude for others and concern, with care as the condition of possibility for the other two: 'It is because being-in-the-world is in its internal structure care that in the previous analysis being preoccupied with ready-to-hand entities could be redescribed as concern [*Besorgen*] and being with the *Mitdasein* of others could be redescribed as solicitude [*Fürsorge*]' (*SZ*: 193). He continues:

> If one were to construct the expression 'care for oneself' [*Selbstsorge*] following the analogy of concern [*Besorgen*] and solicitude [*Fürsorge*] this would be a tautology. 'Care' cannot stand for some special attitude to the self, for the self has already been characterised ontologically by being-ahead of itself, a characteristic in which the other two items in the structure of care, being already in and being alongside have already been jointly posited.

Dasein is always already articulated through care, although usually in a mode in which this is not obvious to it.

In the first section of *Being and Time*, Heidegger distinguishes between positive and negative modes of solicitude: 'Its factical urgency draws its motivation from the fact that *Dasein* maintains itself for the most part and in the first instance in deficient modes of solicitude. Being in agreement or opposed to or being without one another, simply going past one another and not taking the other seriously are all ways of articulating solicitude' (*SZ*: 122). In these ways of articulating solicitude what is missing is a recognition of the difference between care for states of affairs in the world, care for other entities with the structure of *Dasein* and care for self. Even when these distinctions have been made, there are still destructive ways of relating to others:

> It can, as it were, take away 'care' from the other, and put itself in their position; it can leap in for the other. This kind of solicitude takes over the task from the other. The other is thereby pushed to one side and steps back, so that as an afterthought they can take over again what has been achieved as something already ready for use; or indeed shed all connection with it. In such solicitude, the other can become dependent and dominated even if this domination remains tacit and hidden to the one dominated. (*SZ*: 122)

Heidegger adds that this is the most common form of interaction. There is another form of solicitude in which there is no domination but a respect for the other: 'In contrast to this, there is also the possibility of a form of solicitude which does not so much step in place of the other as step forward into their potential, into their existential potentiality for being, not taking away their cares, but returning them for the first time as genuinely their own.' In this relation it is possible to affirm the freedom of self and of the other: 'This form of solicitude addresses genuine care, that means addresses the existence of the other and not simply a content with which the other is concerned, and helps the other to become perspicuous to themselves in their care and to become free for it.' This recognition of the existence and freedom of the other presupposes a recognition of one's own freedom and existence. Only through a relation to oneself is it possible to express genuine care for another, indeed to recognise the concerns of the other as their concerns.

These terms retrieved from the Christian tradition play a crucial role in developing an account of the individual; and the analysis can apply to all human beings, not just to those marked by the Christian tradition, only if these terms and the structures they pick out have universal scope. Now it may be possible that the structures picked out have universal scope, but the impossibility of raising language as spoken, *Gerede*, to the level of a pure historically uncontexted discourse, *Rede*, makes it impossible to name them as such. At this point it becomes necessary to distinguish between the different scopes of analysing human beings in relation to death, which does have universal scope, and the scope of the terms used by Heidegger, which places that analysis between the two traditions in terms of which Heidegger writes: the pagan Greek tradition and the Hebraeo-Christian tradition. This, then, is the truth of Margolis's contention that Heidegger's work reveals a thoroughgoing relativism of judgement. This, however, does not make it impossible to condemn movements such as Nazism on the basis of their disregard for respecting the freedom of others and discouragement of owning one's own existence. The judgement holds within those contexts where respecting the freedom of others and owning one's own existence can be taken to be conditions for engaging in the practice of judgement at all. Such judgement can be condemned as inadequate only on the basis that some other more rigorous criterion is thought to be available; or on the basis that the judgement is deemed not to make sense. Far from undercutting the possibility of judgement, the analysis of *Dasein* shows rather what the entity must be like which can make judgements. It also reveals constraints on the scope and relevance of judgement.

A key issue is that the temporality of judgement is different from the temporality of action, and different again from the temporality of human existence. Judgement brings the cyclical temporal patterns of human existence to a standstill and indeed, as embodied in the death penalty, can bring life to an end. What is judged is actions and characters rendered present at hand as objects of judgement. What is left out of account is how the judge and what is judged arrive in that relation. The world becomes lifeless and the judge takes up the stance of deathlike detachment. The moment of judgement is indistinguishable from the moment of death. The contexts of action and development through which objects for judgement evolve have the temporality of readiness to hand. They have duration, beginnings and ends. They have narrative structure, rather than the simultaneity of juxtaposition required for judgement. Contrasted to an ethics of judgement in the temporal mode of presence at hand and an ethics of action in the temporal mode of readiness to hand, there is a third mode of temporality, of the formation of character, in which individuals set up a relation to themselves and can succeed or fail in modifying their dispositions and behaviour. This temporality of the formation of character provides the basis for bringing together the capacity for judgement and the events to be judged. This is the temporality basic to *Dasein*, as the process of the formation of character and self-discovery which grounds the temporality of judgement and the temporality of action. Thus the temporality of self-discovery is both independent of and ground for these other forms of temporality. Thus ethical theory which analyses judgement and action independently from the questions of individuation and identity is incomplete and ungrounded. Heidegger's analysis could, but does not, reveal how these different temporal structures make judgement both difficult to arrive at and then difficult to integrate back into daily life and into the needs of human beings, which have these divergent temporal structures of duration and incompleteness. This integration is especially hard to achieve when the context of action and judgement is subject to the accelerating rate of change in the age of technology.

Heidegger does not make these moves, but he does make available a set of distinctions between morality, formal ethical analysis, material ethical analysis, a study of character formation and a fifth form of enquiry, which in the 'Letter on humanism' he calls originary ethics. Morality can be understood as the concern with good and evil. Theories of morality attempt to provide derivations of judgements of good and evil from some set of principles. In the mode of formal ethical analysis there is a claim to the universal scope of such principles, concerned with all human beings and seeking to establish the universalisability of judgement. The aim is to demonstrate the possibility of judgement, of actions, both past and future, and of character, as though there were no limit to the availability to a judge of an understanding of what there is to be judged. There is implicit in the claim to universalisability the stance of a perfect knowledge and understanding attributed in the Christian tradition only to God. When Heidegger mentions formal and material ethics (*SZ*: 294), he makes it clear that he intends by these terms the theories of Kant and of Scheler. He does not directly engage with these views, seeking rather to show that there is a prior question of the emergence of a capacity to judge. Even Aristotle's concern with the formation of character presupposes an understanding of the ontological conditions making such a capacity possible. Thus, in *Being and Time*, Heidegger is attempting to spell out the ontological conditions required for Aristotle's concern with the formation of character to make sense.

I contend that such an enquiry is an ethical enquiry and is at work in the analysis of *Dasein* and in the account of the call of conscience. It takes place at a level in advance of the analysis of character, the derivation of principles and the positing of values. It reveals the conditions for such analysis, derivation and positing, and it presumes that there is already such an entity for which values and judgements are an issue. The analysis of *Dasein* reveals what the nature of this entity must be. The call of conscience opens up a kind of ethical concern prior to any division between a concern with judgement and with action. While Heidegger claims that the analysis of *Dasein* is neutral, it is all the same a description of what it is to be human for which there are three central ethical concerns: taking responsibility for oneself, refusing the temptation to take responsibility for others, with the structure of *Dasein*, and recognising differences between self and others. The analysis of concern and care makes Heidegger's fundamental ontology, as a description of what it is to be human, an ethics in the wider, disquotational sense of the two questions of ethics discussed in the first part of his chapter. For this question of ethics, there is a connection between ethical and metaphysical enquiry. The possibility of ethics is conditional on the existence of an entity, for which being is an issue. This entity is the site of a lack of determination, the site of a nothingness, out of which there emerges ethical questioning and the possibility of freedom. If that entity fails to engage in ethical questioning and fails to accept the conditional nature of its freedom, it fails to respond to its own negativity and to accept responsibility for it. The consequence is nihilism and destruction. Moral concern is shown to be derivative from this ethical question, and is possible only because there is an entity for which its own existence is an issue. The description of such an entity is as much an ethical as a metaphysical project; and this is the task undertaken in the published version of *Being and Time*.

There are six key reasons why the ethical nature of Heidegger's enquiries has not been recognised. First, there is the failure to distinguish between producing universal principles, which for the purposes of this discussion has been called moral reflection, and the broader concern with human relations, both self-to-self and self-to-others. This erases the specificity of Aristotelian ethical concerns in favour of a single, general Kantian maxim of universalisability, which imposes sameness at the centre of human existence. Thus, since Heidegger is evidently not producing universalisable moral principles, it is falsely assumed he cannot be concerned with ethics. Second, Heidegger claims his enquiries are not concerned with ethics, because his notion of ethics is restricted to interhuman relations and does not include the relation between human beings and the contexts in which they find themselves. Third, readings of Heidegger fail to stress the systematic linkage of Heidegger's enquiries back to the incompleteness of *Being and Time*. This means that Heidegger's self-interpretative relation has not been made sufficiently central to his readings of the tradition. This self-interpretative relation disrupts his relation to the enquiries of others. This is an ethical relation, and the relation to self, for good or ill, is privileged over the relation to others. Fourth, there is the failure to note the ethical significance of the incompleteness and open-endedness which characterise his enquiries. The linkage from this to his insistence on the finite, transitory and transitional nature of both philosophical enquiry and human existence is not adequately identified or discussed. Fifth, there has been a reluctance to take seriously the relation between Heidegger's thinking in *Being and Time* and the Christian tradition. Heidegger's rejection of theology is permitted to mask the centrality to *Being and Time* of a retrieval of the individualising processes at work in the language of wanting to have a conscience, fallenness and being guilty. The universalising impulse of Christianity is retained without recognising the correlative process of individualisation. Finally, there are the readings of *Entschlossenheit* in terms of Heidegger's speeches for Nazism, which seek to reveal the failure of Heidegger's thinking in permitting such an allegiance. This conceals the centrality of the notion to the enquiries in *Being and Time*; and the ethical content of *Being and Time* is erased in favour of arguing about the morally pernicious status of its author. While the upshot of Heidegger's thinking is to declare philosophy at an end, I suggest that the philosophy which has come to an end is that which pretends to provide a single authoritative answer for all human beings to the puzzlement of existence. The philosophy which remains is that which celebrates the other, multiple Kantian maxim: dare to think. Heidegger's enquiries disrupt the generality of universalisation in favour of this other Kantian imperative.

Notes

1 PREAMBLE: ON ETHICS AND METAPHYSICS

1 See Martin Heidegger: *Sein und Zeit (SZ)*, Tübingen: Max Niemeyer, ninth edition, 1963, translated as *Being and Time* by John Macquarrie and Edward Robinson, Oxford: Basil Blackwell, 1962. The dates given in parentheses after the title of a published work are those of first publication as known to me.

2 See Otto Pöggeler: 'Heidegger's political self-understanding' in Richard Wolin (ed.): *The Heidegger Controversy*, Cambridge, MA: MIT Press, 1993, originally published in Anne-Marie Gethmann Siefert and Otto Pöggeler (eds): *Heidegger und die praktische Philosophie*, Frankfurt am Main: Suhrkamp, 1988.

3 For my discussion of a contribution by Heidegger to the formulation of a postmodern ethics, see Joanna Hodge: 'Genealogy for a postmodern ethics: reflections on Hegel and Heidegger' in Philippa Berry and Andrew Wernick (eds): *Shadow of Spirit: Postmodernism and Religion*, London: Routledge, 1992, pp. 135–48.

4 Martin Heidegger: *Die Selbstbehauptung der deutschen Universität*, Wrocław: Korn, 1935; translated by Karsten B. Harris as 'The self-assertion of the German university' in *Review of Metaphysics*, no. 38, March 1985.

5 For Hannah Arendt's discussion of these Aristotelian categories see *The Human Condition*, Chicago: University of Chicago Press, 1958; for a discussion of the role of Aristotelian categories in the development of the fundamental ontology of *Being and Time* see Jacques Taminiaux: 'The reappropriation of the *Nicomachean Ethics*: *Poiesis* and *Praxis* in the articulation of fundamental ontology' in *Heidegger and the Project of Fundamental Ontology*, Albany: State University of New York Press, 1991.

6 Martin Heidegger: *Hölderlins Hymne 'Der Ister', Gesamtausgabe* vol. 53 (*GA 53*), Frankfurt am Main: Klostermann, 1984. Unless otherwise indicated, the translations of Heidegger are my own.

7 See Martin Heidegger: *What is Philosophy?*, edited by Jean T. Wilde and William Kluback, New Haven: College and University Press, no date.

8 For some of the puzzles about this view see Joanna Hodge: 'Nietzsche, Heidegger, Europe: Five remarks' in *The Journal of Nietzsche Studies*, no. 3, Spring 1992, pp. 45–66.

9 See Martin Heidegger: *Wegmarken (WM)*, second edition, Frankfurt am Main: Klostermann, 1978. The letter is translated in David Farrell Krell (ed.): *Heidegger's Basic Writings*, second edition, London: Routledge, 1993.

10 See Martin Heidegger: *Einführung in die Metaphysik (EM)*, Tübingen: Max Niemeyer, 1953, translated as *Introduction to Metaphysics* by Ralph Manheim, New Haven: Yale University Press, 1959.

11 See Tom Sheehan's excellent discussion of this in 'Heidegger and the Nazis' in *New York Review of Books*, 15 June 1988, pp. 38–47.

12 Hugo Ott's biography: *Martin Heidegger: Unterwegs zu seiner Biographie*, Frankfurt am Main: Campus, 1988, presented material concerning Heidegger's involvement in Nazism which shook some of those who had been of the opinion that the commitment was of no great significance. Ott's book is held to be more reliable on matters of fact than the slightly earlier, and much more controversial book by Victor Farias: *Heidegger et le nazisme*, Paris: Vedier, 1987, translated as *Heidegger and Nazism*, by Paul Burrell and Gabriel Ricci, Philadelphia: Temple University Press, 1989.

13 This is translated in Richard Wolin (ed.): *The Heidegger Controversy: A Critical Reader*, New York: Columbia University Press, 1991. Habermas also discusses Heidegger in his lectures on *The Philosophical Discourse of Modernity*, Oxford: Polity Press, 1988.

14 Published in Jürgen Habermas: *The New Conservatism: Cultural Criticism and the Historians' Debate*, Oxford: Polity Press, 1989; and in Herbert Dreyfus (ed.): *Heidegger: Critical Essays*, Oxford: Basil Blackwell, 1992.

15 See *New German Critique*, no. 45, Fall 1988, edited by Richard Wolin.

16 Reprinted in English translation by William J. Richardson in Thomas J. Sheehan (ed.): *Heidegger: The Man and the Thinker*, Chicago: Precedent Publishing Inc., 1982; and in Gunther Neske and Emil Kettering (eds): *Martin Heidegger and National Socialism: Questions and Answers*, New York: Paragon House, 1990; and in Richard Wolin (ed.): *The Heidegger Controversy: A Critical Reader*, New York: Columbia University Press, 1991. These last two both contain additional material by people other than Heidegger, with that in the former collection presenting Heidegger in a more favourable light and that in the latter bringing together some of Heidegger's most committed critics: Löwith, Marcuse, Habermas, Tugendhat, Bourdieu. Both contain extensive bibliographies of primary and secondary material.

17 Karl Löwith: *Martin Heidegger: Denker in dürftiger Zeit*, Frankfurt am Main: Fischer, 1953; Alexander Schwan: *Politische Philosophie im Denken Martin Heideggers*, Cologne: Westdeutscher Verlag, 1965; and Jean-Paul Palmier: *Les Ecrits politiques de Martin Heidegger*, Paris: Editions de l'Herne, 1968.

18 Rainer Schuerman: *Heidegger: From Principles to Anarchy*; originally published in French, this is translated by Christine Marie-Gros, Bloomington: Indiana University Press, 1987.

19 See Jacques Derrida: *Of Spirit: Heidegger and the Question*, originally published in French in 1987, translated by Geoffrey Bennington and Rachel Bowlby, Chicago: Chicago University Press, 1990; and Philippe Lacoue-Labarthe's essay 'Transcendence ends in politics', in *Typography: Mimesis, Philosophy, Politics* (1989) and Lacoue-Labarthe: *La Fiction du politique*, 1987, translated as *Heidegger, Art and Politics*, Oxford: Basil Blackwell, 1990.

20 Lacoue-Labarthe: 'Neither an accident nor a mistake' in *Critical Inquiry*, no. 15, Winter 1989, pp. 481–4.

21 Martin Heidegger: *Gelassenheit*, Pfullingen: Gunther Neske, 1959; translated in Martin Heidegger: *Discourse on Thinking* by J. Anderson and E.H. Freund, New York: Harper & Row, 1966.

22 *Vorträge und Aufsätze* (*VA*), Pfullingen: Gunther Neske, 1954; translated in *The End of Philosophy*, edited by Joan Stambaugh, New York: Harper & Row, 1973.

23 See Martin Heidegger: 'Vom Wesen des Grundes' in *Wegmarken*, Frankfurt am Main: Klostermann, 1978, and Martin Heidegger: *The Essence of Reasons*, Evanston: Northwestern University Press, 1969, parallel German and English edition, translated by Terence Malick.

24 See Edith Wyschogrod for a discussion of the phenomenon of mass death in relation to the philosophy of Hegel and of Heidegger: *Spirit in Ashes: Hegel, Heidegger and Man-made Mass Death*, New Haven: Yale University Press, 1985.

25 See Martin Heidegger: *Wegmarken*, Frankfurt am Main: Vittorio Klostermann, second

expanded and checked edition, 1978; translated in Martin Heidegger: *Existence and Being*, edited by Werner Brock, London: Vision, 1949; and in David Farrell Krell (ed.): *Martin Heidegger: Basic Writings*, London: Routledge, 1978, second edition, 1993.

26 See Jacques Derrida: *Of Spirit: Heidegger and the Question*, Chicago: Chicago University Press, 1990, for a discussion of the significance of Heidegger's use and abandonment of inverted commas with respect to the term 'spirit'.

27 See Martin Heidegger: *Zur Sache des Denkens* (*SD*), Tübingen: Max Niemeyer, 1969; translated by Joan Stambaugh in Martin Heidegger: *On Time and Being*, New York: Harper & Row, 1972; and in Krell (ed.): *Martin Heidegger: Basic Writings*, London: Routledge, 1978, second edition, 1993. The translation followed here is Stambaugh's, pp. 55, 24.

28 Michel Haar: *Heidegger et l'essence de l'homme*, Grenoble: Millon, 1990; translated by William McNeill as *Heidegger and the Essence of Man*, Albany, NY: SUNY, 1993.

29 Martin Heidegger: *Nietzsche*, two volumes, Pfullingen: Gunther Neske, 1961; translated by Joan Stambaugh, David Farrell Krell and Frank Capuzzi in Martin Heidegger: *Nietzsche*, edited by David Farrell Krell, New York: Harper & Row, 1982, 1987. Martin Heidegger: *Nietzsche: Der Wille zur Macht als Kunst*, edited by Bernd Heimbüchel, *GA* 43, Frankfurt am Main: Klostermann, 1985; Martin Heidegger: *Nietzsches metaphysische Grundstellung im abendländischen Denken: Die ewige Wiederkehr des Gleichen*, edited by Marion Heinz, *GA* 44, Frankfurt am Main: Klostermann, 1986; Martin Heidegger: *Nietzsche: Der europäische Nihilismus*, edited by Petra Jaeger, *GA* 48, Frankfurt am Main: Klostermann, 1986.

30 Martin Heidegger; *Was heißt Denken?* (*WHD*), Tübingen: Max Niemeyer, 1954; translated as *What is called Thinking?* by J. Glenn Gray, New York: Harper & Row, 1968.

31 Martin Heidegger: *Die Selbstbehauptung der deutschen Universität* (*SB*), Wrocław: Korn, 1935; translated by Karsten Harries as 'The Self-assertion of the German university', *Review of Metaphysics* 38, March 1985, pp. 470–80; reprinted in Gunther Neske and Emil Kettering (eds): *Martin Heidegger and National Socialism: Questions and Answers*, New York: Paragon House, 1990, a slightly tendentiously framed translation of the German *Antwort: Martin Heidegger im Gespräch*, Pfullingen: Neske, 1988; and in Richard Wolin (ed.): *The Heidegger Controversy: A Critical Reader*, New York: Columbia University Press, 1991; second edition, Cambridge, MA: MIT, 1993.

32 This essay is published in *Vorträge und Aufsätze*, Pfullingen: Gunther Neske, 1954; and translated in *The End of Philosophy*, edited by Joan Stambaugh, New York; Harper & Row, 1973.

33 Martin Heidegger: 'Die Zeit des Weltbildes' in *Holzwege*, Frankfurt am Main: Klostermann, 1950, translated as 'The age of the world picture' in Martin Heidegger: *The Question of Technology and Other Essays*, translated and introduced by William Lovitt, New York: Harper & Row, 1979.

34 Søren Kierkegaard: *Fear and Trembling*, translated with an introduction and notes by Walter Lowrie, New York: Anchor Books, Doubleday, 1954 [1844].

35 See the parallel German and English text edited by Joan Stambaugh, Martin Heidegger: *Identity and Difference*, New York: Harper & Row, 1969.

36 Martin Heidegger: *Die metaphysischen Anfangsgründe der Logik im Ausgang von Leibniz*, Frankfurt am Main: Klostermann, 1978; translated by Michael Heim as *The Metaphysical Foundations of Logic* (*MFL*), Indiana: Indiana University Press, 1984.

37 See Martin Heidegger: *Kant und das Problem der Metaphysik*, Frankfurt am Main: Klostermann, 1950, translated as *Kant and the Problem of Metaphysics* by James S. Churchill, Bloomington: Indiana University Press, 1962. For an excellent discussion of Heidegger's relation to Kant's philosophy see Frank Schalow: *Imagination and Existence: Heidegger's Retrieval of the Kantian Ethic*, Lanham, MD: University Press of America, 1986.

38 Martin Heidegger: 'Der Ursprung des Kunstwerkes' in *Holzwege* (1950), Frankfurt am Main: Klostermann, fifth edition, 1972, pp. 7–68; translated in Martin Heidegger: *Poetry, Language, Thought* by Albert Hofstadter, New York: Harper & Row, 1971.

39 William J. Richardson: *Heidegger: Through Phenomenology to Thought*, The Hague: Martinus Nijhoff, 1963, preface, p. xv.

40 See Martin Heidegger: *Erläuterungen zu Hölderlins Dichtung*, first edition (*ED1*) 1944, second edition (*ED2*) 1949; and the lectures from 1933-34, *Hölderlins Hymnen 'Germanien' und 'Der Rhein'*, GA 39, Frankfurt am Main: Klostermann, 1980; and the later lectures, *Hölderlins Hymne 'Andenken'*, GA 52, Frankfurt am Main: Klostermann, 1982, and *Hölderlins Hymne 'Der Ister'*, GA 53, Frankfurt am Main: Klostermann, 1984.

41 For a discussion of this see Joanna Hodge, 'Heidegger, early and late: the vanishing of the subject', *Journal of the British Society for Phenomenology*, vol. 25, no. 3, Autumn 1994, pp. 288–301.

2 REASON, GROUNDS, TECHNOLOGY

1 Martin Heidegger: *The Principle of Reason*, translated by Reginald Lilly, Bloomington: Indiana University Press, 1991, from Martin Heidegger: *Der Satz vom Grund (SG)*, Pfullingen: Gunther Neske, 1957. The translations offered here of Heidegger's German text are my own, although I have on occasion improved mine as result of comparing them with those of Lilly.

2 Martin Heidegger: *The Metaphysical Foundations of Logic*, translated by Michael Heim, Bloomington: Indiana University Press, 1984, from Martin Heidegger: *Die metaphysischen Anfangsgründe der Logik, im Ausgang von Leibniz*, Frankfurt am Main: Klostermann, 1978.

3 Martin Heidegger: *The Essence of Reasons*, translated by Terence Malick, Evanston: Northwestern University Press, 1969, from the fourth edition of Martin Heidegger: *Vom Wesen des Grundes*, Frankfurt am Main: Klostermann, 1955. This essay was Heidegger's contribution to a *Festschrift* for Husserl's seventieth birthday.

4 'The age of the world picture' in Martin Heidegger: *The Question of Technology and Other Essays* (*QT*), translated with an introduction by William Lovitt, New York: Harper, 1977, from Martin Heidegger: 'Die Zeit des Weltbildes' in *Holzwege*, Frankfurt am Main: Klostermann, 1952, pp. 69–104.

5 Martin Heidegger: *Identität und Differenz* (*ID*), Pfullingen: Gunther Neske, 1957, translated by Joan Stambaugh as *Identity and Difference*, New York: Harper & Row, 1969.

6 Martin Heidegger: *Unterwegs zur Sprache*, Pfullingen: Gunther Neske, 1959; translated by Peter D. Hertz as *On the Way to Language*, New York: Harper & Row, 1971.

7 For extended discussion of the relation between Heidegger and Hegel, detailing the shifts in proximity and distance between them, see Dennis J. Schmidt: *The Ubiquity of the Finite: Hegel, Heidegger and the Entitlements of Philosophy*, Cambridge, MA: MIT Press, 1988.

8 See Martin Heidegger: 'Hegels Begriff der Erfahrung' in *Holzwege*, Frankfurt am Main: Klostermann, 1972, pp. 105–92; and the lectures from 1930–31, *Hegel's Phenomenology of Spirit*, Indiana: Indiana University Press, 1988.

9 See Jacques Derrida: *Marges de la philosophie*, Paris: Editions de Minuit, 1972; translated with additional notes by Alan Bass as *Margins of Philosophy*, Brighton: Harvester Press, 1982. Derrida's approach to Heidegger is significantly different on the different occasions on which he reads him. These shifts cannot be discussed here, but they are oddly mirrored by Heidegger's own shifts with respect to Hegel.

10 Martin Heidegger: 'Die Frage nach der Technik' in *Vorträge und Aufsätze*, Pfullingen: Gunther Neske, 1954; translated in *The Question of Technology and Other Essays* by William Lovitt, New York: Harper & Row, 1977.

3 HUMANISM AND HOMELESSNESS

1 Ernst Jünger became famous as a celebrant of warfare, on the basis of his book *In Tempests of Steel* (*In Stahlgewittern*, 1921), about his experiences on the Western Front during the First World War. He later wrote a study of the impact on working life of industrialisation, called *The Worker* (*Der Arbeiter*, 1932), which Heidegger used as the basis for seminars. Jünger also wrote a novel, *On Marble Cliffs* (*Marmorklippen*, 1939), in which he depicts the takeover of a rural district by nameless, faceless bullies. Although resonances between Jünger's and Heidegger's thinking are often remarked, it is not usually noted that Jünger, unlike Heidegger, did not join the Nazi party.

2 A parallel English/German edition of *Zur Seinsfrage* was published in 1958: *The Question of Being*, translated and with an introduction by Jean T. Wilde and William Kluback, New Haven, CN: College and University Press, 1958.

3 Martin Heidegger, *Vom Ereignis: Beiträge zur Philosophie* (*GA* 65), Frankfurt am Main: Klostermann, 1989.

4 For lengthy discussion of the status of animals, see the lecture volumes from 1929–1930, Martin Heidegger: *Die Grundbegriffe der Metaphysik* (*GBM*), *GA 29/30*, Frankfurt am Main: Klostermann, 1983.

5 Martin Heidegger: *Gelassenheit*, Pfullingen: Gunther Neske, 1959, translated by J. Anderson and E.H. Freund as *Discourse on Thinking* (*DT*), New York: Harper & Row, 1966.

6 See Georg Lukacs: *The Destruction of Reason*, London: Merlin, 1980, vol. 3, ch. 4: 'The Ash Wednesday of parasitic subjectivism: Heidegger and Jaspers', first published in German in 1954, which gives a sketch of Heidegger's views based on a reading of *Being and Time* and of *Kant and the Problem of Metaphysics*. Granted the complexities of the relation between Jaspers and Heidegger, it is odd to find them thus juxtaposed.

7 This links to Derrida's discussion of writing and his critique of phonocentrism. Derrida's subordination of speech to writing is akin to Heidegger's subordination of the human use of language to the givenness of meaning and language above and beyond human will. See Jacques Derrida: *Speech and Phenomenon*, Evanston: Northwestern University Press, 1972, where this privilege to speech is shown to generate problems in Husserl's account of meaning, and *Of Grammatology*, translated by G.C. Spivak, Johns Hopkins University Press, 1974, where writing is privileged over attributions of meaning based on speakers' intentions. The disruption of appeal to speakers' intentions is further developed in the papers collected in Jacques Derrida: *Limited Inc*, Evanston: Northwestern University Press, 1972, and 3rd edn, 1988. In that collection there appears the following remark (p. 112): 'by addressing myself to you in the form of a letter, I will reduce just a little (but only a little) the essential predicament of all speech and writing, that of context and destination.'

8 See Jean-Paul Sartre: *Critique of Dialectical Reason*, 2 vols, London: Verso, 1991, originally published in French in 1960.

4 WHAT IS IT TO BE HUMAN?

1 See Martin Heidegger: *Erläuterungen zu Hölderlins Dichtung*, *GA* 4, Frankfurt am Main: Klostermann, 1981. This is the fifth edition of a text which has one Nazi edition, in 1944, and three intermediate editions, in which gradually more material on Hölderlin has been included. The differences between the first and second editions will be discussed briefly in the section on 'Heidegger and Hölderlin'. For an English translation of the lecture, see Martin Heidegger: *Existence and Being*, translated and with an introduction by Werner Brock, London: Vision, 1949.

2 I have great difficulty with the relation between Heidegger and Hölderlin, and indeed in getting to grips with Hölderlin at all. David Constantine's lectures on Hölderlin and his book, *Hölderlin*, Oxford: Oxford University Press, 1988, have been a great help; Andrzej Warminski: *Readings in Interpretation: Hölderlin, Hegel, Heidegger*, Minneapolis: University of Minnesota Press, 1987, sets up the distinction between interpreting and reading the text of the other. There is also an illuminating discussion of Heidegger and Hölderlin in Christopher Fynsk: *Heidegger: Thought and Historicity*, Ithaca: Cornell University Press, 1986. I shall make references to other works I have consulted in the course of the discussion.

3 This is published in German in Martin Heidegger: *Holzwege*, Frankfurt am Main: Klostermann, 1950, fifth edition 1972, and in English in *The Question of Technology and Other Essays*, translated and introduced by William Lovitt, New York: Harper & Row, 1977.

4 See Martin Heidegger: *Die Grundbegriffe der Metaphysik: Welt – Endlichkeit – Einsamkeit*, *GA* 29/30, edited by Friedrich Wilhelm von Herrmann, Frankfurt am Main: Klostermann, 1983.

5 See 'Das Ding' (1950) in Martin Heidegger: *Vorträge und Aufsätze*, Pfullingen: Neske, 1954, translated as 'The thing' in *Poetry, Language, Thought*, New York: Harper & Row, 1971; and 'Die Kehre' (1950) in Martin Heidegger: *Die Technik und die Kehre*, Pfullingen: Neske, 1962, translated as 'The turning' in *The Question of Technology and Other Essays*, New York: Harper & Row, 1977.

6 For a remarkable discussion of memory and reminiscence, see David Farrell Krell: *Of Memory, Reminiscence and Writing: On the Verge*, Bloomington: Indiana University Press, 1990.

7 See Friedrich Nietzsche: *Untimely Meditations*, (1874), essay three, Cambridge: Cambridge University Press, 1989; and Martin Heidegger: *Sein und Zeit*, p. 396.

8 See Beda Allemann: *Hölderlin und Heidegger*, Freiburg: Atlantis, 1954, p. 95.

9 Martin Heidegger: 'Hölderlin und das Wesen der Dichtung' in Martin Heidegger: *Erläuterungen zu Hölderlins Dichtung*, *GA* 4, Frankfurt am Main: Klostermann, 1991, translated in Martin Heidegger: *Existence and Being*, edited by Werner Brock, London: Vision, 1949.

10 Martin Heidegger; 'Der Ursprung des Kunstwerkes', in Martin Heidegger: *Holzwege*, Frankfurt am Main: Klostermann, 1950, fifth edition, 1972, translated in *Martin Heidegger; Basic Writings*, edited by David Farrell Krell, London: Routledge, second edition 1993.

11 See William Richardson: *Heidegger: From Phenomenology to Thought*, The Hague: Martinus Nijhoff, 1964, pp. 562–3; for Richardson's assessment of the 1943 afterword to 'What is metaphysics?' as a first draft for the 'Letter on humanism', see p. 473.

12 See Beda Allemann: *Hölderlin und Heidegger*, Freiburg: Atlantis, 1954, pp. 91–111.

13 Martin Heidegger: *Unterwegs zur Sprache (US)*, Pfullingen: Neske, 1959, translated by Peter D. Hertz as *On the Way to Language*, New York: Harper & Row, 1971.

14 See the three volumes of lectures, published as volumes of the complete works under the titles: *Hölderlins Hymnen 'Germanien' und 'Der Rhein'*, (1934–35), *GA* 39, 1980; *Hölderlins Hymne 'Andenken'* (1941–42), *GA* 52, 1982; and *Hölderlins Hymne 'Der Ister'* (1942), *GA* 53, 1984.

15 See Martin Heidegger: *Erläuterungen zu Hölderlins Dichtung*, Frankfurt am Main: Klostermann, 1944; and Martin Heidegger: *Erläuterungen zu Hölderlins Dichtung*, second edition, Frankfurt am Main: Klostermann, 1951. The second edition contains two additional essays and slightly different editorial notes. Some of these differences are identified and discussed in what follows. The third edition (1953) is a reprint of the second edition, but the fourth edition (1971) republished as volume 4 of the complete works (1981) contains two further essays, including a lecture from 1959, 'Hölderlin:

Himmel und Erde', and a quantity of supplementary material, some of it taken from the first edition and left out in the second edition.

16 For some details of this, see the introduction to Beda Allemann's discussion in *Hölderlin und Heidegger*, Freiburg: Atlantis, 1954.

17 For an outstanding treatment of Heidegger's thinking about the relation between language, truth and poetry, see Gerald L. Bruns: *Heidegger's Estrangements: Language, Truth and Poetry in the Later Writings*, New Haven, CN: Yale University Press, 1989, who argues convincingly that there is a shift from the reading of Hölderlin in the middle years as revealing how poetry may reveal a word for being to the view in the postwar years that even the expressive powers of poetic language are held back by the withdrawal of being. Bruns would not approve of my insistence on the philosophical character of Heidegger's thinking.

18 See Martin Heidegger: *Vorträge und Aufsätze*, Pfullingen: Neske, 1954; and Martin Heidegger: *Early Greek Thinking*, edited and translated by Frank Capuzzi and David Farrell Krell, New York: Harper & Row, 1975.

19 See Martin Heidegger: *Vorträge und Aufsätze*, Pfullingen: Gunther Neske, 1954; and translated as 'Poetically man dwells' in Martin Heidegger: *Poetry, Language, Thought* (*PLT*), translated and edited by Albert Hofstadter, New York: Harper & Row, 1971.

20 See Karl Löwith: 'Meine letzte Begegnung mit Heidegger in Rom, 1936' in *Mein Leben in Deutschland vor und nach 1933*, Stuttgart: Metzler, 1986; translated in Richard Wolin, (ed.): *The Heidegger Controversy: A Critical Reader*, New York: Columbia University Press, 1991; and in G. Neske and Emil Kettering (eds): *Martin Heidegger and National Socialism: Questions and Answers*, New York: Paragon House, 1990.

5 FREEDOM AND VIOLENCE

1 This is available in English in both Günther Neske and Emil Kettering (eds): *Martin Heidegger and National Socialism: Questions and Answers*, New York: Paragon, 1990, and in Richard Wolin (ed.): *The Heidegger Controversy: A Critical Reader*, Cambridge, MA: MIT, 1993.

2 These lectures were given in the winter semester of 1935/36 under the title 'Grundfragen der Metaphysik'. They were published in 1962, under the title *Die Frage nach dem Ding: Zu Kants Lehre von den transzendentalen Grundsätzen* (*FD*), Tübingen: Max Niemeyer, 1962, translated as *What is a Thing?* by W.B. Barton, Jr. and Vera Deutsch, Chicago: Henry Regnery Company, 1977.

3 Karl Löwith wrote a series of essays on Heidegger's accounts of history and nature after the Second World War, which are collected in *Martin Heidegger: Denker in dürftiger Zeit*, Frankfurt am Main: Fischer, 1953.

4 Martin Heidegger: *Schellings Abhandlung über das Wesen der menschlichen Freiheit (1809)*, Tübingen: Max Niemeyer, 1971.

5 *GA 31*, Frankfurt am Main: Klostermann, 1982.

6 Versions of both of these papers are included in Martin Heidegger: *Wegmarken*, Frankfurt am Main: Klostermann, second edition, 1978. 'On the essence of truth' is translated in both Werner Brock (ed.): *Existence and Being*, London: Vision Press, 1949, and David Farrell Krell (ed.): *Martin Heidegger: Basic Writings*, London: Routledge, revised and expanded edition, 1993.

7 Martin Heidegger: 'Die Sprache' in *Unterwegs zur Sprache*, Pfullingen: Neske, 1959, pp. 9–35, translated as 'On the way to language' in *Poetry, Language, Thought*, ed. Albert Hofstadter, New York: Harper & Row, 1971.

8 See Martin Heidegger: 'Die Zeitbegriff in der Geschichtswissenschaft' in *Frühe Schriften*, Frankfurt am Main: Klostermann, 1972.

9 Martin Heidegger: *The Concept of Time*, translated by Will McNeill, Oxford: Basil Blackwell, 1992. This was first published in German by Klostermann in 1989, but was published in French translation in 1983 in *Cahiers de l'Herne*, volume 45: *Martin Heidegger*, edited by Michel Haar. Karl Löwith refers to it in his book, *Martin Heidegger: Denker in dürftiger Zeit.*

10 Martin Heidegger: *Prolegomena zur Geschichte des Zeitbegriffs*, GA 20, Frankfurt am Main: Klostermann, 1979. It appeared in a second corrected edition in 1988. The English edition, *The History of the Concept of Time*, was translated by Theodore Kisiel, Indiana: Indiana University Press, 1985.

11 Published in *Holzwege*, Frankfurt am Main: Klostermann, 1950, fifth edition, 1972, pp. 7–69, and translated in *Poetry, Language, Thought* by Albert Hofstadter, New York: Harper & Row, 1971.

12 See Martin Heidegger: 'Vom Wesen und Begriff des *phusis*, Aristoteles, *Physik* B, 1' in *Wegmarken'*, Frankfurt am Main: Klosterman, 1967, second edition, 1978, pp. 237–301.

13 See Martin Heidegger: 'The rectorate 1933/34: facts and thoughts' in G. Neske and E. Kettering (eds): *Martin Heidegger and National Socialism: Questions and Answers*, New York: Paragon House, 1990, pp. 15–32.

6 BEING AND TIME

1 See Robert Bernasconi: *Heidegger in Question: The Art of Existing*, New Jersey: Humanities Press, 1993, especially essays 1, 2 and 12.

2 Martin Heidegger: *The Metaphysical Foundations of Logic*, translated by Michael Heim, Bloomington: Indiana University Press, 1984.

3 Martin Heidegger: *Basic Problems of Phenomenology*, translation, introduction and lexicon by Albert Hofstadter, Indiana University Press, 1982, revised edition, 1988.

4 See von Herrmann's recently published essay '*Being and Time* and the *Basic Problems of Phenomenology*' in John Sallis (ed.): *Reading Heidegger: Commemorations*, Indiana University Press, 1993, pp. 118–36.

5 I cannot here go into Derrida's discussion of Kant's diagnosis of the resulting death of philosophy. See J. Derrida: 'On an apocalyptic tone newly adopted in philosophy' in Harold Coward and Toby Foshay (eds): *Derrida and Negative Theology*, Albany: State University of New York Press, 1992 [1982].

6 J. Derrida in *Of Spirit: Heidegger and the Question*, translated by Geoffrey Bennington and Rachel Bowlby, Chicago: University of Chicago Press, 1989 [1987], analyses Heidegger's use of quotation marks and the disquotational effect. While his discussion centres on the term 'Geist', this also brings into view the importance of Heidegger's use of quotation marks in *Being and Time* with respect to the terms 'metaphysics' and 'ethics'.

7 See Ernst Tugendhat: *Der Wahrheitsbegriff bei Husserl und Heidegger*, Berlin: de Gruyter, 1970.

8 See his essay 'Discarding and Recovering Heidegger' in Tom Rockmore and Joseph Margolis (eds): *The Heidegger Case: On Philosophy and Politics*, Philadelphia: Temple University Press, 1992.

9 See the essay 'An Introduction to Heideggerian Existentialism', printed as chapter 3 of Leo Strauss: *The Rebirth of Classical Political Rationalism: An Introduction to the Thought of Leo Strauss. Essays and Lectures*, selected and introduced by Thomas L. Pangle, Chicago: University of Chicago Press, 1989.

Bibliography

WORKS BY HEIDEGGER

[1914–16] *Frühe Schriften, GA* 1, Frankfurt am Main: Klostermann, 1972.

[1919–61] *Wegmarken*, Frankfurt am Main: Klostermann, second expanded and revised edition, 1978.

[1924] *Der Begriff der Zeit*, Frankfurt am Main: Klostermann, 1989. *The Concept of Time*, translated by Will McNeill, Oxford: Basil Blackwell, 1992

[1925] *Prolegomena zur Geschichte des Zeitbegriffs, GA* 20, Frankfurt am Main: Klostermann, 1979. *The History of the Concept of Time*, Bloomington: Indiana University Press, 1988.

[1927] *Sein und Zeit*, Tübingen: Max Niemeyer, ninth edition, 1963. *Being and Time*, translated by John Macquarrie and Edward Robinson, Oxford: Basil Blackwell, 1962.

[1927] *Die Grundprobleme der Phänomenologie, GA* 24, Frankfurt am Main: Klostermann, 1986. *Basic Problems of Phenomenology*, translation, introduction and lexicon by Albert Hofstadter, Bloomington: Indiana University Press, 1982, revised edition, 1988.

[1928] *Metaphysische Anfangsgründe der Logik im Ausgang von Leibniz, GA* 26, Frankfurt am Main: Klostermann, 1978. *The Metaphysical Foundations of Logic*, translated by Michael Heim, Bloomington: Indiana University Press, 1984.

[1929] *Kant und das Problem der Metaphysik*, Frankfurt am Main: Klostermann, 1950, fourth edition, 1973. *Kant and the Problem of Metaphysics*, translated by James S. Churchill, Bloomington: Indiana University Press, 1962.

[1929] *Vom Wesen des Grundes*, Frankfurt am Main: Klostermann, 1955. *The Essence of Reasons*, parallel German and English edition, translated by Terence Malick, Evanston, IL: Northwestern University Press, 1969.

[1929–30] *Die Grundbegriffe der Metaphysik: Welt – Endlichkeit – Einsamkeit, GA* 29/30, edited by F. W. von Hermann, Frankfurt am Main: Klostermann, 1983.

[1930] *Vom Wesen der menschlichen Freiheit: Einleitung in die Philosophie, GA* 31, Frankfurt am Main: Klostermann, 1982.

[1930–31] *Hegel's Phänomenologie des Geistes, GA* 32, Frankfurt am Main: Klostermann, 1988.

[1933] *Die Selbstbehauptung der deutschen Universität*, Wrocław: Korn, 1935. 'The self-assertion of the German university', translated by Karsten Harries, *Review of Metaphysics* 38, March 1985, pp. 470–80.

[1934–35] *Hölderlins Hymnen 'Germanien' und 'Der Rhein', GA* 39, Frankfurt am Main: Klostermann, 1980.

[1935] *Einführung in die Metaphysik*, Tübingen: Max Niemeyer, 1953, third edition, 1966. *An Introduction to Metaphysics*, translated by Ralph Manheim, New Haven: Yale University Press, 1959.

[1935–36] *Die Frage nach dem Ding: Zu Kants Lehre von den transzendentalen Grundsätzen*, Tübingen: Max Niemeyer, 1962. *What is a Thing?*, by W. B. Barton, Jr. and Vera Deutsch, Chicago: Henry Regnery Company, 1967.

[1936] *Schellings Abhandlung über das Wesen der menschlichen Freiheit (1809)*, Tübingen: Max Niemeyer, 1971.

[1936–37] *Nietzsche: Der Wille zur Macht als Kunst*, edited by Bernd Heimbüchel, *GA* 43, Frankfurt am Main: Klostermann, 1985.

[1936–38] *Vom Ereignis: Beiträge zur Philosophie*, *GA* 65, Frankfurt am Main: Klostermann, 1989.

[1937] *Nietzsches metaphysische Grundstellung im abendländischen Denken: Die ewige Wiederkehr des Gleichen*, edited by Marion Heinz, *GA* 44, Frankfurt am Main: Klostermann, 1986.

[1940] *Nietzsche: der europäische Nihilismus*, edited by Petra Jaeger, *GA* 48, Frankfurt am Main: Klostermann, 1986.

[1941–42] *Hölderlins Hymne 'Andenken'*, *GA* 52, Frankfurt am Main: Klostermann, 1982.

[1942] *Hölderlins Hymne 'Der Ister'*, *GA* 53, Frankfurt am Main: Klostermann, 1984.

[1944] *Erläuterungen zu Hölderlins Dichtung*, *GA* 4, Frankfurt am Main: Klostermann, 1981.

[1950] *Holzwege*, Frankfurt am Main: Klostermann, fifth edition, 1972.

[1951–52] *Was heißt Denken?*, Tübingen: Max Niemeyer, 1954, second edition, 1961. *What is Called Thinking?*, translated by J. Glenn Gray, New York: Harper & Row, 1968.

[1954] *Vorträge und Aufsätze*, Pfullingen: Neske, 1954.

[1955] *Was ist das – die Philosophie? What is Philosophy?*, parallel German and English edition, translated by Jean T. Wilde and William Kluback, New Haven: College and University Press, 1958.

[1955–56] *Der Satz vom Grund*, Pfullingen: Neske, 1957. *The Principle of Reason*, translated by Reginald Lilly, Bloomington: Indiana University Press, 1991.

[1956] *Zur Seinsfrage*, Pfullingen: Neske, 1956. *The Question of Being*, parallel German and English edition, translated by William Kluback and Jean T. Wilde, New Haven: College and University Press, 1958.

[1957] *Identität und Differenz*, Pfullingen: Neske, fifth edition, 1978. *Identity and Difference*, parallel German and English edition, translated by Joan Stambaugh, New York: Harper & Row, 1969.

[1959] *Gelassenheit*, Pfullingen: Neske, 1959. *Discourse on Thinking*, translated by J. Anderson and E. H. Freund, New York: Harper & Row, 1966.

[1959] *Unterwegs zur Sprache*, Pfullingen: Neske, 1959, sixth edition, 1979. *On the Way to Language*, translated by Peter D. Hertz, New York: Harper & Row, 1971.

[1961] *Nietzsche*, 2 volumes, Pfullingen: Neske, 1961. *Nietzsche*, 4 volumes, edited by David Farrell Krell, translated by Joan Stambaugh, David Farrell Krell and Frank Capuzzi, New York: Harper & Row, 1979–87.

[1962] *Die Technik und die Kehre*, Pfullingen: Neske, 1962.

[1969] *Zur Sache des Denkens*, Tübingen: Max Niemeyer, 1969. *On Time and Being*, translated by Joan Stambaugh, New York: Harper & Row, 1972.

Translations of essays and lectures

Existence and Being, edited by Werner Brock, London: Vision, 1949.

Poetry, Language, Thought, edited and translated by Albert Hofstadter, New York: Harper & Row, 1971.

The End of Philosophy, translated by Joan Stambaugh, New York: Harper & Row, 1972.

Early Greek Thinking, edited and translated by Frank Capuzzi and David Farrell Krell, New York: Harper & Row, 1975.

The Question Concerning Technology and Other Essays, translated and introduced by William Lovitt, New York: Harper & Row, 1977.

'The rectorate 1933/34: facts and thoughts', in Günther Neske and Emil Kettering (eds): *Martin Heidegger and National Socialism: Questions and Answers*, New York: Paragon House, 1990, pp. 15–32.

Basic Writings, edited by David Farrell Krell, London: Routledge, 1978, second edition, 1993.

SECONDARY SOURCES

Allemann, Beda: *Hölderlin und Heidegger*, Freiburg: Atlantis, 1954.

Arendt, Hannah: *The Human Condition*, Chicago: University of Chicago Press, 1958.

Bernasconi, Robert: *Heidegger in Question: The Art of Existing*, New Jersey: Humanities Press, 1993.

Berry, Philippa and Andrew Wernick (eds): *Shadow of Spirit: The Religious Sub-text of Contemporary Western Thought*, London: Routledge, 1993.

Bruns, Gerald L.: *Heidegger's Estrangements: Language, Truth and Poetry in the Later Writings*, New Haven: Yale University Press, 1989.

Constantine, David: *Hölderlin*, Oxford: Oxford University Press, 1988.

Coward, Harold and Toby Foshay (eds): *Derrida and Negative Theology*, Albany: State University of New York Press, 1992.

Derrida, Jacques: *Writing and Difference*, translated by Alan Bass, London: Routledge, 1978 [1967].

—— *Speech and Phenomenon*, Evanston, IL: Northwestern University Press, 1972.

—— *Of Grammatology*, translated by Gayatri Chakravorty Spivak, Baltimore: Johns Hopkins University Press, 1974 [1967].

—— *Limited Inc*, Evanston, IL: Northwestern University Press, 1988.

—— *Marges de la philosophie*, Paris: Editions de Minuit, 1972. *Margins of Philosophy*, translated by Alan Bass, Brighton: Harvester, 1982.

—— *De l'esprit: Heidegger et la question*, Paris: Editions Galilée, 1987. *Of Spirit: Heidegger and the Question*, translated by Geoffrey Bennington and Rachel Bowlby, Chicago: University of Chicago Press, 1989.

—— 'On an apocalyptic tone newly adopted in philosophy' in Harold Coward and Toby Foshay (eds): *Derrida and Negative Theology*, Albany: State University of New York Press, 1992.

Dreyfus, Herbert and John Harrrison (eds): *Heidegger: Critical Essays*, Oxford: Basil Blackwell, 1992.

Farias, Victor: *Heidegger et le nazisme*, Paris: Vedier 1987. *Heidegger and Nazism*, translated by Paul Burrell and Gabriel Ricci, Philadelphia: Temple University Press, 1989.

Foucault, Michel: *The Order of Things*, London: Tavistock, 1973 [1966].

—— 'Omnes et singulatim' in Sterling M. McMurrin: *The Tanner Lectures on Human Value*, vol. 2, Cambridge: Cambridge University Press, 1981, pp. 223–54.

—— 'The subject and power', in Herbert Dreyfus and Paul Rabinow: *Michel Foucault: Beyond Structuralism and Hermeneutics*, Brighton: Harvester, 1981, pp. 208–26.

—— 'On governmentality', *Ideology and Consciousness*, no. 6, 1979, pp. 5–21.

Fynsk, Christopher: *Heidegger: Thought and Historicity*, Ithaca, NY: Cornell University Press, 1986.

Gethmann Siefert, Anne-Marie and Otto Pöggeler (eds): *Heidegger und die praktische Philosophie*, Frankfurt am Main: Suhrkamp, 1988.

Haar, Michel (ed.): *Cahiers de l'Herne*, vol. 45: *Martin Heidegger*, Paris: Editions de l'Herne, 1983.
—— *Heidegger et l'essence de l'homme*, Grenoble: Millon, 1990.
Habermas, Jürgen: *The Philosophical Discourse of Modernity*, Oxford: Polity, 1988.
—— *The New Conservatism: Cultural Criticism and the Historians' Debate*, Oxford: Polity, 1989.
Hodge, Joanna: 'Nietzsche, Heidegger, Europe: Five remarks', *The Journal of Nietzsche Studies*, no. 3, Spring 1992, pp. 45–66.
—— 'Genealogy for a postmodern ethics: reflections on Hegel and Heidegger' in Philippa Berry and Andrew Wernick (eds): *Shadow of Spirit: The Religious Sub-text of Contemporary Western Thought*, London: Routledge, 1993, pp. 135–48.
—— 'Heidegger, early and late: the vanishing of the subject', *Journal of the British Society for Phenomenology*, vol. 25, no. 3, Autumn 1994, pp. 288–301.
Krell, David Farrell: *Of Memory, Reminiscence and Writing: On the Verge*, Bloomington: Indiana University Press, 1990.
—— *Daimon Life: Heidegger and Life Philosophy*, Bloomington: Indiana University Press, 1992.
Lacoue-Labarthe, Philippe: *Typography: Mimesis, Philosophy, Politics*, edited by Christopher Fynsk, introduced by Jacques Derrida, Cambridge, MA: Harvard University Press, 1989.
—— *La Fiction du politique*, Paris: Bourgois, 1987. *Heidegger, Art and Politics*, Oxford: Basil Blackwell, 1990.
Löwith, Karl: *Martin Heidegger: Denker in dürftiger Zeit*, Frankfurt am Main: Fischer, 1953.
—— *Mein Leben in Deutschland vor und nach 1933*, Stuttgart: Metzler, 1986.
Lukacs, Georg: *The Destruction of Reason*, volume 3, London: Merlin, 1980 [1973].
Neske, Günther and Emil Kettering (eds): *Antwort: Martin Heidegger im Gespräch*, Pfullingen: Neske, 1988. *Martin Heidegger and National Socialism: Questions and Answers*, New York: Paragon House, 1990.
Nietzsche, Friedrich: *Untimely Meditations*, Cambridge: Cambridge University Press, 1989 [1874].
Ott, Hugo: *Martin Heidegger: Unterwegs zu seiner Biographie*, Frankfurt am Main: Campus, 1988.
Palmier, Jean-Paul: *Les Ecrits politiques de Martin Heidegger*, Paris: Editions de l'Herne, 1968.
Pögeller, Otto: 'Heidegger's political self-understanding' in Herbert Dreyfus and John Harrison (eds): *Heidegger: Critical Essays*, Oxford: Basil Blackwell, 1992.
Richardson, William J.: *Heidegger: Through Phenomenology to Thought*, The Hague: Martinus Nijhoff, 1963.
Rockmore, Tom: *On Heidegger's Nazism and Philosophy*, Brighton: Harvester, 1992.
Rockmore, Tom and Joseph Margolis (eds): *The Heidegger Case: On Philosophy and Politics*, Philadelphia: Temple University Press, 1992.
Sallis, John (ed.): *Reading Heidegger: Commemorations*, Bloomington: Indiana University Press, 1993.
Schalow, Frank: *Imagination and Existence: Heidegger's Retrieval of the Kantian Ethic*, Lanham, MD: University Press of America, 1986.
—— *The Renewal of the Heidegger–Kant Dialogue: Action, Thought and Responsibility*, Albany: State University of New York Press, 1992.
Schmidt, Dennis J.: *The Ubiquity of the Finite: Hegel, Heidegger and the Entitlements of Philosophy*, Cambridge, MA: MIT Press, 1988.
Schuerman, Rainer: *Heidegger: From Principles to Anarchy*, translated by Christine Marie-Gros, Bloomington: Indiana University Press, 1987 [1986].
Schwan, Alexander: *Politische Philosophie im Denken Martin Heideggers*, Cologne: Westdeutscher Verlag, 1965.

Sheehan, Thomas J. (ed.): *Heidegger: The Man and the Thinker*, Chicago: Precedent Publishing Inc., 1982.
—— 'Heidegger and the Nazis' *New York Review of Books*, 15 June 1988, pp. 38–47.
Stambaugh, Joan: *The Finitude of Being*, Albany: State University of New York Press, 1992.
Strauss, Leo: *The Rebirth of Classical Political Rationalism: An Introduction to the Thought of Leo Strauss. Essays and Lectures*, selected and introduced by Thomas L. Pangle, Chicago: University of Chicago Press, 1989.
Taminiaux, Jacques: *Heidegger and the Project of Fundamental Ontology*, Albany: State University of New York Press, 1991.
Tugendhat, Ernst: *Der Wahrheitsbegriff bei Husserl und Heidegger*, Berlin: de Gruyter, 1970.
Warminski, Andrzej: *Readings in Interpretation: Hölderlin, Hegel, Heidegger*, Minneapolis, University of Minnesota Press, 1987.
White, Stephen K.: *Political Theory and Postmodernism*, Cambridge: Cambridge University Press, 1991.
Wolin, Richard: *The Politics of Being*, New York: Columbia University Press, 1989.
—— (ed.): *The Heidegger Controversy: A Critical Reader*, New York: Columbia University Press, 1991; second edition, Cambridge, MA: MIT Press, 1993.
Wyschogrod, Edith: *Spirit in Ashes: Hegel, Heidegger and Man-made Mass Death*, New Haven: Yale University Press, 1985.
Zimmerman, Michael: *Heidegger, Modernity, Technology*, Bloomington: Indiana University Press, 1991.

Index